I LOVE YOU BUT ...
YOU ALWAYS PUT ME
LAST

Why the Kids-First
Approach to Parenting
Is Hurting Your
Marriage—and
the Proven Plan
to Restore Balance

ANDREW G. MARSHALL

author, *I Love You But . . . I'm Not In Love With You*

Health Communications, Inc.
Deerfield Beach, Florida

www.hcibooks.com

The Library of Congress Cataloging-in-Publication Data

Marshall, Andrew G.
    I love you but you always put me last : why the kids-first approach to parenting is hurting
your marriage—and the proven plan to restore balance / Andrew G. Marshall.
        pages cm
    ISBN-13: 978-0-7573-1790-3 (Paperback)
    ISBN-10: 0-7573-1790-1 (Paperback)
    ISBN-13: 978-0-7573-1791-0 (ePub)
    ISBN-10: 0-7573-1791-X (ePub)
    1. Parenthood—Psychological aspects.   2. Married people—Psychology.
3. Man-woman relationships—Psychological aspects.   I. Title.
    HQ755.8.M357297 2014
    306.874—dc23

                                                                                    2013048070

© 2014 Andrew G. Marshall

HCI, its logos, and marks are trademarks of Health Communications, Inc.

Publisher: Health Communications, Inc.
        3201 S.W. 15th Street
        Deerfield Beach, FL 33442–8190

Cover image ©iStockphoto
Cover design by Dane Wesolko
Cover and interior design by Lawna Patterson Oldfield

Contents

Introduction

I've spent almost thirty years helping couples resolve their arguments, turn around their relationships, and fall back in love again. I've written eleven books, answered countless letters sent to my website, given talks, and appeared on numerous radio and TV shows. However, in all that time, I've never really addressed one of the most fundamental issues that is driving so much of the misery I encounter: how to stop your children from ruining your marriage. My silence is not because I've got nothing to say—as you'll discover, I've got a whole book—but because I know from experience that most parents don't want to hear my message. Unfortunately, it goes against much of our contemporary culture and all the received wisdom. So I scout around the edges, approach the problems from another angle, and deal with the fallout. What, then, has made me finally decide to speak out?

Every hour at my practice in London, the doorbell rings and a couple or an individual sits opposite me and pours out feelings. On one occasion, I had a thirty-one-year-old woman sobbing about her parents' divorce more than twenty years ago and why she couldn't find a lasting relationship. Even though she was a top-flight government adviser, it felt like I had a small child in the room as she looked up from her pile of crumpled tissues and asked, "Why did nobody think about me?"

My next clients were a deeply unhappy couple, on the point of divorcing, who were fighting about weekend joint-custody visits. He thought she was turning their three children against him. She was angry that he was bailing out of their marriage—he had found another woman—without even trying to sort out their differences. Suddenly, I had a mental fast-forward to twenty years later and saw one of this couple's daughters sitting in the seat opposite me. Despite my clients doing everything in their power for their children to be happy, confident, and successful (the best schools, extensive extracurricular activities, and all the latest gadgets), they had exhausted first their marriage and then themselves—so running away and starting again seemed the only way for the husband to reclaim his identity. What made this story doubly tragic is that they used to have such a happy relationship.

When we explored what went wrong, the problems could be traced back to choices made when their children were small. I knew from my work with the single client mentioned previously that her fear that she was "too much for anyone to handle" was a result of decisions made by her parents when she was a small child. On the train home that night, I decided to break my silence and write this book so that I could help people protect their marriages and avoid turning their children into my future clients.

There's another reason I haven't written about parenting before. I've never had children, so what right do I have to give advice? I've had no firsthand experience in arguing about whose turn it is to get up for the baby, what time small children should go to bed, or how to stop teenagers from smoking. However, I *am* an expert on relationships. I know how easy it is to lose sight of being husband and wife when you become Mommy and Daddy and how that breeds not only unhappy parents but fractious and desperate kids. Time and again, the first sign that my clients have turned the corner in therapy is when they report that their children are much happier, because kids thrive when their parents are in harmony and tackle problems as a team. In addition, after thousands of hours listening to adults talk about their childhood, I also have a clear idea of what can go wrong and how to help your children grow up to be happy, balanced, and resilient.

If you've recently had a baby, this book will give you a sense of the road ahead and how to avoid the pitfalls. I also cover the effect on your family of the second child and subsequent children. If your family is complete and your children are older, my argument is just as relevant whether they are eighteen months or eighteen years old. Please don't skip the early chapters, though, because they will help you diagnose where any problems might have started and direct your energy toward where it will be most effective.

Ultimately, this is a positive book. Having children is a great opportunity to grow and change. It can help put pain from your own childhood behind you and bring you closer to your own parents. It can also deepen the bond with your partner, because there's nothing more awesome than creating a new life together. However, you do need good relationship skills and to know how to communicate effectively, even when you're tired and stressed—in fact, especially then! But don't worry, I have lots of practical advice and tips that will help you talk, listen to each other, and find a solution that's acceptable to both of you. There's also information on how to foster a great relationship with your children and therefore provide good emotional support. At the end of each chapter, there is specific advice on how to strengthen your relationship with your partner, and because I know you are busy and juggling lots of different tasks, I've summed everything up in ten golden rules (which are at the end of the book).

Although I've used the word *marriage* in the subtitle for this book, I don't think you have to be married to have a secure relationship or raise happy children. It's just that *marriage* makes it clear what kind of relationship I'm discussing. I also want to stress that this book is just as much for fathers as for mothers; both women and men can feel that their partners put them last. Unfortunately, there's a tendency in our society (I'm thinking particularly of politicians) to blame everything on mothers. No wonder mothers can feel under attack and sometimes hear criticism when none is intended. So let me be clear: I believe in *equal* parenting responsibilities, and when relationships hit a problem, it is generally six of one partner and half a dozen of the other.

The case histories come from my practice as a marriage counselor as well as interviews with mothers and fathers not in counseling. I have changed details and sometimes merged two or three cases so nobody can be recognized. Finally, I would like to thank my clients for their generosity in allowing me to share what we have learned together.

—**Andrew G. Marshall**
www.andrewgmarshall.com

1

Getting Your Priorities Right

Although bringing up the next generation is possibly the most fulfilling and life-affirming thing anyone can do, babies and small children do seem to have a mission to destroy everything they come into contact with, from your clothes and furniture to your nerves, your sex life, and sometimes even your marriage. Even when they're older, children have so many needs and make such demands on your time that it is easy to lose sight of your partner.

Fortunately, it does not have to be like this. During almost thirty years as a marriage counselor, I've seen many couples whose relationships have been beaten into submission by the child-rearing years, but I've helped many more turn their sons and daughters into the glue that binds them together. So what makes the difference? In a nutshell, it's about getting your priorities right and balancing three key elements: your marriage, your children's welfare, and your own needs.

1

When you first fell in love, you had eyes only for your beloved. He or she was the center of your universe, the light of your life, and the reason you got up in the morning. When you walked down the aisle or joined hands in the office of a justice of the peace, it was impossible to believe that anything would ever come between you. You had discussed that you wanted children at some point, but in the abstract, they would bring you together and be a living and breathing proof of your devotion, and there would be more than enough love to go around. So it came as a complete surprise when, in the hurly-burly of bringing up a family—earning enough to provide food, clothing, and shelter—you dropped on each other's list of priorities, until one of you complained, "You always put me last."

Men find that they come after the children, housework (especially when their wives won't come to bed, and potentially have sex, because they're wiping down the kitchen counters), the wives' jobs, and maybe even the dog. Women discover that they come after their husbands' work, the children (because when the men come home, they are happy to play with their kids, which is fine because their wives want them to be good fathers, yet the wives can't help feeling ignored), and sometimes even a favorite football team.

> *After the seductive promise of romantic love, the everyday grind of babies and small children comes as a nasty shock.*

After the seductive promise of romantic love, the everyday grind of babies and small children comes as a nasty shock. In an ideal world, the partners would talk about their disappointments, regrets, and losses; cuddle; and support each other through the adjustment from lovers to parents without losing sight of either role. Unfortunately, many couples get into a downward spiral in which the husband feels excluded at home, so buries himself in his work (after all, it pays the bills and keeps the show on the road), and since the wife hardly ever sees her husband (because he's working late, catching up on his e-mails, or away at a conference), she buries herself in the minutiae of her children's lives (because what is more important than raising the next generation?). Perhaps the problems start because she has always felt secondary to his work. So the arrival of a baby—for whom she is definitely number one—bolsters her self-confidence, and she throws herself further into this demanding but rewarding new role. Whatever way everything starts, a couple can withdraw further and further into the stereotypes of what it means to be a man, a woman, a father, or a mother and find it harder to reach out to each other and be a team.

With so much unspoken resentment, it is not surprising that people prioritize family time over couple time. Not only is there less chance of a fight with the children around, it is easy to hide behind the comfortable intimacy of being Mom and Dad together and forget the problems of being husband and wife.

Fortunately, it doesn't have to be like this.

Revolutionary Ideas

At the center of this book is a radical idea—so radical that I will be surprised if you accept it. So please feel free to say, "Yes, but . . . ," or complain that I don't understand; maybe you'll even think that I'm mad, bad, and dangerous. However, I hope that you'll suspend your judgment for a while and mull over my suggestions rather than dismissing them out of hand. So what is this idea?

You should put your children second.

Of course, there will be times when the children need you—perhaps they are ill or it's their first day at school. What I'm talking about is on an everyday basis; your husband or your wife should be your number one priority. I know this is a tough idea to swallow, particularly when you have a helpless baby on your lap, but children are just passing through, whereas marriage should be forever. (I know this stands today's perceived wisdom on its head, that marriages come and go but being parents together endures.)

Before you throw the book or the e-reader across the room, know that I'm not saying that you should prioritize your partner just because it will be good for your marriage; I'm saying it because it will be good for your children, too. A happy marriage means happy children. If you put your

> *A happy marriage means happy children. If you put your children first— as a matter of course, day in and day out—you will exhaust your marriage.*

children first—as a matter of course, day in and day out—you will exhaust your marriage. Children sense the unhappiness, so they try to build bridges for their parents and then get drawn into things they are too young to understand; or, worse still, they think the problem is because of them in some way. Time and again, I have seen that the couples I'm counseling turned a corner because they reported that the children were happier.

What happens if you *do* put your child or children first? Amanda is forty-one and married with a three-year-old daughter. "We do a lot of things on the weekend that are very child-oriented and focused on her," she explained. "I'll make arrangements with people we're not particularly friendly with or have much in common with but who have children of the same age, because I believe that being an only child is unfair on our daughter. For example, last night, I had six children over for her to play with and set up craft activities—decorating a card and making snacks—on the kitchen table."

Amanda's determination to provide plenty of opportunities for her daughter to mix with other children came at a cost, however. "If we were going out for dinner or I had made arrangements for my husband and I to meet friends without our daughter and I got a phone call for a playdate, I would cancel the adult event—without a second thought," she admitted.

Obviously, I was interested in the effect this had on her husband. "Regardless of whether he will be stuck having a conversation with a guy he's only just met, I never say no," Amanda said. "Sometimes he says, 'Can't just the three of us do something?'"

Although I can easily imagine the look on her husband's face when he comes home after a long day to find six strange children in the kitchen, it is Amanda's last sentence that really worries me. Not only is her husband very aware of how low he is on his wife's list of priorities, he can't even ask, "Can't just the *two* of us do something?"

When I explain about putting each other first, my clients often look at me blankly, almost as if they can hear my words but can't quite process them. Of course, they don't want to neglect their marriage, but they want to give their children every opportunity in life and (although they don't necessarily use this word) be *perfect* parents. If that involves putting your relationship on autopilot during your child's crucial formative years, isn't it worth it?

At this point, I should introduce the accompanying idea to *Put your children second*, and that is *Be a good enough parent*. Unfortunately, *good enough* is not a popular idea, either. We want the very best for our children. So perhaps I should explain what I mean by *good enough*. Donald Winnicott (1896–1971) was one of Britain's most influential pediatricians and child psychiatrists. He believed that if by some miracle we could fulfill all our children's needs on the spot, they would have the illusion that the world revolved around them. Worse still, they would never need to overcome any obstacles and would therefore not have the opportunity to test things out for themselves, make mistakes, grow, and become independent. Obviously, neglecting a child is equally dangerous, so he proposed a middle way: being *good enough*. In other words, you look out for your children but do not micromanage them.

There are two advantages to taking this concept to heart. First, it will help you keep your sanity, since it accepts that every parent makes mistakes and it's not necessarily the end of the world. "I'd forgotten that our son needed a costume for World Book Day at his playgroup on Monday morning, and all the shops were closed," explained Muriel, age thirty-two. "In my mind, I could see him upset about being the only one who hadn't dressed up or, worse still, bullied because he had a third-rate costume. So I went online and fortunately found a Thomas the Tank Engine outfit on eBay."

However, buying it involved driving halfway across London and out to one of the towns outside the city, a round-trip of at least three hours. "Aiming to be a perfect mother," Muriel reported, "I packed my husband, my son, and my one-year-old daughter into the car and set off. Nobody was in a good mood, and the tension in the car started to grow and grow." Fortunately, Muriel and I had already covered *good enough* in counseling, so instead of fighting, Muriel and her husband, Neil, stopped the car and started talking.

"I wondered if going to Chelmsford was the best way to spend our Sunday," said Neil in therapy.

"And I began to question if the journey was really necessary," added Muriel. "I could try to make the costume. Did it matter if he went in something homemade? So we turned around and went out for something to eat instead."

In the end, Muriel made a good enough costume and her son enjoyed helping her to turn a hat into a funnel. In the next couple of weeks, Muriel became less and less anxious about being perfect and allowed herself time off—for example, to have a nap—rather than pushing herself to be ever present and always "on top of my game."

Equally important, *good enough* stops you from competing with other parents. Rachel, who had given up her career to focus on her child, found that she transferred her natural competitiveness from her work to her son. "It was like the mothers at playgroup were all engaged in some kind of arms race," she described. "It wasn't just whose child reached all the landmark events first. If one of us started something like baby yoga, it suddenly became necessary for everyone else to go or in some way we'd be 'neglecting' our babies. When I opted out and start laughing at how anxious they all became, I not only relaxed and started really enjoying my son, I also had funny anecdotes to share with my husband, David."

Returning to Amanda, what had been the effect on her daughter of aiming to be the perfect mother (and compensating for the lack of siblings) rather than merely good enough? "Yesterday, when we had the other children over to play," she replied, "my daughter was bossing everybody around, even though she's only three and one of her playmates was nine years old. If they weren't doing what she wanted, she'd send them to the 'thinking corner,' which is where I send her when she misbehaves." A worried tone entered Amanda's voice. "I'm also at risk of turning our daughter into a very unpleasant person because she'll expect to always be the center of attention."

Thus, combining my two revolutionary ideas—*Put your partner first* and *Be a good enough parent*—is best for your marriage *and* your children. I know this takes a bit of getting used to, so don't worry. I will return to these two central themes and explore them in each chapter.

There is a third idea that runs through this book, but I wouldn't describe it as revolutionary. In fact, most people would accept it, but some parents lose sight of it during the first five years of their child's life.

You have needs, too.

Unfortunately, in the rush to be perfect parents, the easiest person to neglect is yourself. If you do stop and think, *What about me?*, it's hard not to feel guilty or even think you're a bad parent, because there is a trusting, beautiful baby whose immediate need for food, nurturing, and protection must trump your selfish needs. By the time you reach the end of this book, I hope you will have stopped thinking in such black-and-white terms and realize that completely burying your needs only brings on long-term problems—not just for your personal welfare but, crucially, for your marriage, too.

What Are Your Priorities?

This exercise is about taking stock of your priorities and understanding where, on an everyday basis, you rank each of your responsibilities. The exercise is best done as a couple but can also be completed alone.

1. Look at the following list of priorities, which I use with my clients, and check that nothing important in your life is missing. If there is, please add it to the list.

Self	Partner	Children
Work	Friends	Parents
Siblings	Hobbies	Fitness and health
Fun	Home	Pets
Status	Personal development	
Sex	Intellectual nourishment	

2. Make up a series of cards, one for your partner and one for yourself. Write each item of your list on one card.

3. Independently of each other, you and your partner should put your own set of cards in order from most important to least important. Let me stress that there are no right or wrong answers. It is a matter of opinion and personal choice.

4. When you've finished ranking your everyday priorities, explain the reasoning behind your choices to your partner.

5. Listen while your partner takes you through his or her priorities.

6. Discuss each other's rankings and whether they were a surprise or what you expected.

What Happens When You Put the Children First?

At this point, I don't expect you to have accepted my idea that children come second, especially since I haven't yet explained how this translates into everyday life. So don't worry if you've made the children your number one priority. Most marriages will survive this choice, especially if both partners agree and find ways to mitigate the effects on their relationship. I hope that the previous exercise started this discussion. Unfortunately, most couples never talk about their priorities and blindly fall into one or more of the following five common traps: taking each other for granted, fusing your personal interests with your children's interests, developing a midlife crisis, experiencing a lack of sexual intimacy, and becoming vulnerable to an affair.

Taking Each Other for Granted

Christine and Mark had been married for fifteen years and had three children. Although they both worked in London, they had moved to the countryside because they thought it was best for their children. "In our previous house, they would run out the back door and hit the garden wall in about five steps," explained Christine. "We wanted space for them to play and have a carefree time, climb trees, and be able to ride their bikes without the risk of being mown down by the traffic." Unfortunately, it meant at least a two-hour commute in the morning and the evening for Mark and only a marginally shorter one three days a week for Christine. Worse still, the logistics of getting the children anywhere meant that Christine had to hold huge amounts of information in her head at any one time.

"Our youngest will be going swimming, which is twenty-five minutes away, and the middle one will need new shoes, and the eldest will have a piano lesson," she recited. "I don't think Mark understands just how tough it can be running a family. All it takes is for him to be half an hour late coming home or for the dog to be sick and have to go to the vet, and all the complicated arrangements come tumbling down."

Mark retorted, "I don't think Christine understands the pressure of getting up each morning at six, entertaining clients, and getting the last train home. Sometimes I don't get into bed until two in the morning."

Each of them felt exhausted and taken for granted. I had a picture of them living life on 98 percent capacity, so that even the smallest problem could send them into a spiral of resentment. When I did the priorities exercise with them, Christine put children first, then work, and then home. She put Mark fourth, fun fifth, and self at ten. When Mark looked at her priorities, he was surprised that he wasn't a lot lower.

"I do consider you," Christine explained, "but maybe you don't notice it. If there are two shitty jobs to be done, I always take the worst one myself— like going to the supermarket for the weekly food shopping—while you stay home and look after the kids."

I could understand how Mark might not have noticed this type of consideration or felt particularly cherished.

Meanwhile, Mark had made work his number-one priority, followed by home, children, partner, status, and self. When Christine looked at the rankings, she was surprised that self was not higher.

"I don't really get much pleasure out of my work," Mark explained. "It pays the bills, and of course I went after a promotion, because I thought it would give the children a better future—certainly if we're going to send them to the best schools—but it doesn't feed me. It's not me. I do it for you and the children."

Once again, I could understand that Mark's sacrifice, the long commute, going for extra responsibility, and the stress was more for the money than because he was passionately interested in his work. It must have been tough spending so many hours doing something that did not inspire him.

However, I could equally understand how this kind of caring did not make Christine feel particularly cherished, either.

During the next few months, I worked on their communication skills and helped them find more visible ways of showing that they cared about each other. For example, Mark offered to stay home and deal with a particularly difficult child-care problem during the school holidays, and Christine organized a weekend away, for just the two of them, in Paris. When I repeated the priorities exercise with them, the situation had begun to change. Christine put self third and personal development fourth. Mark put children first, partner second, and work third. Self and status had dropped dramatically.

Fusing Your Personal Interests with Your Children's Interests

There is no right or wrong place to put yourself on your list of priorities, although I am concerned if someone puts it fifth or lower. At that point, a subtle but deadly phenomenon kicks in. If you consider yourself a low priority, you will find it hard to ask for what you need, whether it is something practical ("Please fix my computer; it seems to have a bug in it") or something emotional ("I really need a hug and a back rub"). However, it is very difficult to live without care, consideration, and the feeling of being appreciated.

> *It is very difficult to live without care, consideration, and the feeling of being appreciated.*

So what do people do? This happens entirely unconsciously, but they ally themselves closely with something that does come higher up on their partners' priorities: the children. Instead of asking for something for themselves, which they expect to be refused, they ask for something for the children that also fulfills some of their needs. For example, Amanda's husband requested time as a family (without other people's children) rather than couple time (what he really wanted). Christine was pleased that Mark offered help with child care (because it made her life easier), but what she really needed was a spontaneous gesture that would make her feel special (for example, Mark turning up at her workplace and taking her out for lunch).

Not only does fusing your interests with those of your children mean that you get only some of your needs met, you also risk your partner misunderstanding your request and rejecting it. For example, Amanda could easily respond to her husband by saying, "It's important for our daughter's development to mix more with children her own age." He would have been more likely to succeed if he'd been direct: "I think it's really important for our marriage for just the two of us to have a night out."

Ciara and Thierry, in their late thirties, had two children under five and came into counseling because of arguments that were never resolved. Ciara felt particularly resentful because Thierry, a freelance consultant, had gone away on a job just two months after their youngest child was born.

"But you didn't tell me not to go," said Thierry angrily.

"I shouldn't have to tell you," Ciara retorted.

I had a very clear idea of how their fights escalated at home. "How would Thierry know that you wanted him to stay?" I asked Ciara.

"I explained how our eldest needed his dad because he was unsettled by the new arrival," she replied, "and I explained how difficult it is to breastfeed a baby while a toddler is trying to get your attention."

"But you had your mother staying," Thierry noted, "so she could help. It was not like you were all alone."

"You know how she bosses, how she takes over," Ciara insisted. "I'll turn around and she'll be going through the cupboards, throwing away everything that's past its sell-by date."

"What would happen," I asked, "if you'd just said, 'I'm lonely, frightened, and worried about whether I can cope, and I need your support and love'?"

At this point, Ciara burst into tears. When she stopped crying, she explained that she didn't dare risk being rejected and that she secretly feared that Thierry didn't truly love her. He was able to reassure her, and the counseling turned a corner.

However, until we could uncouple her interests and the children's interests, it was difficult to have an honest and open discussion.

Developing a Midlife Crisis

The next trap for couples who put their children first is closely related to the previous one. If you fuse your interests with your children's, you are also likely to encourage or expect your partner to do the same. And here is the dangerous twist: you can use that love for the kids to control him or her and get your own way—but without appearing to be doing that.

Here's how it works. A wife will say, "You don't want to play golf now that you're a father" or "You've got to stop going out with the guys, because you've got responsibilities." Of course, she is half right. He does want to be with his kids. She does need extra help. However, instead of putting all the issues up front—"I don't like your friends" or "Four hours is a big chunk of time on the weekend"—where they can be debated, negotiated, and resolved through compromise, the conversation is closed down by implying that anything else would mean "You don't love me and the kids" or "You're a part-time dad."

Obviously, it's not a game that just women play; men are equally adept. For example, "Do you really want to retrain? Because all that extra studying will mean you've got less time for the kids" or "Our youngest is having a bad time at school, so I don't think now is a good time for you to go away for the weekend." And how do you challenge such a reasonable approach, especially if you're putting your children first and your own interests sixth or seventh? Nobody wants to feel like a bad mother or father, so parents are easily manipulated into burying their needs.

Perhaps you're thinking, *What's wrong with being altruistic and thinking of others?* My answer is nothing, if that's your choice. By all means put the children first. But I would question whether you have the right to make that choice for your partner. Whatever the rights and wrongs, on a short-term basis there isn't a major problem, especially when the children are small and really do need a lot of care. However, it can quite easily become a habit, and before you know it, five, ten, or fifteen years have passed.

One morning you wake up and think, *There's got to be more to life than this.* Perhaps your partner's father has died and your partner is reminded that we have only a fixed time on this planet. Maybe both of you have reached forty; your life is possibly, or at least nearly, half over, and you're thinking about what comes next. Obviously, these are perfectly natural feelings. It can be really healthy to take stock from time to time, but if you've buried your needs, if even questioning the supremacy of your children is forbidden, what should be a midlife adjustment quickly turns into a midlife crisis.

"We got together when my husband was seventeen and I was twenty-two," Vicky wrote to my website. "After five years, we moved in together and shortly afterward got married and had two boys, who are now ages six and five. He said that he felt like in the blink of an eye, it was seventeen years later and he didn't know what he'd done with his life. It sounded like a typical midlife crisis to me—his life had gotten humdrum, work had become particularly pressured (and in a way made him powerless), and he seemed to blame me for his lot in life. He thinks that he made all these sacrifices for me, but I gave up a lot for him, too—I just wasn't as audible about it, nor was I keeping score. I gave up on the notion of pursuing the career I had always wanted—for him—mainly because it would have meant that I had to give up my role as breadwinner and go to college. The things he 'gave up' for me were things like going to meat-only restaurants without good vegetarian options for me. It's not like he still doesn't get to eat meat."

In the next part of the e-mail, Vicky described how her husband prioritized communicating with the children over talking to her.

"Just before he moved out, he started to really mess with me. Even on the day we'd agreed was his moving-out day, he decided to move it back a week, saying that he'd told the boys that he'd stay for the week—but he hadn't told me! I know that he is in turmoil, but he's turned into someone else I don't recognize."

I can quite believe that Vicky's husband seemed like a stranger, but after years of putting the children first and downgrading his own needs, he imploded and started an affair. I have met many men and plenty of women who, after years of thinking of others, felt entitled to put themselves first for once. So although it seems admirable to put your children first, it can rebound with the most extraordinary acts of selfishness.

Experiencing a Lack of Sexual Intimacy

Jack and Layla, both in their early forties, agreed on one thing: "The children are the center of our lives." After one session, Jack insisted on showing me a photo on his phone of his two sons climbing all over him. It was the first time in almost thirty years of counseling that I'd seen a picture of a client's children. Although it was only a snapshot, probably taken on a vacation after a dip in the pool, it could have been an advertisement for fatherhood from a magazine. Everybody was laughing and jostling for position, and I could picture Layla taking the shot and smiling. There was just one problem with this happy family: Jack and Layla had had sex on only a handful of occasions since their youngest son had been born—six years ago.

"I had a difficult birth and complications," Layla explained. "I was breast-feeding and not getting enough sleep, and when I look back, I probably had postpartum depression, too."

"I told you as much at the time," Jack interjected.

"So starting sex was the last thing on my mind, I suppose," said Layla.

Although I could understand the initial problem, we were talking about six years later!

"I had two small children hanging on me," Layla continued. "I didn't want Jack mauling me too."

"Motherhood is very physical," I reflected, "feeding babies, washing them, changing their diapers—with lots of skin-to-skin contact. You can almost get all your needs for intimacy met."

Obviously, there's nothing wrong with enjoying cuddles with your kids, but it can become a way of compensating or feeling less alone when the central relationship between husband and wife is not being fed. Unfortunately, instead of talking about their lack of sexual intimacy—and getting help earlier—Jack and Layla had been able to hide behind being "great parents" and "doing what's best for the kids." Consequently, months and then years had gone by.

By the time I met them, Jack had told Layla, "I love you, but I'm not *in* love with you," and Layla was furious because she suspected that Jack was having affairs while off on business trips—something that he strenuously denied.

They reminded me of another client, Lucy, a thirtysomething single woman whose parents had split up when she was six years old. "Years later, when I had a long chat with my father," she told me, "he admitted, 'I fell out of love with my wife and in love with my daughter.'" Is this what had happened to Jack and Layla?

Becoming Vulnerable to an Affair

Martin and Sarah, both forty-three with three children under twelve, came into counseling after Martin discovered some intimate texts on Sarah's phone from a contractor who had been helping them remodel their house. Although the affair had not gone further than kissing and cuddling, Sarah had fallen deeply in love with the other man. She wanted to save her marriage but was not certain if she could get back her feelings for Martin.

"I'd felt lonely and undervalued for a long time," Sarah explained, "and this man listened. He seemed genuinely interested in what I had to say. It wasn't just that we talked; we shared similar values and a friendship together." Over the next few weeks, I helped Martin deal with his panic, stop pressuring Sarah for reassurance, and tackle the everyday issues between them rather than sweeping them under the carpet.

When I did the priorities exercise with them, Martin placed self first, status second, children third, and partner fourth. In contrast, Sarah put children first and partner second but self seventh and fun eleventh. It was therefore not surprising that she had felt so unhappy.

"I was like an alcoholic desperate for a drink," Sarah stated, "or in my case, love, affection, and a little attention. But I was fearful that if I had even a drop, I would never be able to quench my thirst."

"And if I was brutally honest with myself," Martin added, "I was aware that Sarah was miserable, but I thought there was nothing I could do about it, so I told myself, selfishly, 'Get on with it, because I'm not going to let you drag me down with you,' and I got on with my life."

Very few people go looking for affairs, but if they feel unappreciated and not valued at home—or (like Sarah) have completely neglected their own needs—they become vulnerable to the attention of other people. "It was almost like this man finding me special allowed me to accept that I might be someone more than a wife and a mother," Sarah said. "I had needs, and that was okay."

> Very few people go looking for affairs, but if they feel unappreciated and not valued at home—or have completely neglected their own needs—they become vulnerable to the attention of other people.

In most cases, affairs start innocently enough: through a simple working relationship or by going on the Internet to relax and forget everyday troubles. Someone who feels cherished and a priority at home will find it easy to back off before any harm is done. However, if you feel that your partner routinely puts you last, it is not surprising that a "special" friendship becomes so important so quickly and causes so much pain.

How Strong Is Your Marriage Right Now?

It is difficult to balance being a parent and a partner, especially if you're dealing with a multitude of other pressures. To get a sense of how resilient your marriage might be and how well you deal with conflict, I've devised a test and some tailor-made advice for your situation.

1. Which of the following statements describe your relationship? Check off as many as apply.

   a. We were childhood sweethearts and have had no other serious relationships.
   b. One of our parents died in the last twelve months.
   c. One of us is dreading or recently experienced a fortieth birthday.
   d. One of us travels a lot for work involving overnight stays.
   e. One of us has a lot of extra stress at the moment.
   f. We're moving or are about to move.
   g. There's an elderly relative who requires help.
   h. We have two children under five.

2. Which of the following statements are true? Check off as many as apply.

a. I can name at least five of my partner's friends.
b. I can name five or more people at my partner's place of work (or, if fewer than five coworkers, name all of them).
c. I can explain my partner's life philosophy.
d. We have talked in the last twelve months about our dreams for the future.
e. I can name someone who has irritated my partner recently (besides me!).
f. I can name three of my partner's favorite TV shows.
g. We both know the names of all of our children's current best friends.
h. My partner knows what's been worrying me lately.

3. If you already have children, which of the following best describes your attitude to free time? (If you're expecting or don't have children yet, please skip this question.)

a. We make certain that we have nights out as partners and weekends away on our own.
b. We might aim to go out without the kids, but it's not often practical or affordable.
c. We'd rather go out as a family, and it feels strange on the rare occasions when it's just the two of us.
d. We both work and alternate child care. Generally, we're too tired to do anything beyond ordering take-out food and watching a movie.

4. At a party, an attractive stranger shows a lot of interest in you. Nothing happens beyond sharing a laugh and a joke, but you have a really good time. On the way home, your partner asks about it. How do you reply?

a. Tell the truth: "I enjoyed the attention because it made me feel special."

b. Make a sharp comment: "It's been a long time since you've noticed me like that."
c. Deny everything: "Don't be so stupid. You're imagining it."
d. Go on the attack: "That was nothing compared to how you leer at everybody."

5. How often does your partner let you know how much he or she appreciates you by saying "thank you" or "I love you" or by giving you a compliment?

a. I'm sure he or she means to do it, but it gets lost in the hurly-burly of day-to-day living.
b. All the time.
c. Only when he or she is after something or trying to sweet-talk me after a fight.
d. On special occasions, when I've made a special effort, or when I've dropped pointed hints.

6. When there is a major dispute between the two of you, how is it most likely to be resolved?

a. I will back down and keep the peace.
b. My partner will huff and puff but will generally accept when I have the stronger case.
c. We talk it through, and although it takes time, we find a compromise.
d. It doesn't generally get resolved, and we have several subjects we avoid.

7. When your partner does something irritating, like forgetting to pick up something on his or her way home or make an important phone call, what do you think?

    a. Get your act together.

    b. Why did I trust you? I should have done it myself.

    c. If you really loved me, I wouldn't be such a low priority.

    d. You're really busy and have a lot on your mind.

8. If your partner was being honest, which of the following statements would best describe how he or she often feels?

    a. Sometimes I just can't win.

    b. Deep down, I know I'm appreciated, but it would be nice to hear it more often.

    c. I feel supported, loved, and cherished.

    d. I sometimes feel like sex is rationed out and used as a reward for good behavior.

9. Which of the following statements best describes how you would rate the level of intimacy in your relationship?

    a. To be honest, nothing much would happen if one of us didn't take the initiative.

    b. There's something in bed that I'd really like to do, but my partner is not interested.

    c. I feel cherished and loved the majority of the time.

    d. We should do more casual touching outside the bedroom, like cuddling on the sofa or holding hands.

10. What happens when there is an important decision to be made about the children's welfare, such as concerning school or discipline?

    a. One of us does the necessary research but consults the other before making a decision.

    b. We're a team, and everything is done jointly.

   c. The parent who is on the spot or who knows most
      about the topic makes the call.
   d. There's a lot of arguing and resentment.

11. When your partner is stressed out, how does he or
    she deal with it?

   a. Unloads it on friends or family.
   b. Bottles everything up.
   c. Talks it over with me.
   d. Forgets by having a drink, going for a run, playing a
      computer game, eating, or engaging in some other
      distraction.

12. How has your relationship been in the past six months?

   a. We've been really close.
   b. We've had the usual ups and downs.
   c. We've been incredibly busy. We've barely had time to
      talk beyond functional conversations about running
      the house or what time to pick up the kids.
   d. Difficult. One of us has been prickly, dismissive,
      or out more than usual.

Score Your Results

Use the following guide to determine your score:

1. Score 2 points for each description that you checked off. If
   b, c, d, or e applied to you and your partner, score 4 points.
   If none of the descriptions fit your relationship, score 0.

2. Subtract 1 point for every statement you agree with. If none
   of them are applicable, add 2 points.

3. a. 1   b. 2   c. 4   d. 3

4. a. 1   b. 2   c. 3   d. 4

5. a. 2   b. 1   c. 4   d. 3

6. a. 3   b. 2   c. 1   d. 4

7. a. 3   b. 2   c. 4   d. 1

8. a. 4   b. 2   c. 1   d. 3

9. a. 3   b. 2   c. 1   d. 3

10. a. 2   b. 1   c. 3   d. 4

11. a. 2   b. 3   c. 1   d. 4

12. a. 1   b. 2   c. 3   d. 4

Add up your points to discover the state of your relationship, but read all the categories below to put your relationship in context.

Up to 15: High Resilience

Congratulations, your relationship is in great shape! Although you have your fair share of stress and the problems that life throws at you, you're involved in each other's lives, understand each other's problems, and work as a team. Be aware that certain circumstances—like two children under five or approaching forty and wondering about the paths not taken—can put a marriage under extra strain. If that's the case, it is important to communicate clearly and effectively. Fortunately, this book will provide an opportunity to improve your skills and add new ones to your repertoire.

16 to 28: Good Resilience

This score is like going to the doctor and being told everything is fine. However, there's *fine* in the sense of "Go home and don't worry about a thing" and *fine* in the sense of "Let's keep an eye on things to be on the safe side." Your relationship falls into the second category. You've got good communication skills, but they might need a little fine-tuning.

It is particularly important to ask rather than assume, especially if you have lived with your partner for a long time or you were childhood sweethearts. Under these circumstances, it is easy to imagine that you *know* what he or she is thinking or why he or she has done something. That's fine when you're relaxed and in a good mood, because those interpretations are largely positive. For example, "He didn't mean to upset me." However, when you're stressed and fed up, your interpretations can easily become negative. For example, "She did that on purpose to upset me." Before you leap to conclusions, ask your partner, "Why did you . . . ?" or "Are you angry with me?" It could be that your partner is just annoyed or maybe preoccupied with something else.

29 to 39: Okay Resilience

I'm pleased that you've bought this book, because it can have a big effect on your relationship. When you have children, and thus more demands on your time and energy, it's important to have good communication skills in order to deal with the ups and downs. However, you probably believe that connection, chemistry, and really loving each other guarantee a happy relationship and that with those elements in the bag, you can coast along and concentrate on more immediate concerns like getting the youngest to sleep, arranging a playdate for your eldest, and checking on supper.

Nevertheless, a relationship is a living thing and needs tending. Think of a potted plant. It's fine if you don't water it for a while, but pretty soon it will begin to wilt. If you don't keep an eye on it, it can develop a nasty fungal infection. Fortunately, I have lots of ideas for tending your relationship. Unfortunately, you're likely to be resistant to my ideas, especially the notion that children should come second, because you think that if your partner loves you, he or she should understand.

It's words like *should* and *must* that really drive anger and turn a minor spat into a full-blown fight. Who says, for example, that a man *should* fix things around the house or that a woman *should* have the house clean when her husband comes home? The government? The pope? All right-thinking people? What you really mean is "*I* think . . ." or "My parents always did ____, therefore I believe ____" (fill in the blanks with your particular *shoulds*). If you start your sentences with "I think," you and your partner can discuss the pros and cons and probably find an amicable solution. In sharp contrast, *should* makes you right and your partner wrong (and both of you angry).

40 or Higher: In Danger of Being Overwhelmed

Your relationship is suffering from one or more of these toxic problems: an inability to communicate, a general dissatisfaction with each other, or a strategy of putting your heads in the sand. You might hope for the best and tell yourself that it will get better when X or Y happens, but your partner could easily be slipping into depression or inappropriate coping strategies—or perhaps it's you who's at the end of your rope.

If a problem seems insoluble, most people come up with only two possible ways forward: to walk away (which seems drastic) or to put their heads down and soldier on (which keeps the peace but resolves nothing). If you, your partner, or both of you have chosen the second option, then the only way to cope with the daily stress of work, the demands of a small baby, financial worries, or the feeling of being unloved is to switch off (and risk becoming clinically depressed) or blank out your feelings and self-medicate with alcohol, fattening food, pornography, or maybe the attention of someone else.

I know the situation looks bleak, but let's focus on the positives. You have recognized that your relationship isn't working, and buying this book is proof that you want to do something about it. That's not only brilliant, it's also the first step toward changing. So what should you do next?

If you're the one who is feeling overwhelmed, anxious, or depressed, please speak to your doctor or other health provider. My guess is that you're a perfectionist and that asking for help is hard, because it means admitting that you're not a perfect parent. I hope you have begun to consider the idea of *good enough* and imagine what it might mean for you.

If your partner is the one who is self-medicating or you suspect him or her of an inappropriate relationship, it is important to tackle the issue calmly rather than accusing. Talk about what has been going wrong in your relationship and what you'd like to change, and then bring up your concerns about his or her behavior. Finally, discuss how to make things better, rather than issuing ultimatums, which will only make things worse. (For the issue of infidelity, see my book *How Can I Ever Trust You Again?*)

How to Put Your Partner First

At the end of each chapter, I give practical ways of showing your partner that he or she is a priority in your life and of strengthening your relationship. I call this chapter's first tip *Guarding comings and goings*.

Returning to Christine and Mark, who had taken each other for granted: Toward the end of our counseling, I repeated the priorities exercise, and they both put partner first, children second, fun third, and self fourth. Next we had to change these from mere aspirations into day-to-day behavior.

"Who do you speak to first when you get home?" I asked Mark. "Christine or the kids?"

"The children are normally in bed," he replied, "but if they're not, my eldest daughter opens the door because Christine is bathing the younger kids."

"I know it's tough," I said, "because she probably wants you to 'just look at this,' but what would happen if you said, 'In a minute, I've just got to say hello to Mom' and went to find Christine, say hello, give her a kiss, and then attend to your daughter?"

"It would make a powerful statement," Mark admitted.

"We already don't let them interrupt us when we're chatting," Christine added. "I'll say, 'Hang on a second, I'm talking to Dad.'" (I thought this was a brilliant idea, so I'm passing it on to you.)

How does *Guarding comings and goings* work in practice? If your partner is already home when you get there, go immediately to where he or she is and give him or her a kiss (rather than settling down for a drink in front of the TV or fixing something for your son or daughter). If your partner is with the children, it is doubly important to greet him or her first. I know your children will be excited to see you, and your partner will be busy doing stuff, but getting off to a good start sets up an evening of cooperation and pleasure in each other's company, rather than your partner feeling like part of the furniture.

Guarding comings and goings is particularly important when you have a baby. It is very easy to greet or tickle your son or daughter under the chin, because babies are designed to bring out our protective instincts and to encourage us to pick them up—and thereby completely ignore the other person holding him or her! For the first few days, it takes a bit of willpower to greet your partner first and *then* cuddle the baby, but soon it'll become second nature.

If you're the person already at home, I'm not asking you to drop everything and go to the door—although that would be nice. (I know it's not always practical, though, because you're busy cooking, feeding the children, or supervising something potentially dangerous.) However, you can stop what you're doing for a second to give your partner a kiss and maybe a quick hug. You might also like to exchange the headlines of your news about what happened that day.

Guarding your goings is as important as guarding your comings. When you leave the house, give your partner a kiss and, if it's not obvious, tell him or her where you're going and when you'll be back. You might like to throw in a compliment like "I love you," "Can't wait to get back," or "You smell nice." If you just disappear, even for ten minutes, without saying good-bye, it sends the message that your partner is not important or that you don't see the two of you as a team. After all, if you're going to a store, you could pick up something your partner or someone else in the family needs, too.

My second tip takes the concept of guarding one stage further: *Put a lock on your bedroom door.* This is seldom a popular idea. Somehow parents think they have to be 100 percent available, all the time, whatever the circumstances.

> Put a lock on your bedroom door. *This is seldom a popular idea. Somehow parents think they have to be 100 percent available, all the time, whatever the circumstances.*

"What if the children need us?" they ask.

"If there is an emergency, your children can knock or shout '*Fire!*'" I always reply.

A locked door sends an important message. It will make your children think twice before demanding attention and help them realize that even parents need a private space. As my clients who have teenagers admit, even though they would never dream of entering their sons' or daughters' rooms without knocking, they allow their children to just wander into *their* bedroom whenever they wish.

If you've done the priorities exercise in this chapter, you have already started on my third tip for putting your partner first: *Discuss your priorities.* Nobody minds temporarily dropping on the list if there is an emergency— for example, your mother is in the hospital and needs extra support. But your partner needs reassurance that it won't last forever and needs to feel able to discuss the day-to-day implications. Most important, he or she needs not to fear negative consequences from saying, "What about me?"

So set aside a regular time to talk to each other—such as over your evening meal, or switch off the TV or computer for fifteen minutes after the children have gone to bed—and explain the current demands on your time. Once again, I'd like you to guard this time to unwind together and not let it get trumped by work demands or a pressing need to empty the dryer. Time together says, "You're important to me; I'm interested in what's happening in your life, and I want to share what's going on in mine."

Summary

When you first said "I love you" to your partner, you never imagined that it could be followed by "but." When you walked up the aisle, you never thought you would let your relationship drift. Of course children are wonderful and give your life shape and meaning. Unfortunately, it is easy to get carried away, put your children first, and run yourself ragged trying to be perfect parents. Fortunately, you don't need to be perfect—just good enough. And the good news is that's better for your children as well as your marriage.

> When you first said "I love you" to your partner, you never imagined that it could be followed by "but."

I know it is tough being a parent, feeling torn in two and having little spare time. That's why I have condensed my advice into ten golden rules (listed at the end of the book) and designed some simple exercises to help. However, it is important that you stop taking each other for granted and start nurturing your love for each other again. Your children's, your partner's and your own happiness are all at stake.

2

How Did We Get Here?

"Having our daughters has been one of the best experiences of my life," said Blake, thirty-seven, whose youngest was just three months old when he started couples counseling with his wife Emily. "I'd never known unconditional love before. If anybody asked, I'd definitely recommend starting a family, but I'd warn them that they'd better have a rock-solid relationship first." It is great advice, and in an ideal world, we would all be sure of our partners, our relationships, and ourselves. Unfortunately, we don't live in an ideal world, and most people go into parenthood hoping for the best, worried about what sort of parent their partners will be, or secretly frightened that they won't measure up themselves.

What do you need for a rock-solid relationship? Most people think the answer is love: if you *truly* love each other, you can withstand any pressures, from outside or within. I would certainly agree, but only up to a point.

What makes the difference between growing closer and being split apart during the years you're raising children is *good communication*. That's why I have devoted this chapter to understanding how, despite the best intentions, things can go wrong; this is a theme I will return to throughout the book.

When Is the Right Time to Have Children?

The debate in the media and in parenting forums is normally about whether it is best to have your children when you are younger (when you have more energy and are more flexible) or when you are older (when you have more self-knowledge and are better established). However, I think this overlooks the most important element: How long have you and your partner been together? Love changes over time and goes through six distinct stages: blending, nesting, self-affirming, collaborating, adapting, and renewing. These stages, each of which has its own particular joys and challenges, will help you understand how minor problems can escalate into major ones and why you might have stopped prioritizing your partner.

Blending: The First Six to Eighteen Months

Falling in love is a magical experience. It is almost like walking on air, and you spend half of your time sighing or thinking about your beloved. I call this stage *blending* because you want nothing more than to be together. When that's not possible, you're either talking about your beloved (until your friends want to throw things) or thinking about this person, imagining, for example, what he or she would think of the TV program you're watching. The intense feelings are so different from the everyday love of a couple that has been together longer—partners who can't afford to spend every waking minute thinking about each other—that psychologists have coined a specific word for it: *limerence*.

The significance of the influence of limerence is that it emphasizes what is truly admirable about the other person ("He really wants to help me reach my potential" or "She wants to make me happy") and downgrades what might be a problem. For example, it doesn't matter that he slurps his tea ("because it's really cute") or that she is not very confident ("because I can boost her self-esteem"). In contrast, for a settled couple, making noises while drinking is irritating or disgusting, and it can be exhausting to always be giving compliments and feeling terrified of saying anything negative in case it is heard as criticism.

During the blending stage, the partners accentuate their similarities and minimize their differences so that the two individuals can merge into a couple. It is a heady time, because sex is easy and plentiful and each partner feels completely understood. No wonder songwriters and poets talk about the blindness, madness, and ecstasy of falling in love: "I only have eyes for you," or "Can't take my eyes off you," and "All you need is love."

Unfortunately, limerence does not last for ever. In my experience, it lasts somewhere between six months and three years. It is interesting to note, in this regard, that neuroscientists have found that the chemicals associated with bonding—dopamine, oxytocin, and phenyl ethylamine—are at their height for eighteen months to three years.

Problem

When Natasha, thirty-eight, arrived in my counseling room, she was almost seven months pregnant and extremely angry. Her partner, Josh, thirty-two, was sheepish and looked ready to head out the door at any moment.

"I'm just not getting any support from Josh," Natasha complained. "I know he has to work hard, and it is difficult to coordinate when we can talk."

"I'm working shifts in India," Josh explained, "and when I finish, it's the middle of the night in the UK. So I go out for a couple of drinks to unwind with my friends, so by the time Natasha calls, I'm merry, and she either gets angry or I'm tired and don't want to hear her moan."

"It's hard being apart," Natasha confessed. "I get tearful. My back hurts. I feel very alone."

Natasha and Josh had been a couple for eighteen intense and exciting months, flying back and forth between Europe and Asia. Under the influence of limerence, overcoming the obstacles of different continents and time zones had been part of the attraction. However, as the peak of the passion had begun to wear off, everyday realities were becoming more and more of a problem.

In addition, I wondered whether the baby had been planned.

"We both wanted this baby," said Natasha firmly.

"Sure." Josh shifted in his seat.

"We had talked about having children," Natasha cut in before Josh could say anything more.

Under the influence of limerence, people say what their partners want to hear, such as "Of course I want children" when what they really mean is "I'd like to have children *someday*." It doesn't necessarily mean that that day has arrived yet.

Natasha and Josh had indeed "talked," but in very much the same way that they had discussed living in the same country, going backpacking in the Andes, and renovating a villa in Tuscany. In the heady days of blending, everything is possible, reality has not yet intruded to spoil the fantasy, and partners want to please each other. So Natasha did not spell out that she was about to turn forty and needed to get pregnant sooner rather than later. Josh did not explain that forging a career was his number one priority and that he would need to be based abroad, at least for the next three years.

There is a third way that limerence and the blending stage can set up problems for the future. At the very beginning of a relationship, an argument feels like the end of the world, because a new couple has no experience of falling out and making up. So the partners tend to bury their issues and leap into bed instead. Not only was this option not available to Natasha and Josh, because they spent so much time apart, but their differences were also too great to overcome with a kiss and a cuddle (however passionate).

Turning It Around

I don't want to knock limerence, because it helps us overcome our fear of getting hurt and allows us to throw our lot in with people who are, after all, complete strangers. Our desire to be with our partners can make us try out new hobbies or experiences and find enduring interests. Love can also help surmount what seem like impossible odds. However, you should take promises made during this heady phase with a grain of salt—much as you would check out whether someone really meant something said under the influence of alcohol. So if you have a contentious topic, and your understanding of your partner's views is based on conversations during blending, it is best to revisit it. It is certainly hard to hear the caveats that might have been added, but it's better to have the issues out in the open. Later in the chapter, I will explain how to resolve any differences.

Nesting: A Year and a Half to the Third Year

When partners decide to move in together, their home becomes an expression of their love for each other. Whereas blending capitalized on the attraction and minimized the differences, *nesting*, or living together full-time, brings issues to the surface, and a couple will begin to risk arguing over small and manageable questions, like what color to paint the bedroom or the best way to grout tiles. Desire is reduced to a more manageable level, rather than making love two or three times a day.

However, limerence has not disappeared completely, and it can help smooth over the transition out of blending—especially as friends and family become more important again and familiarity can breed annoyance. Long-term tracking by the University of Texas found that a courtship of eighteen months to three years is the optimum preparation for a happy marriage.

Problem

"It seemed the most natural next step to move in together," explained Justine, thirty-six. "I spent most weekends and several nights during the week at Murray's flat, and it was much more convenient for work than mine. So it would have happened anyway, but my getting pregnant just moved it up."

However, Justine and Murray had been dating for only eleven months when they "officially" started to live together. Almost immediately, a few cracks began to show in their relationship.

"I found that Justine did not respect my standards," said Murray, forty-one. "I know I'm set in my ways, and it's not like Justine is particularly untidy, it's just everything has its place and I like structure and order. I can't relax otherwise."

"And I respected that when we were just seeing each other," Justine stated. This is typical of blending, because partners try to appear as similar as possible. "However, it's my home now, too, and I need to relax. I can't if you're hovering, about to take my coffee cup away before I've finished."

After the initial excitement of the birth of their daughter had worn off, the cracks began to turn into chasms.

"Sometimes I worry that Murray doesn't want me and Chloe there." Justine had tears in her eyes. "I feel that we've upturned his nice orderly bachelor lifestyle."

"I gave up my study so we could turn it into a nursery," Murray interjected, "but that's not enough. I come home and find Chloe's stuff all over the house."

Unfortunately, the usual territorial issues—especially when one partner moves into the other's home—had been exacerbated by having a baby. The stakes had been raised, and Justine and Murray had still not learned to disagree, find a compromise, and move on. Instead Justine would back down or Murray would be resentful, and the next time they argued, all the old unresolved issues came back up again.

Turning It Around

Arguing is one of the most intimate things you can do with your partner. This is going to sound a little strange, but arguing shows that you care, instead of just sweeping the issue of contention under the carpet. There's another bonus to arguing:

> *Arguing is one of the most intimate things you can do with your partner.*

sorting everything out and overcoming a small but manageable amount of adversity can bring back a momentary flutter of limerence. For example, the woman smiles after an argument and it feels like the sun has come out again, or the man admits that he overreacted and it seems he does understand, after all. In many cases, all it takes to resolve a problem is to keep arguing a bit longer and resist the temptation to throw in cold cases—even if they seem like part of a pattern—because this will only make your partner more defensive and less likely to budge.

Self-Affirming: Third or Fourth Year

By the *self-affirming* stage, partners realize that they don't have to do everything together. After all, it doesn't take two people to go to the hardware store and buy a pack of nails. Whereas the emphasis was previously always on *we*, in this stage, each partner begins to remember that there is a *me*, too. So one partner can go off fishing for the day without the other feeling compelled to try it out or take a book to read by the lake. On another weekend, the other partner will sign up for a course, even though it will reduce the precious time they might otherwise have spent together.

Not only is it *natural* for individual habits, traits, and characteristics to reemerge, a relationship *needs* each partner's individuality to grow and develop. Otherwise, a couple will have only shared interests, like eating out or going to the movies—things they both enjoy but do not necessarily feel passionate about. If there is no room for private space or interests, one partner can end up feeling stifled or, even worse, controlled.

Problem

The self-affirming stage is the trickiest of all the stages of love. After being "everything" to each other, you might easily worry that you are falling out of love. (Indeed, one of the most common times that people say "I love you, but I'm not in love with you" is at three years, when limerence is definitely on the wane.) Lots of partners find it hard to balance the needs of the relationship with their individual needs. If you have low self-esteem, it is easy to see your partner's natural desire for personal time as a reflection on you (and become clingy or anxious) or as a threat to your relationship (and bury your personal needs or pretend they don't matter but end up secretly resenting your partner). It is not uncommon for a couple to have power struggles, some really nasty fights, and lots of long talks into the night to sort out a workable solution.

It should go without saying that this is probably the worst time to have a baby. Unfortunately, people are waiting longer to settle down. This means that lots of thirty-five-year-old (and older) couples feel the need to start having children almost immediately. So they find themselves struggling with self-affirming *and* baby issues at the same time.

"I really resented Matt doing anything out of the house," said Alice, thirty-seven. "I knew he had to go to work, but surely if he loved us, he wouldn't want to miss a moment more." Everything came to a head when

Matt's parents came to visit one Sunday, and, after cooing over his grand-child, Matt's father suggested that he take his son to a bar. "Matt just got his coat, as if it was the most natural thing in the world to go out for a drink while his wife and his mother cooked lunch. I wanted to scream, and I did when they had gone. How dare he!"

"It was just for forty minutes," Matt defended himself. "My dad and I haven't talked for ages. And if *you* cared so much about going for a drink, *I* would have looked after the baby while you and my mom went out."

"I thought we were going to do this as a team, equal partners," Alice protested.

It is not uncommon for issues about men's and women's roles to come to the forefront during the self-affirming stage, but these are particularly difficult if a couple has not yet begun to balance reasonable personal needs (like talking to your father without distraction) and couple needs (like your wife wanting support and to know that she is loved and cherished).

Turning It Around

In many ways, just knowing about the self-affirming stage—that it is a natural phase rather than something wrong with your relationship—can be immensely reassuring. It might be disappointing after the magic of limerence to realize that you are two different people with different strengths and interests. Fortunately, however, bringing up children requires complementary skills rather than just being carbon copies of each other.

Collaborating: The Fifth to Fourteenth Years

After the worry of blending (will your love be returned, or will an argument prove fatal?), the shock of nesting (when you have to accept that your partner is not perfect), and the stormy waters of self-affirming (and reasserting your individuality), you have really gotten to know each other. A couple can use the greater security within the relationship and the stronger individual sense of selves to launch successful projects. This is the *collaborating* stage. The projects can be something outside the relationship, like a new job or further education, but each partner brings the excitement, freshness, and new friends back home. More likely, a couple starts a new project together, like establishing a business, renovating a house, or traveling. The most common choice at the collaborating stage is, of course, having a baby. Whatever the choice, it will help to revitalize your relationship.

Problem

This is the best time to have a child. However, I sometimes see partners who have been together for five or more years but have gotten stuck in self-affirming rather than truly moving on to collaborating. Although they should have been ready for parenting, they were still struggling with getting the right balance between being an individual and half of a couple. Blake and Emily, mentioned at the beginning of this chapter, had lived together for nine years before starting their family. Blake was an artist, and although he had had some success, he was still struggling to get properly established.

"My painting is not just something important to me," he said, "it's how I see the world. Sometimes I struggle with being a father and a husband because it takes up so much of my time, energy, and thinking space that I should be channeling into my art. Don't get me wrong, because I love my daughters to bits, but I have to be honest: I need to focus on my career."

Meanwhile, Emily came from a family where her parents were always arguing and caught up in their own problems. "I was constantly trying to please my mother and father and keep the peace between them," she recalled. "When that didn't work, I started shoplifting to get some attention.

I truly believed that they must have adopted me, because I felt they didn't love me."

For Emily, the closeness of blending and subsuming her identity into being a couple had been completely intoxicating. However, she found it hard to express her needs during self-affirming. "I've never really stopped and thought what I want, just what would make Blake happy."

My job was to help them find a balance so that Emily could ask for what she needed and Blake could stop focusing only on the painting currently on his easel and see the bigger picture. In this way, they would truly start collaborating.

Turning It Around

Although it might be sad to give up some of your old, preparent ways, a relationship needs to grow and change, or it will stagnate and become boring. By this stage, you can think you know each other so well that communication has been condensed to shorthand. However, this can easily allow you to slip into assuming you know what your partner is thinking. So instead of taking something for granted, try asking.

Adapting: The Fifteenth to Twenty-Fourth Years

A couple in the *adapting* stage are busy adjusting to external changes rather than dealing with changes within the relationship. Demands from outside can include the parents getting older and needing more support, the upheaval of having a teenager in the house, or the onset of the "empty-nest syndrome," when the youngest child leaves home for college. Each partner has given up the fantasy of changing the other partner and thinks, *He will always be like this*

Once someone accepts who we are, we are more likely to bend and change.

or *Actually, the way she is is quite sweet.* Perversely, once someone accepts who we are, we are more likely to bend and change.

Problem

The empty-nest syndrome can be particularly difficult for parents who have prioritized the children, exhausted their relationship, and learned to relate to each other as coparents rather than as partners. Now they find it hard to relate as partners again.

Tracey and Gregory had been married for twenty years and had three children. The oldest had gone off to college, and Tracey could see the day coming when she would be needed less by the others. "I don't have a role anymore," she said worriedly. "I've spent years being a mom, and I don't resent that, but I'm beginning to wonder who I am. Sometimes, I feel I don't get any support from Gregory, who is either at work, dealing with work-related problems, or too tired to do anything. I hate to think what it will be like when it's just the two of us, because all the conversations now are either about the children or the business."

The problem had come to a head because Gregory also felt unsupported. "My mother died last year, after a long illness," he said, "and I spent much of the past year driving back and forth on the highway. My father is eighty, and he's finding it hard to manage on his own. He doesn't really cook, and when he has the slightest problem, he's on the phone to me."

"I did all the catering for your mother's funeral," countered Tracey. "I ran myself ragged."

"I know, and I'm grateful," Gregory responded, "but there were times when I really needed you—particularly toward the end. It was really tough sitting by my mother's deathbed. My father was in pieces."

"But it was our daughter's school play," Tracey reminded him.

Gregory sat there glumly, staring into space.

Turning It Around

When your partner is struggling to cope with a crisis, it is vital that you are 100 percent behind him or her, especially if you routinely put the children first. Otherwise, you are likely to prioritize the run-of-the-mill needs of your children over the extraordinary needs of your partner. In particular, do not underestimate the trauma of losing a parent, however expected the death may be—your partner will definitely need extra support.

> *When your partner is struggling to cope with a crisis, it is vital that you are 100 percent behind him or her, especially if you routinely put the children first.*

Renewing: The Twenty-Fifth Year and Beyond

Many people look back to the beginning of a relationship as the best of times, but what most don't realize is that twenty-five years together can be just as good—if not better. In many ways, the final stage of love is an echo of the first stage. During blending, the bond is heightened by the promise of a future together, whereas *renewing* is all about the reality of that shared life. After the battles of earning a living and raising a family, all the attention is focused back onto the relationship, as in the early days of courting, and the partners become everything to each other again. In addition, they can look back with a real sense of achievement for weathering the storms and enjoy shared memories or private jokes.

Problem

It is not surprising that I see only a few couples who have been together twenty-five or more years. There are occasionally health problems that cast a shadow, or unresolved issues from the adapting stage, but generally this is the best of times. Recently, however, I have started seeing parents in their sixties struggling with their grown-up sons' and daughters' emotional crises (which, in some cases, have brought the kids back home again).

"It's clear that our son is having problems with his wife," explained Martha, sixty-two. "He visited us with the grandchildren on his own last weekend. I gave him the chance to open up and talk to me, but I don't think we've ever been that kind of family."

"We've been talking about whether we could afford to support him more financially," added her husband, Tony, sixty-three, "without adversely affecting our retirement plans."

"I can't help wondering if we let our children down because we were too wrapped up in our own problems," said Martha. Tony had traveled constantly for work and had been unfaithful on several occasions.

"I have lots of regrets," Tony told Martha, "and I wish we'd been able to communicate better with each other and as a family."

Although there was sadness between them in my counseling room, there was none of the bitterness of similar arguments from younger couples, who have not been together as long and can't fall back on the evidence that their love has overcome plenty of obstacles. Fortunately, Martha and Tony were tackling their son's problems as a team rather than tearing into each other.

Turning It Around

When you are stuck in the trenches of child rearing, it is easy to think that the good times are behind you. However, I ask my clients to think of their marriages as being U-shaped. There is a high when two people first get together, but older couples are often the most romantic partners. It's the time in the middle—rubbing each other the wrong way and bringing up children—that's hard. If you're currently immersed in a tough patch in your relationship, talk about it; remind each other about the bright times ahead (for example, an upcoming holiday) so you don't feel stuck in this place forever. If you're struggling with your grown-up children's problems, don't forget that they are indeed adults. Of course, you should be supportive, but don't feel responsible for solving their problems.

Communicating Better

If circumstances meant that you did not start your family during the collaborating stage, don't worry. There is no reason you can't still have a great marriage and raise happy and contented children. The secret is to be able to communicate well. In this way, problems are solved rather than ignored or allowed to come up repeatedly. The following exercise will help with one of the most important components, listening:

1. **Know your weakness.** It's easy to think you're good at listening, but do you fall into one of the following traps? *Interrupting*: Before your partner has even finished his or her case, you're speaking up to rebut something. *Preparing your case*: You're silent but not really listening because you're marshaling your evidence. *Discounting something your partner says*: You *meant* to buy the milk on the way home, so therefore your partner's fury that you forgot to do it is unjustified. Or when your partner brings up something from the past, you think it doesn't count because it happened years ago. *"Yes, but . . ."*: You don't acknowledge your partner's anger before launching into your own defense. *Second-guessing*: You think your partner is angry about one thing, but actually the argument is about something else.

2. **Flip a coin to decide who goes first.** The winner has as long as it takes to state his or her case about something contentious— without interruption. You might fear that your partner will talk forever, but I've yet to meet someone who talks for more than five minutes. Most people need only thirty seconds.

3. **Summarize.** The person who has been listening proves that he or she has been paying attention by simply summarizing the main points, and *only* summarizing. The chance to respond will come soon.

4. **Give feedback.** The talker gives feedback about the summary. How accurate was it? What was missed? Was anything exaggerated?

5. **Switch roles.** The listener becomes the speaker and finally has the chance to refute the partner's case and make any fresh points. Afterwards, the new listener summarizes (but does not respond), and the speaker offers feedback about the accuracy.

6. **Repeat as many times as necessary.** Keep going until each of you feels truly heard. With a better understanding of each other's position, you are ready to start discussing possible solutions. If the negotiations turn nasty, flip a coin and start the whole process again.

How Disagreements Pile Up

Every relationship has sensitive topics. Maybe she earns more than he does, or he really dislikes her mother. However, most couples avoid talking about these topics because they cause a lot of upset and, in normal everyday life, they are easy to circumnavigate. For example, she will ask his permission before spending money, and he will go fishing when her mother comes to visit. I call these topics "buried bodies" because we know where the problems are, but through an unspoken agreement we choose not to disturb them.

Unfortunately, becoming parents will often bring the buried bodies up to the surface. For example, can the couple cope on just the husband's salary? If child-care issues mean that one partner should work part-time, who should try to arrange this work schedule first? These are hard enough topics even without years of unspoken resentment. In addition, babies bring other family members center stage. So even though the husband could use his love of fishing to avoid his mother-in-law in the past, if she's coming around three times a week, this is no longer practical.

How do you tackle these underlying problems? The answer, of course, is good communication. If you're new parents, you obviously need to focus on your baby's needs first, but be aware of any relationship issues and make a note of discussing them after the all-consuming first few weeks. If you're already a parent, it's never too late to exhume your buried bodies and put them properly to rest.

Simon, twenty-seven, had met Belinda, thirty-five, when he was twenty, and they had gotten married shortly afterward. She already had two children from a previous marriage.

"They call me Dad because they don't see their father, and I'm all they've ever known," explained Simon.

The couple had finally decided to have children, and Belinda was five months pregnant.

"He really gets on my nerves, following me around the house like a sick puppy," said Belinda. They had been having a lot of arguments lately. "It's like he's begging me to stop being angry and make up."

"You've had a really difficult pregnancy—there was that scare and you had to spend time in the hospital," Simon declared, trying to appease her.

"You keep on messing up my systems and putting your two cents in where it's not wanted," Belinda objected. "It's beginning to affect the kids, too; they don't know whether they're coming or going."

It didn't take long to discover the buried body in Belinda and Simon's relationship. He had moved into her house, with her children and her rules.

"I was young and inexperienced, so I accepted that she knew best," Simon admitted. "Obviously, I left the discipline up to her. But I want a greater say with *my* child, and although Belinda's a great mom and the kids are a credit to her, I want to be more hands-on."

"But I'll be negotiating with our eldest about what time she has to be home," Belinda pressed on, "and you'll keep sticking your nose in."

"I'm trying to back you up," Simon protested.

"But you're just parroting back what I'm saying," Belinda snapped.

In effect, they were dealing not only with the buried body of how to raise their unborn child but also with years of swallowing their differences, sweeping contentious issues under the carpet, and occasionally exploding when everything got to be too much. At first glance, the problems seemed almost overwhelming, but I knew that if I could help them communicate better, they could begin to solve their everyday squabbles before they became so destructive.

We are not taught how to resolve our differences at school, so if your parents divorced (as Belinda's did), avoided issues (Simon's mother smoothed over his father's nasty temper), or fought like cats and dogs, you won't have learned at home, either. Most people are left hoping that love will save the day or looking for mythical soul mates who "get" them on such a profound level that all differences melt away. Unfortunately, it's impossible for two people to live together without having disagreements, however much they

> *We are not taught how to resolve our differences at school, so if your parents divorced, avoided issues, or fought like cats and dogs, you won't have learned at home, either.*

love each other. The only answer is to roll up our sleeves and start talking. Yet not only is it hard to ask for what we want, we also don't know how to deal with the conflict when our needs and beliefs don't match those of our partners. The result is that most people muddle along using one of three unhelpful strategies: being passive, being domineering, or alternating between the two.

Being Passive

When there are conflicting desires, your needs, wants, and beliefs are of *less* importance than those of your partner. It could be that you're a people pleaser and hope that if you meet other people's needs, then they will meet yours. You could hate conflict so much that you will do anything to avoid it, or maybe you feel uncomfortable if you stick up for yourself (and therefore prefer to fold). Finally, you might be incredibly generous and get your pleasure from making other people happy. Whatever the combination of motives, *your* needs are of secondary importance.

Simon hadn't stood up for his rights as a parent to his stepchildren—even though he was paying for the food on the table and the roof over their heads—because he thought his wife was the expert on child rearing (and therefore his opinions were of no consequence), he hated conflict (because he had often suffered from his father's sharp tongue), and he generally thought that Belinda was wonderful. "She's a great mother and I would do anything to please her."

The problem with being passive is that you seldom get your needs met (which leads to long-term resentment), and if nobody (not even yourself) asks what you want, you can easily lose touch with what makes you happy. All too often, passive people are boiling over with unexpressed anger that slips out through sighs, pointed comments, and outright sarcasm.

Being Domineering

In sharp contrast to someone who is passive, if you are being domineering, you believe that your needs, wants, and beliefs are of supreme importance. It could be that you're always right (as Belinda supposedly is) and your partner is wrong (so his or her needs can be downgraded and ignored). Perhaps you've never given much thought to your partner's needs, wants, and beliefs; maybe he or she is passive and has therefore never told you about them; or maybe your parents brought you up to believe that your needs were of paramount importance and trumped everybody else's. Being domineering does not necessarily mean being aggressive and demanding; getting your own way can just as easily be achieved with charm, sweet-talking, or bribery. Men sometimes buy off their wives with expensive baubles, and women will offer sex to get their way.

Belinda liked to be in control. She had her way of doing the dishes and knew how the sink should be left afterward—where a bowl should go and where the cloth to wipe down the surfaces should be left to dry. She would lose her temper if Simon did not follow her rules to the letter. She simply could not accept that there might be another way.

On the surface, being domineering seems a better option than being passive—at least you get your needs met. Unfortunately, you can also lose respect for your partner, because most people want an equal relationship rather than someone who trots a couple of paces behind saying, "Yes, dear."

Alternating Between Being Passive and Being Domineering

When it comes to who's in charge, most couples divide up the responsibilities, so one partner takes charge in one area (being domineering) but lets the other be in charge in another (being passive). For example, Simon would make decisions about what car to buy, where to service it, and who their insurance provider should be. Belinda would control their social life and decide whom to invite, when to invite them, and how often to see family. Whichever way responsibilities are divided in your home, be aware that having a baby can upset these cozy arrangements. Unlike smaller domains (e.g., washing, gardening, shopping, recycling, buying gifts), the care and well-being of a child is a huge responsibility and demands so much time that it does not easily fit into one or the other person being in charge.

Another common way of alternating between being passive and being domineering is to put up with something for years without saying anything (and thereby downgrading your needs, wants, and opinions), until suddenly you explode and demand a change (overnight your needs, wants, and opinions become of supreme importance). For example, Simon had been in charge of the couple's finances, but during an argument Belinda exploded about it.

"You're really cavalier with our money," she accused. "You never shop around for an alternative price for anything, you just accept the first figure. That's just plain lazy. You could probably save seventy or eighty dollars— that's one bill at the supermarket for me." She had always been worried about money because there was never enough to go around when she was growing up.

Belinda was also angry about the amount of time Simon spent at work, that he let his boss take advantage of him, and that he could have been earning more elsewhere. However, until this argument, she had not said anything about it.

"I can't manage anymore. You're going to have to get another job," Belinda demanded.

The third common pattern involves being both passive and domineering at the same time. For example, Simon seemed to go along with Belinda's rules on bedtimes for their elder children, but when she was out, he allowed them to go to bed when they chose but to "make this our little secret." This is called being *passive-aggressive*. On the surface, you might give the impression that your opinions don't matter and readily agree to complete a task (being passive), but then you go your own sweet way (being aggressive) because you do believe your opinions count but are not able to debate your case openly.

Another combination of being passive and aggressive is playing the martyr: "Don't worry about me, I'll just sit here in the dark." On the surface it seems someone's needs are of no importance, but the person is actually demanding in a passive way. People can also be manipulative by using behavior that might seem passive but is actually quite controlling: "My husband thinks he's in charge because he has come up with a great plan, but I've only *let* him think it's his plan."

Being Assertive

Fortunately, there is a middle way to deal with conflicts of interest: being assertive. Let me explain exactly what I mean, because some people mix up being demanding and being assertive. With assertiveness, your needs, wants, and beliefs and those of your partner are *equally* important. You both have the right to ask for what you want, but there is a second part of the equation that is equally important: you both have the right to say no. In this way, it is a request, not a demand.

But what happens when, inevitably, your needs, wants, and beliefs clash? Here's what you have to do:

- **Compromise.** You listen to each other's case and find a middle way. For example, you want to see one film and your partner wants to see another. Instead of one of you sitting through a film that he or she would not enjoy, you choose a third film that is acceptable to both of you.

- **Negotiate.** You listen to both cases and make a deal in which each of you gets something you want. For example, this can be a trade ("If we watch your film, can we go to my favorite restaurant afterward?") or taking turns ("I'll watch your superhero movie this time, but next week we'll see my romantic comedy").

- **Back down.** Once again, you both listen to each other's needs, wants, and opinions, but one partner has a compelling case, and the other partner, it turns out, does not care that much. However, this is different from one partner simply demanding or deciding and the other person automatically agreeing. Returning to our couple going to the movies: One movie is based on a book that is being discussed at the woman's book club, and she'd like to be able to compare and contrast. The man might find, with a closer look at the poster, that one of his favorite actresses is in a supporting role or after hearing his partner talk more about the story, he decides it sounds interesting after all.

- **Agree to differ.** After a long discussion, it might be that you still have different views but it actually doesn't matter. For example, you might decide it is more important for each of you to see your preferred choice of film than be sitting side by side in the dark for an hour and a half—after all, you're going out for supper together afterward. This option can work only if both parties believe they have made their case, each partner has acknowledged the other's feelings, and their opinions have merit.

After I explained being assertive to Simon and Belinda, they returned the next week with this example: Simon needed to send a letter by registered mail, and the post office was opposite their son's school.

"I asked if I could take him to school," Simon said, "so he and I could spend some time together."

"The school run is one of the highlights of my day," Belinda replied. "I see other mothers and catch up on the gossip."

Simon had exercised his right to ask, and Belinda had exercised hers to say no. At this point, a lot of people fold. Fortunately, Simon had used an assertive skill: *explaining your request better*. "I'm not asking to do this on a regular basis," he pointed out, "it's just that I need to go to the post office tomorrow."

Belinda stood firm, however. "That's all very well, but I promised to give one of the other mothers something."

So Simon used another assertive skill: *changing your request*. "Could you take the letter to the post office for me, then?"

Belinda readily agreed, and although Simon did not get everything he wanted, he did get something. Previously he would have backed down immediately (because his needs, wants, and opinions didn't count) and felt resentful when he had to stop opposite the school and register the letter. There was another positive effect that came out of this discussion. In the evening, Belinda used an assertive skill: *offering something different*.

"I told him that if he really does want to be more involved," she said in therapy, "it would be really helpful if he could take our daughter swimming on Saturday, since it is a real rush for me to fit everything in."

Simon had readily agreed, and both parties were happy.

Assertiveness Rights

Assertiveness training has gotten a bad name because many people associate it with being aggressive. However, a good training course stresses the importance of both parties having rights and responsibilities. These are listed in the two tables on the following page.

Rights

My Rights	My Partner's Rights
To ask for what I need or want.	To refuse my request.
To be listened to and taken seriously.	To be listened to and taken seriously.
To be myself and have space and time to fulfill my needs, wants, and interests.	To rely on me for love, support, and consideration.

Responsibilities

My Responsibilities	My Partner's Responsibilities
To judge my own behavior, thoughts, and emotions.	To judge his or her own behavior, thoughts, and emotions.
To ask: Is my request reasonable?	To ask: Is it reasonable to say no?
To be responsible for the consequences.	To be responsible for the consequences.

How to Put Your Partner First

The best way to show your partner that you truly value him or her is to give his or her concerns serious consideration. So instead of trying to dismiss your partner's feelings, rationalize them, or soothe them away, accept that it is natural to worry, feel sad, or be angry from time to time—especially if you're new parents or your children are moving on to another life stage (e.g., starting school, becoming teenagers, or leaving home).

When partners start communicating better, they normally find that their fears are incredibly alike, just expressed differently. For example, Simon discovered that Belinda was worried that if she didn't control every aspect of child care and housekeeping, he would be stressed out and annoyed and might even leave her (which is what her first husband had done).

Meanwhile, Simon was worried about whether he would be a good enough father and feared being squeezed out if he didn't make the grade. *She would have completed her family and wouldn't need me anymore,* he thought. In their different ways, both Simon and Belinda were terrified of being abandoned. Acknowledging this fact was the breakthrough in their counseling.

When partners start communicating better, they normally find that their fears are incredibly alike, just expressed differently.

So how are good communication skills and being assertive connected to putting your partner first? If your partner is domineering and seems to put his or her or your children's needs, wants, and opinions before yours, it is important to learn to stand up for yourself and state your requests in an assertive manner. If your partner is passive and puts everybody else's needs first, he or she needs to learn these skills, too.

It's a good idea to read this book as a couple and discuss what changes you need to make. However, if your partner is not really a reader (or is taking forever to get past page 3), don't worry. By modeling the sort of behavior you'd like to see, you will be encouraging your partner to follow suit, rather than punishing the behavior that you don't want and starting a downward spiral in which he or she retaliates with something equally unpleasant.

Here are five concrete ways of showing your partner that you are interested in his or her feelings, opinions, and needs:

- **Value your partner's communication style.** In most relationships, one partner takes on the role of raising issues (so they can be resolved) and the other contains or keeps a sense of proportion (so that small problems do not spiral out of control). Unfortunately, it is easy to downplay the benefits of your partner's communication style or, worse still, think that his or her way is the problem. So the "We need to talk" partner thinks the other is ducking the issues and the "Let's not make a mountain out of a molehill" partner thinks the other is sucking all the joy out of the relationship. However, you need both styles for a fulfilling marriage.

- **Help your partner open up.** If your partner tends to contain rather than communicate, you can invite him or her to talk about a potentially contentious issue by acknowledging this before asking. For example, "I know it's been difficult since [fill in], but I'd really like to understand what it's been like for you."

- **Take seriously what your partner has to say, even if it makes little sense to you.** This is especially important if you contain rather than talk. Ask questions, nod to show you're listening, get clarification, and discover why your partner feels this way. Your partner's experience of being a parent will be different from yours but no less valid.

- **Keep calm.** If your partner says something upsetting, try reporting how you are feeling ("I'm angry that you said that" or "I feel misunderstood") rather than acting out (shouting, slamming doors, or making sarcastic comments) or becoming overwhelmed (bursting into tears or leaving the room). If you are calm and report your feelings, your partner will feel okay about disagreeing and will be less likely to be passive (and clam up) or domineering (and escalate the discussion into a fight).

- **Fully discuss an issue rather than rush to a conclusion.** If your partner is prone to being passive, you might also like to give permission to say no: "Are you sure?" or "I'd much rather you were truly behind the idea." If your partner is prone to being domineering, try rephrasing your position rather than automatically backing down. Time and again in my counseling room, I find couples resolve issues when they argue for a few minutes longer than usual.

Summary

When you feel taken for granted or that your partner puts you last, it is easy to think that he or she doesn't love you enough or, worse still, that there's a fundamental flaw in your relationship. However, the problems could be caused by moving from one stage of love to another or by simple miscommunication. The temptation is to keep busy and look the other way. However, suppressing or avoiding issues is never the answer. If you can talk honestly and listen, really listen, there are few problems that can't be solved. In fact, if you take away just one idea from this book, I would choose this one: *Happy marriages are built on good relationship skills.* And that's an optimistic message, because those skills can be learned.

3

The Shock of Becoming a Parent

Having a child is a journey into the unknown, even if you've had one, two, or more before. Not only is each birth and each baby different, but each changes the family dynamic in a different way. So no matter how much you read and prepare or how experienced you might be, there will be surprises. Many of them will be pleasant, but some will not be so welcome.

There are two approaches to the unknown. The vogue in modern self-help is to focus on the bright side, with positive visualizations of perfect births, happy babies, and contented mothers. This upbeat approach is very reassuring. Yet optimism can also be a double-edged sword. When your mother or a more experienced friend says, "Don't worry" or "You'll cope," there is a wonderful moment of calm. However, it lasts only a short while, and soon you're back looking for more and more reassurance.

"It's all going to be fine" and positive thinking in general also encourages the idea that parenting is natural. So not only can it be doubly shocking if things don't live up to your rosy expectations, you can also easily feel like a failure or a bad mother or father. Fortunately, there is an older tradition that takes a very different approach.

The Power of Negative Thinking

Stoicism is an ancient Greek philosophy that seeks tranquility not by chasing enjoyable experiences or through endless reassurance but by cultivating a calm acceptance of what has happened. Seneca (4 BC to 65 CE), one of the most important thinkers from this school of thought, counseled dwelling on worst-case scenarios. He believed that we are most hurt by what we don't expect. If we expect blue skies, smiling faces, and no lines to stand in, then when things don't go according to plan, we can feel weighed down by personal misfortune rather than just dealing with the inevitable setbacks, annoyances, and problems of being human.

> *If we expect blue skies, smiling faces, and no lines to stand in, then when things don't go according to plan, we can feel weighed down by personal misfortune.*

"What need is there to weep over parts of life?" Seneca wrote. "The whole calls for tears." The French writer Nicholas Chamfort (1741–1794) put it more wittily: "A man should swallow a toad every morning to be sure of not meeting with anything more revolting in the road ahead."

Although stoicism is not a popular approach, I believe that facing up to any possible downside is better than pretending it won't happen. Not only does denying something never quite banish the thought from our heads, but our fears lurk in the shadows, gaining strength and power over us. More important, when we examine and name our fears, they are never quite as catastrophic as we imagined.

Let's return to Natasha from Chapter 2, who became pregnant nine months into her relationship. In the second counseling session, when Josh had returned to his job in India, she started to voice her worries. "What if he deserts me?" she asked.

Her friends had told her, "Don't be stupid," "He really loves you," and "Didn't he fly all this way just to be with you?" So instead I opted for the opposite approach and asked her to talk about what such a desertion might be like.

"It would be too horrible," she said, and dissolved into tears.

"Would you be penniless?" I asked after a brief pause.

"No, he would never leave me short of money."

"Are you worried that he wouldn't come to the birth?"

"No, he's booked plenty of time off work, and I could get the baby induced if need be."

"So what is it?" I pressed.

"He might be too engrossed in his phone."

"What could you do then?"

"Ask him to switch it off?" Natasha laughed at herself. "But I suppose I worry that he'll start to drift off into the distance and then out of our lives."

"What would you do then?"

"My mother is very supportive. I have friends." She thought for a second. "I'd cope. I'd have to."

And that's the advantage of stoicism: it gets us in touch with our own resources, a belief that problems can be overcome, and a lasting calmness. In contrast, positive visualizations and positive thinking provide only a fleeting relief, which ultimately feeds our anxieties.

A Fixed Mind-Set Versus a
Growth Mind-Set

So let's accept that babies are not easy sailing and help you prepare for the inevitable problems and how best to overcome them. At this point, I want to introduce you to another important idea that will improve the way you approach parenting and any other challenge. Carol Dweck is a social and developmental psychologist from Stanford University in California who has dedicated her career to studying why some people achieve their full potential and others don't.

In the mid-1970s, she conducted a famous experiment on how fourth-grade students responded to an unsolvable problem on a math test. The students who identified themselves as hopeless at math were unable to complete simple questions later in the test—even though they had solved problems of a similar level of complexity earlier. In effect, they had retreated to a first-grade level, and worse still, some took days to recover their confidence. These pupils had basically told themselves, "I'm not good at math, and this proves it" and had simply given up.

Dweck divided these "hopeless" students into two groups. In the first, she challenged the idea that talents were something inherent—you either had them or you didn't—and introduced the idea that ability is something that *has to be developed*. She encouraged the students to attribute an obstacle to insufficient effort ("I need to try harder") or the need for more skills ("I haven't learned how to do that yet"). In the second group, she conducted a neutral session on memory. When the experiment was repeated, the pupils in the first group made huge strides in their math scores while those in the control group continued to do poorly.

Dweck believes that how you respond to a challenge—such as becoming a parent—depends on your mind-set: your beliefs about yourself and your most basic qualities. Do you believe that talent is innate and fixed at birth and that stars in any field are therefore born rather than made? In that case, you will tend to give up easily when faced with an obstacle or hand the problem over to someone else who does have ability in that area. Dweck called this a *fixed mind-set*. The alternative is believing that talent and ability have to be developed and nurtured. In that case, when something goes wrong, you're a problem solver who tries something else or gets advice. Dweck called this a *growth mind-set*.

Although Dweck described two mind-sets, I think it is better to imagine a continuum with fixed at one and growth at the other. To use a personal example: I'm a firm believer that effort, practice, and developing skills breeds success and that in important matters, like love and relationships, we certainly shouldn't give up. So it would seem I have a growth mind-set. However, I've branded myself hopeless at math and believe that I don't have any natural talent. My hand-eye coordination is poor, and I'm no good at sports. So in these specific areas, I have a fixed mind-set. However, if I stop and think, I realize I *can* succeed at math, if I put my mind to it. I have a degree that involved a statistics paper, and I have a diploma in market research, which also involved statistics. I didn't do too badly at sports, either; I played tennis for the school's second team. So although I have a growth mind-set, I have some fixed views about myself that I need to challenge from time to time.

There is more about mind-sets, how they affect your attitude to parenting, and a quiz to discover where you fall on the continuum in the following exercise. Since no mind-set is completely set, there is also advice on how to improve yours.

What's Your Mind-Set?

To get an insight into your mind-set, look at the following questions and rate how strongly you agree or disagree with them:

1. Talent is something that just needs to be discovered.
   ❏ Strongly agree ❏ Agree ❏ Disagree ❏ Strongly disagree

2. Criticism is a gift.
   ❏ Strongly agree ❏ Agree ❏ Disagree ❏ Strongly disagree

3. When I get stuck, I often think, *What's the point of beating a dead horse?*
   ❏ Strongly agree ❏ Agree ❏ Disagree ❏ Strongly disagree

4. I'm not excessively worried by change.
   ❏ Strongly agree ❏ Agree ❏ Disagree ❏ Strongly disagree

5. Effort is always necessary.
   ❏ Strongly agree ❏ Agree ❏ Disagree ❏ Strongly disagree

6. I get defensive when other people make critical remarks.
   ❏ Strongly agree ❏ Agree ❏ Disagree ❏ Strongly disagree

7. I tend to avoid challenges when I think I won't do well.
   ❏ Strongly agree ❏ Agree ❏ Disagree ❏ Strongly disagree

8. Although I have my weak areas, I can generally understand enough to ask intelligent questions or supervise someone else.
   ❏ Strongly agree ❏ Agree ❏ Disagree ❏ Strongly disagree

9. I need to look smart and perform well at all times.
❏ Strongly agree ❏ Agree ❏ Disagree ❏ Strongly disagree

10. I often attribute other people's success to luck or money.
❏ Strongly agree ❏ Agree ❏ Disagree ❏ Strongly disagree

11. I set goals for myself.
❏ Strongly agree ❏ Agree ❏ Disagree ❏ Strongly disagree

12. I don't think as much in terms of passing or failing as of learning opportunities.
❏ Strongly agree ❏ Agree ❏ Disagree ❏ Strongly disagree

13. If I'm not good at something, I get someone else to do it rather than making an attempt at it myself.
❏ Strongly agree ❏ Agree ❏ Disagree ❏ Strongly disagree

14. If I put my mind to it, I could pass most subjects at school.
❏ Strongly agree ❏ Agree ❏ Disagree ❏ Strongly disagree

Score Your Results

For questions 1, 3, 6, 7, 9, 10, and 13: strongly agree = 3, agree = 2, disagree = 1, and strongly disagree = 0.

For questions, 2, 4, 5, 8, 11, 12 and 14, strongly agree = 0, agree = 1, disagree = 2, and strongly disagree = 3.

The closer you are to the maximum score of 42, the more you have a fixed mind-set. The closer you are to the minimum score of 0, the more you have a growth mind-set.

28 or Higher: Fixed Mind-Set

If you think that intelligence and ability are static and that you are just the way you are, you are likely to approach becoming a parent in the same way. You will need to look smart and perform well and thereby prove that you are a "natural" mother or father. That's great, but there is a downside. Sometimes you will avoid challenges—often easier for fathers than mothers to do—because it might affect your self-image, or you'll stick to what you know you can do well.

You are equally likely to give up easily when faced with obstacles because you tend to see effort as fruitless. After all, what's the point if you'll just be back at square one? Once again, it is easier for men to bow out and tell their wives, "I don't know how," "You're the expert," or "You're a woman, so you should know"— as though caring for a baby were a skill that women are born with. Obviously, any feedback, for both men and women with this mind-set, is heard as negative. This is because someone is not commenting just on how you bathed your baby but on whether you are a good parent.

When men have a fixed mind-set, they can easily become helpers for their wives rather than copartners in looking after their baby and thus set up a lifetime of being the "reserve" parent. (It should go without saying that this will have a detrimental long-term effect on their relationship.) Women with a fixed mind-set can become very isolated, not only because they find it hard to ask for help—for fear of what people might think—but also because other people tend to keep quiet when they think their helpful advice will be heard as "sticking their noses in."

If this is you, to move more toward the middle of the continuum, think back to times in the past when you have persevered with something important and achieved a reasonable competence. Remember, there is no need to be a perfect mother or father—just good enough.

15 to 27: Combination Mind-Set

A lot of people fall somewhere between a fixed mind-set and a growth mind-set. In our specialized world, where we don't have to excel at everything, this is perhaps a good place to be. For example, I employ an accountant to file my tax returns. Of course, part of the reason is my attitude from school that "I'm no good at math," but it is also a result of pragmatism: I'm better off putting my energy into writing books and seeing clients than struggling to fill out tax forms and get the figures right. There is a certain amount of truth in the fixed mind-set that doing something well shouldn't involve too much sweat. However, as Dweck noted, "The fallacy comes when people generalize it into a belief that effort on any tasks, even hard ones, implies low ability."

The closer you are to a purely fixed mind-set, the more likely you are to feel threatened by the success (or happy children) of others, since they become a benchmark that makes you look bad. Under these circumstances, you are likely to criticize other people or make poisonous remarks, such as "Of course it's easy for her, with all that money." Meanwhile, the closer you are to the growth mind-set, the more other people's success is a source of inspiration rather than a threat.

There is a key skill to help you move more toward the growth mind-set end of the continuum: dealing with criticism. Try not to judge whether comments are helpful or not so helpful, because that will make you be defensive or misunderstand what's being said. For example, you might hear "You were too preoccupied with work on our vacation" when the real message might be "The kids really enjoyed it when you played badminton and swam in the pool with them, but they were disappointed that you brought work with you."

Criticism often comes with a corresponding compliment, so be sure you don't miss that. Once you've really listened, heard the whole message, and weighed the truth (did you really need to work?), you can fully respond. On many occasions, criticism is a gift, since it helps us look at ourselves and our motivations from a fresh perspective.

Under 15: Growth Mind-Set

If you think intelligence and ability can be developed, you are more likely to embrace change, since you view obstacles as something that can be overcome and as a chance to develop new skills or refine existing ones. With this mind-set, problems are not a sign of failure but an opportunity. Not only will you see effort as something necessary, but that setbacks can be treated more philosophically as well. So a crying baby seems less a personal failure than, more stoically, "These things happen" or "Some babies cry more than others." When you need to solve these problems, you are more likely to accept feedback and learn from criticism because it is not about you, it's about your current abilities (which can be improved).

Although it is really helpful to have a growth mind-set, don't lose sight of how much our culture pushes the fixed mind-set and downplays the hard work behind success. On TV talent shows, successful contestants are painted as being as ordinary as possible so we can relate to them, but this means that details like being in drama school or having studied at the Berklee College of Music are edited out of their backstories.

So when you're tired, stressed, and worried by the demands of a baby, it is easy to fall into the trap of thinking that other people have inherent skills and lose touch with your growth mind-set. Good parenting is the result of trial and error; nobody "just knows" how to do it.

Common Shocks

Life is full of ups and downs, and even the most joyous events, like having a baby, involve disappointments and problems. In the spirit of Seneca, let's look at some of the possible obstacles so it won't seem quite so shocking if they do occur and, equally important, to help you get in touch with your growth mind-set and be ready to overcome them.

Childbirth Can Be Traumatic

Even a natural, uncomplicated birth is a massive physiological challenge for a woman's body, and it takes time, rest, and a slow rehabilitation to recover. In 1931, W. Blair Bell, the first president of the British College of Obstetricians, estimated that 10 percent of mothers were "more or less crippled as a result of childbearing." He said that 70 percent of new mothers had lesions, and 35 to 40 percent of these lesions were disabling.

Although much has changed since the experiences of women two or three generations ago, as recently as 1991 the *Health After Childbirth* report, which followed the health of 11,000 new mothers, found that nearly half (47 percent) had at least one health problem (such as backache, frequent headaches, migraine headaches, or bladder problems) six weeks after giving birth. More alarming, two-thirds of these women still had their problems thirteen months after giving birth. Today mothers have more choices and benefit from the latest advances in aftercare, but childbirth remains a physically challenging experience.

Why It Is a Shock

In our celebrity-obsessed culture, we have almost become inured to how much time and space is devoted to poring over women's bodies and analyzing their supposed failings. However, there is a new phenomenon: hot, famous women and their babies. Magazines and the Internet are full of supermodels and celebrities who have dropped sixty pounds and gotten their figures back after giving birth with just "cardio and sculpting sessions five times a week." One celebrity trainer made a DVD showing other mothers how to achieve this goal just six weeks after her daughter was born by cesarean section.

This phenomenon is so widespread in the United States that a new term has been coined for such a supermother: *momshell* (a combination of *mom* and *bombshell*). Not only does this culture leave lots of ordinary mothers feeling guilty, it also creates an expectation that women will recover quickly from giving birth. As a result, family and friends leave them to care for their baby alone, even though many new mothers feel physically and emotionally shaken.

Turning It Around

There are two ways to confront this problem. First, stop reading celebrity magazines or visiting websites that pore over other women's alleged imperfections. Although you might think that seeing famous women looking flabby will make you feel better about your own body, the boost is only short-lived at best and ultimately feeds self-loathing. "I worry more about my body now than I did before," explained Gemma just three weeks after giving birth. "I compare how I look to other new moms to gauge how we're coping with the roller-coaster journey." Keep reminding yourself that most mothers take months to reshape their bodies after pregnancy, and your figure is not an indication of how well you are coping with motherhood.

I know this is asking a lot, but please don't compare yourself to other mothers or fathers. If you can pull this off, it will make your life much easier—especially since the Parenting Olympics have only just started. (Next it will be whose baby is sleeping best, eating most, crawling first, and, before you know it, getting a place at the best university.) Just because other people have entered the competition doesn't mean that you're obliged to join in. Keep quiet when other parents are boasting; walk away or turn it into a private joke between you and your partner. It will help you enjoy this special time rather than missing something because you've been too busy looking over your shoulder.

Second, if you are a new parent and did not expect to need extra support, it's not too late to ask—especially if there were complications from the birth. Don't feel guilty or ashamed. In the eighteenth century, women were considered ill and therefore expected to "lie in" at special facilities while other people did the chores and the mothers could bond with their babies. Even today, in Malaysian villages, new mothers spend forty days being cared for by other women, away from their families, before rejoining their communities. In some Asian cultures, especially China, confinement is still popular, and postpartum houses are set up even in U.S. cities to cater to new immigrants who don't have practical support from their families.

Speak to your mother, your father, or your in-laws and explain that you need some extra muscle—just a few hours a week can make a huge difference. Remember the friends who said, "Let us know if there's anything we can do" and turn their offer into something concrete. Lots of people in your circle will want to help but might feel awkward about offering or not be aware that you need help. Even if it is only an occasional afternoon or evening visit, this can still be a boost and make you feel emotionally supported even when no long-term practical assistance is offered.

Your Carefully Constructed Identity Can Crumble

Children can provide a sense of purpose and belonging and make us feel needed, but they can also turn our lives upside down. It is particularly destabilizing when the stories we tell ourselves, to make sense of the world and our place in it, are challenged.

For example, Karen, thirty-eight, had always believed that "I can cope with whatever is thrown at me," and her career in information technology had given her plenty of examples. "When everybody else is running around screaming," she related, "I can keep calm, go back to basics, and slowly work through everything and isolate the problem." It wasn't just work that had forged this identity, however; it stemmed from her childhood. "My mother was a borderline alcoholic and my father was away at work a lot. I was the eldest of three children, and we could never predict how my mother would be, so from about the age of seven, I'd fix my brother and sister breakfast and help them get dressed and ready for school."

When I asked her to imagine herself having superhero qualities, she pictured herself as Atlas holding up the world. Unfortunately, her husband had a great career opportunity just two weeks after their second son was born, and he needed to be out of the country for six weeks. In the debate over whether he should go, Karen's arguments were formed by her Madam Atlas identity: "I can cope." The result was that her husband went off with her blessing. Unfortunately, Karen found that she couldn't manage alone with a toddler and a newborn, and she slipped into depression.

Although most men continue to work full-time, which props up their old, preparent self-image, their identities can also be severely challenged by the arrival of a child. Karen's husband, Edward, thirty-six, had always seen his job as regulating the mood in the house. "If there's a bad atmosphere," he said, "I try to suck it up, keep positive, and help everybody else get on to an even keel. Normally it works because I've got a sunny disposition, but I couldn't shift the black cloud over Karen. I felt helpless and, for the first time ever, a bit hopeless, too."

When I asked Edward to name his superhero, he dubbed himself the Great Absorber (he had also tried to keep the peace between his parents, who were always quarreling). Edward was feeling particularly bleak when he arrived in counseling. "If I'm not the Great Absorber, who am I?" he asked.

Other common identities that babies and toddlers challenge include "I'm in charge" and "my beautiful life" (in which looking good, having nice clothes, and living in a beautiful house are paramount to your identity).

Sometimes the shock comes when the children are older, start school, become teenagers, or leave home. If you are the principal caregiver, being a great mom or a superdad can be the core of your identity. So what happens when the children don't need you so much?

"I suppose I was one of the first dads in our town who gave up work to look after our three children," said Mike, forty-three. "My wife had a career with a pension fund and promotion prospects while I just pushed paper on a desk for local government, so I was pleased to leave it all behind. It was strange at first because the moms at the school gate were a bit wary, but I got involved with the school—listening to the kids read—and quickly made a circle of friends.

"The mothers were always so complimentary: 'I wish my husband was like you.' When I helped our eldest bake for home economics, you'd think I'd invented a cure for cancer. The kids really liked me being at home, and my wife was relieved that I took up the most of the strain. I suppose I became 'Wonder Mike,' the man who knew the name of all the children's teachers. Now, however, the eldest is going off to college and the youngest is entering middle school, so I'm no longer needed so much. If I'm not the ideal dad, who am I? What do I want to do with the rest of my life?"

Why It Is a Shock

Generation Y is particularly ill equipped to become new parents. It was normative for women several generations ago to grow up in large, tight-knit families and take care of their younger siblings or help an aunt with her children, but today many expectant mothers and fathers have no experience of being left in charge of a baby. A significant number have not even held one before being handed their own.

In the meantime, the hysteria about child abuse means that only people who have been vetted are allowed anywhere near children, and thus the average person's contact has been even further reduced. In addition, people are having children at a much later age and have therefore had longer to create myths about themselves and their roles in the world, and these have become more deeply entrenched. No wonder the transformation from being childless to being a parent can be difficult, and the journey out of the parenting years equally fraught.

Turning It Around

It is healthy to update your self-image from time to time, but first you need a clear idea of how you see yourself. Ultimately, problems arise when you have a narrow or too rigid self-image.

Think about the questions I asked Karen and Edward and how you might respond. If you had superhero qualities, what would they be? If you were a superhero, what would you be called? Where does this image come from? How accurate is it today? How realistic is it?

Next, consider what might happen if you failed to live up to this identity. Would it really be the end of the world?

Some new mothers and fathers get a pleasant surprise and find that being a parent really suits them, providing a significant boost to their confidence. This can often be the case for people who have been striving to find a place in the world or whose careers were not particularly satisfying. In these circumstances, new mothers and fathers can become so focused on caring for the child and get so great a reward that they lose sight of some of their other identities—like partner (which can be a nasty shock for the spouse).

If becoming a parent has been challenging to your carefully constructed image of yourself, don't try to be everything to your child; concentrate on your strengths and be prepared to delegate responsibility from time to time. Karen learned, slowly but surely, that it was okay to ask Edward for help when she needed it rather than seeing this as failure on her part. The biggest turning point was when she went away for a short vacation on her own. "It not only gave me a chance to catch up on my sleep and truly relax, possibly for the first time in years," she enthused, "but I learned that the world didn't collapse if I wasn't there to hold it up."

> *If becoming a parent has been challenging to your carefully constructed image of yourself, don't try to be everything to your child; concentrate on your strengths and be prepared to delegate responsibility from time to time.*

Unconditional Love Is Difficult

There is a nasty secret that most parents would rather die than confess: sometimes they resent their children. The taboo is so strong that many people won't even admit it to themselves. After all, parents are supposed to love their children unconditionally from the moment they set eyes on them. Unfortunately, there are always conflicts between the needs of a parent and the needs of a child, and we wouldn't be human if we didn't resent the self-sacrifice from time to time.

Fiona, a thirty-three-year-old artist, has a nine-year-old son, and although she expected support from her partner, he disappeared from their lives (except for occasional visits) a few months into her pregnancy. "I love my son," Fiona said. "Don't get me wrong—he's the center of my life, but he significantly curtails my options. I'll have an idea for a painting and I'll want to start on it. However, my son will want me to play, and I can't always say, 'Why don't you go across the street and see what Granny and Grandpa are doing?' Most of my creative friends don't have children, so I don't get to see them that often (since there's only so many times I can ask my parents to babysit), and I don't really fit into the young mothers' dinner-party circle where they only want to talk about new kitchens and vacations in Tuscany."

Why It Is a Shock

Many of us have been brought up on images of the Madonna and Child, not only on Christmas cards but also through updated versions in advertising and popular culture. The message is always the same: be self-sacrificing, accepting, and devoted. Yet before becoming parents, we are encouraged to set goals for ourselves, focus on them, and be ruthless in our determination to reach them. What is prized most is being autonomous and independent and having the ability to control the agenda. Going from standing up for yourself to being self-sacrificing is a 180-degree turn, and you're expected to achieve it just by "unconditional love." However, parents—and even more shocking, mothers—still have needs, too.

Turning It Around

It is fine to resent your children. It does not make you a bad mother or father. In fact, it could make you a better one. Any feeling that is

> *It is fine to resent your children. It does not make you a bad mother or father. In fact, it could make you a better one.*

suppressed does not simply disappear but either gathers power in the shadows or simply pops up somewhere else. In fact, this is one of the biggest causes of bitterness that I see between new parents. No mother can easily say, "I resented my baby today," and after all, it's not the baby's fault that you're tired, stressed, and upset. He or she is small, innocent, and needy. So it's much easier to take your resentment out on your husband, who "doesn't understand" or has been "having fun" at work all day.

Similarly, a husband can't come home and see his wife and baby in their dreamy little world of two, breast-feeding, cuddling, or tickling, and not feel a little bit excluded. He can't say, "I'm jealous," because what sort of monster would resent his own child? So he takes it out on his wife by being snappy or behaves in a passive-aggressive manner (such as by playing games on his computer or drinking too much).

The week after I told Fiona that most parents resent their children from time to time, she felt as though a weight had been lifted off her shoulders, and we could begin to negotiate a compromise between her own needs and those of her son.

"In the evening," she explained, "he'll want my attention but I'll want to be doing my stuff. For example, I'll try to catch up with my friends on Facebook (because I never see them in the flesh) and he'll always be interrupting. I worry what will happen when he goes to bed later and my time is completely swallowed up."

I had the picture of neither party feeling satisfied. Her son never quite had her undivided attention (no wonder he was needy), and she could never be in anything other than mother mode (no wonder she felt resentful).

"What would happen if you put down your work or whatever when he came home and focused entirely on him, listened to what he'd done, asked questions, and maybe did something together for an hour?" I asked.

Fiona admitted she had only half heard his stories about school, because she was working or "looking for something more interesting online."

"Afterward," I continued, "he has to entertain himself for a while, watch TV, read, or do his homework, and you can focus on your stuff."

The experiment was a huge success; furthermore, Fiona began to include her son in some of her weekends away, when there were other children around. Their relationship became even closer, but first she had to admit that she had different needs from those of her son and sometimes resented her sacrifices.

Your Parents Return to Center Stage

We spend our teens and early twenties distancing ourselves from our parents, becoming our own people and creating our own lives. The journey back into the fold often starts with getting married, which turns a private arrangement (like living together) into something public as you and your spouse join each other's extended families—albeit at a manageable level, like holidays and cousins' weddings. However, having a baby brings your parents back to the center of your life—they provide support and advice, whether or not you've asked for it. This could be financial help, babysitting, an experienced shoulder to cry on, or even all going on vacation together, but what used to be an arm's-length relationship is a decidedly more intimate one. This can be wonderful, but it can also bring up issues that you thought were long buried or make existing problems more acute.

Why It Is a Shock

Having a child brings back your own childhood and all the raw emotions associated with it. "When I held my son in my arms, I couldn't stop crying," explained Derek, thirty. "He seemed so small, so trusting, and he needed me to be there to look after him." Unfortunately, Derek's own father had always been a shadowy presence—more a friend than a father. He had left Derek's mother before Derek was one year old and had had a series of transitory relationships with other women.

"I'd always thought I don't need a dad because my mom is amazing—a mom and a dad rolled into one," Derek said, "but now I feel this great big gaping hole. I phoned my dad and he congratulated me, but he joked that I'd gotten the full ball and chain." Derek wondered how he could be a good father when he'd never had a father himself.

It is easy to dump your old childhood fears onto your baby. For example, Carrie, twenty-nine, had been labeled the "ugly one" by her mother in comparison with her younger sister, who was the "pretty one."

"When the midwife told me I'd had a baby girl," Carrie recalled, "my heart gave a huge lurch. Would she be ugly like me? Her face was all crumpled and she had a bit of jaundice. The midwife thought I was crying with joy, but the tears were about all the jibes my daughter would get on the playground because people can be cruel. It took a couple of days to realize this was not about my daughter, who, after recovering from the trauma of arriving in the world, is a really cute baby; it's about me and the messages from my mother. I know she didn't intend to be mean, but how could she do that to me?"

Turning It Around

Although you might revert to your old relationships with your parents—and regress every time they walk through the door—it is important to recognize there has been a shift. You and your partner and your child are at the core, whereas your parents' old omnipotence as Mom and Dad will dwindle as they become Grandma and Grandpa. Moreover, you have an extraordinary opportunity to heal the scars from your childhood and transform your relationship with your parents.

If there are incidents from the past that you need to discuss with your parents, it is best to broach them as questions rather than accusations— for instance, "What was happening in your life when I was born?" rather than "You never had time for me." As a parent yourself now, you might find it easier to understand their perspective and view past traumas from another angle.

However, I find in most cases that there is no need to confront your parents and that improving your day-to-day communication is enough. To achieve this goal, I use transactional analysis, a way of looking at how we interact based on the ideas of Canadian psychologist Eric Berne (1910–1970). He believed that we have three modes of operating: parent, adult, and child. We need access to all these modes: the parent nurtures, the adult solves problems, and the child is creative and fun. The problem arises when people get stuck in one particularly poisonous transaction: the critical parent and the adapted child.

We all immediately recognize the critical parent ("I wouldn't do that if I were you" or "Here you go again"), but the adapted child needs more explanation. It includes sulking, throwing a tantrum, being a people pleaser (going along with something even when you don't agree), rebelling, playing the martyr, and being passive-aggressive (slamming doors or agreeing to do something but never getting around to it). In a disagreement with someone—like your mother, partner, or work colleague—you will switch back and forth between the critical parent and the adapted child. Here is an example:

> Person A (playing the critical parent): I've been waiting here for half an hour. You could have called.
>
> Person B (playing "poor me" and being the adapted child): I've had a horrible day and now you're giving me a hard time!
>
> Person A (switching into "martyr" mode and the adapted child): I don't know why I say anything.
>
> Person B (playing the critical parent): If you didn't leave everything to me, perhaps I would be on time.

As you can imagine, this type of interaction can go on for hours, even years. Fortunately, there is an alternative: if you go into adult mode, the other person will switch into that mode, too. The adult mode is rational, questioning, problem solving, and assertive. For example: "What are the facts?," "What seems to be the problem?," and "How can we solve this problem?" Adult mode is also about what's happening now or will happen in the near future rather than what happened in the past. It avoids loaded words like *always* and *never*. Here is an example of how staying in adult mode—even when the other person responds in child mode—will encourage the other person to match you in adult mode:

Person A (adult mode): How can we ensure that everybody has a good time when we come over to your house on Sunday?

Person B (sulkily, in adapted child mode): It has nothing to do with me; your wife is always so sensitive.

Person A (resisting the temptation to slip into critical parent mode): What could we do differently?

Person B ("poor helpless me," still in adapted child mode): I don't know; I've tried everything.

Person A (using a question to remain in adult mode): How could I help?

Person B (finally in adult mode): Perhaps if you arrived earlier, so we didn't have to sit down immediately for lunch, we could take the children to the park and burn off some energy.

Person A: That sounds like a great idea; let's try it. How much earlier are you suggesting?

So next time you feel yourself slipping into the adapted child and critical parent dynamic with your mother or father, check yourself and switch into adult mode. It might take you a couple of statements in adult mode, but your mother or father will respond and switch into adult mode, too, and slowly but surely your relationship will change. (There is more about transactional analysis in my book *Help Your Partner Say Yes*.)

Telling the Story of Your Childhood

Your childhood has shaped not only you but also your understanding of what it means to be a mother or a father and your fears about the future. To turn these from something nebulous into something concrete that can be discussed, tell your partner a story about a fierce moment from your childhood, then listen to him or her tell you a similar story.

What do I mean by *fierce*? It could be something dramatically charged (for you or somebody else in the story). It could be the moment that everything changed, or its power might come from being very ordinary but emblematic of something that happened repeatedly. Don't take too long thinking about it: if something pops into your head, go with it and tell the story. Here are a few pointers on what to include:

- How old were you?
- Set the scene. Where were you? Who was there? What time of year was it? What could you see? (This will not only draw your partner into the story but also help you step back in time and inhabit the story.)
- What happened?
- How did you react? Why did you do that? How did you feel?
- What about the other people? How did they respond to the incident and to your reaction?

When you've finished telling your story, let your partner ask questions and truly understand the significance of it. Ask what strikes him or her as interesting. Consider why you chose this story, what it reveals about your role in your family, and the messages you were given as a child. Finally, return to the issues that have been troubling you in the past months—especially if you're about to become a parent for the first time. What light does this story shed on those concerns?

Next, listen while your partner tells his or her story. Once it's over, think about the following questions:

- How much do you recognize the dynamics revealed by the story?
- What surprised you?
- What is missing?
- What are the differences between your family and your partner's family?
- What does the story tell you about being a father or a mother?

Finish by thanking each other for the story, and since it's probably been quite emotional, give each other a big hug. Remember what you told each other and use it to understand why you both behave the way you do. It is easy to think that your partner does something because "he's selfish" or "she doesn't love me enough," but more often than not, it's because your partner is wrestling with his or her ghosts rather than deliberately trying to annoy you. Knowing the real reasons for any behavior will allow you to respond more sympathetically and, instead of arguing, have a constructive discussion about other ways of a tackling the issue.

Help! I'm Turning into My Parents

One of the biggest shocks about becoming a parent is finding yourself doing the things your parents did and using the same put-downs you promised yourself you'd never inflict on your own children. To illustrate just how deeply ingrained the parenting we received is, and how strongly it informs the parenting we give ourselves, I'm going to use a personal example.

My sister and her two children were visiting our parents, and I had joined them for the weekend. My niece was about ten or eleven, and despite her normally sunny disposition, she was being extremely cranky. It felt like one false move and she would explode, so everyone had been putting themselves out to accommodate her. If she wanted to play cards, we played cards, and if she wanted to go to the swimming pool and jump off the high diving board all day, that's what we did.

On the final morning, my niece and I were alone in the kitchen. We couldn't follow her desires to the letter, and she stuck out her bottom lip and said, "We never do anything I want." Instead of allowing my niece to open up or asking her a question, such as "Why do you feel like that?," I did exactly what my mother would have done. (In my defense, I was sitting in my mother's seat at the table where I'd eaten every meal from ages seven to eighteen.)

Despite all my training and my awareness of this trap, I laughed—a horrible, mocking laugh. It seemed to come from nowhere, and it was out of my mouth before I could stop it. I didn't really know what was going on in my niece's life beyond this weekend, and I didn't even understand the last few days from her viewpoint. Instead of allowing her to express her feelings, I stopped her dead in her tracks. It was the same message I'd been given when I was young: Shut up and get on with it. (No prizes for guessing why I decided to become a therapist!)

I want to stress that I'm not blaming anyone. I know my mother was on the receiving end of that laugh from my grandmother, and who knows how many generations had used it before that. However, understanding your parents' parenting style and looking out for the same behavior in yourself is better than simply copying it or being so determined not to make the same mistakes that you fall into a different trap.

Below I list eight common problematic parenting styles that I've identified and explain how they might have affected you. The first four tend to be exhibited by fathers and the second four by mothers, but they can be adopted by either men or women. If you have trouble recognizing which category your parents fall into, try completing these sentences: "Mom will always . . ." and "Dad will always . . ."

If you're still finding this hard because your parents were loving and supportive, don't think of just their everyday parenting style; think of how they behaved when they were tired or stressed. However much we, as adults, understand their behavior, the words or actions will still have hurt and left wounds. I know this is difficult. A lot of my clients feel guilty about criticizing their parents because they did their best, but it is important to have a balanced picture of your childhood.

Here are the descriptions of the eight problematic parenting styles.

The Supreme Ruler

The supreme ruler is the man who would be king. He works hard, and his wife and kids should be grateful and behave like loyal subjects. He rules by decree, and if there's any dispute, it's settled by him declaring, "It's my house" or "I pay the bills."

Sons of this parenting style are likely to grow up and expect the same deference from their wives and children. Daughters of this parenting style may automatically expect their husbands to be domineering and acquiesce to it because it is all they have ever known. Having been parented in such a way is less of a problem before you have children as money is not so tight (so each partner can pretend to be a benign ruler and buy off any opposition) and there is enough free time to pursue both individual and couple goals (so who's in charge is less of an issue).

Many men don't feel ready to have children in their twenties and thirties, and their wives sense this deep down. The supreme ruler will try to keep the focus on him and the messy, exhausting parts of parenting to a minimum. Unfortunately, this can lead to women feeling resentful or, when they fail to achieve the impossible, becoming depressed.

The Critic

The critical father (or sometimes mother) is full of frustration and anger because nobody can ever do anything "right." He is a perfectionist and has a great talent for spotting what other people have done wrong. His comments might be meant as helpful, because he wants you to do things better, but the tone is always dismissive and undermines his wife's and his children's confidence.

Sons and daughters of the critical parenting style can be left feeling not good enough or worthy of praise, time, or tenderness. Not only will they be sensitive to any criticism themselves—because even the mildest reproach will be heard as a character assassination—but they are also likely to be critical of others, too.

The Passive Parent

The passive father gives his power over to his wife, his children, and his boss. At home, he does not interrupt, interact, or show much interest in what his children have been doing. If he did complain, he would be ignored or verbally beaten down, so he disappears into alcohol, TV, or his garden shed.

The sons of passive men grow up to hate passivity in other men, in their sons, and in themselves. They take on too much, won't let others share the burden, and behave like a supreme ruler. If they lose their jobs or feel defeated by life, their self-loathing becomes overwhelming and they become severely depressed or self-medicate with alcohol, pornography, computer games, and the like.

Daughters of passive men often grow up with such an abhorrence of passive men that they either marry supreme rulers or become so finely tuned to passivity in their partners or sons that they will spot the slightest slip, exaggerate it in their minds, and get angry completely out of proportion to the "crime."

The Absentee Parent

The absentee father is simply not there. It might be because of work commitments or divorce, but he misses sports events, school concerts, and other significant days in the lives of his children because he is too busy or has other priorities. He might think he's doing the best for the family by paying the bills and providing a good lifestyle, but the message he gives is one of indifference.

Sons of an absentee father have no idea how to be father themselves because they received such little fathering. They will either go to the opposite extreme and become superdads (overinvolved in their children's lives) or throw themselves into the role of being chief provider and spend so much time at work that their marriages suffer. If they are not careful, they will try so hard not to be their father that they become him anyway.

Daughters of absentee dads have a tendency to fall for men who are either emotionally or physically unavailable, so as mothers they are left carrying the majority of the day-to-day responsibility for raising the children.

The Smothering Parent

This mother (and sometimes father) is always there for the children. She is still tying their shoelaces years after they can do it themselves. She is ready to fight their battles with friends, teachers, and bosses and is interested in every detail of their lives. I once had a client who was about to drive two hours to her daughter's university to search for her daughter's passport because the daughter was too busy to do it herself. Fortunately, the daughter found it behind a bookcase and saved her mother the trip.

If you were smothered as a child, there is a strong possibility that you could become too involved in your own child's life, especially since modern parenting culture encourages this phenomenon. The son of a smothering mother can develop a strong sense of entitlement and become a supreme ruler. The daughter of a smothering mother may become a smothering mother herself or try to be different but forever feel guilty that she's not doing enough.

If you rebelled as a child and withdrew so that your mother could not invade your emotional space, you will be self-contained and tend to keep other people at a distance. In that case, the experience of having a baby and its overwhelming emotional demands can be very frightening.

The Control Freak

There is only one way to do things, and that's the controlling parent's way. She (or he) knows best what time to leave for school, who your friends should be, and how to do your school project. Although fathers can be equally controlling (see "The Supreme Ruler"), they tend to be most interested in controlling the major areas of their children's lives (such as mealtimes, bedtimes, curfew times, where to go to school, or what career to choose).

Controlling mothers, in contrast, are interested in every little detail of their children's lives, both emotionally and practically. For example, I had a client, a successful career woman in her forties, whose mother was forever trying to get her to buy a different bedspread because she thought white was too impractical. It is usually tempting to go along with what a controlling parent wants, partly to have a calm and peaceful life, but mainly because doing something different is taken as a personal affront—and who wants to upset his or her mother?

If you were raised by a controlling parent, you are likely to want to be in charge of every last detail, too—especially since this is encouraged by contemporary culture—and feel very uncomfortable when events spiral out of control. It is especially challenging when your baby won't stop crying or your partner has different ideas about child rearing. It is easy to see everything as black and white, where you are right and your partner is wrong rather than just being two people with different opinions.

The Martyr

There is a lot of crossover between the martyr and both the smothering and controlling mother—especially if she doesn't get her own way. "After all I've done for you! But it doesn't matter, I'll be fine on my own" is a common refrain. Sometimes these women have good reason to feel like martyrs—perhaps life has dealt them a tough hand, and they are coping with illness or bringing up their children alone because their husbands are passive, alcoholic, or absent. Whatever the circumstances, rather than being assertive and asking for what they need, martyr mothers and fathers manipulate other people by playing the "poor me" card or remaining silent but deeply resenting all the sacrifices they are making.

If you have been raised with the martyr parenting style, you will do your utmost not to fall into this trap. However, when you're tired and overwhelmed (something that's not uncommon after having children), you are likely to find yourself behaving just like your mother.

The Timid Parent

Timid mothers are frightened of the world and tend to lead constricted lives, normally centered in the home. They always fear the worst and are pessimistic or anxious about how something might turn out. Sometimes they have good reasons to be frightened, because they are trying to hide the full effect of a husband's infidelity, gambling, or violence from their children. A timid mother often has a different relationship with her children when her husband is not around. If he is a supreme ruler or a critic, she may try to appease him behind the scenes.

The children of timid parents tend to be cautious themselves and become anxious mothers and fathers. Once again, this is encouraged by our modern society, especially with the news media's saturation coverage of every child that is missing, murdered, or abused.

The Power of a Fulsome Apology

If reading about parenting styles has made you cringe because you have inadvertently reproduced your father or mother's behavior with your partner or your children, please don't be too tough on yourself. Everybody makes mistakes, and what counts is how you recover. That's why I am a great believer in the fulsome apology. There are three parts to it:

1. Identify the unhelpful behavior.
2. Identify the effect on the other person.
3. Express your sorrow.

For example, "I'm sorry I laughed when you said nobody does anything you want. It must have made you feel belittled and not taken seriously. I really regret it and want to apologize."

There are two ways that people lessen the power of a sincere apology. The first is by explaining the behavior. By saying, for example, "It's something my mother did to me," you sound like you are making excuses or asking for sympathy. The second is going overboard with expressing sorrow. For example, "I haven't been able to sleep properly" or "I've been so worried."

Instead of the apology being something about the other person, it has become about you (and he or she could feel obliged to forgive you).

Don't worry about whether your apology is accepted. Give the other person the chance to respond, but if he or she has nothing to say, let the topic drop. (If you don't normally apologize, the other person could be in shock!)

It is particularly powerful when a father or a mother apologizes to a child—for example, "I'm sorry I lost my temper. It was nothing to do with you, and it must have made you feel that you'd done something wrong. That's not the message I wanted to give you, and I'm sorry"— because it models the sort of behavior you would like the child to use with his or her brothers, sisters, and friends.

A sincere apology provides the opportunity to move on, and if you fall into the same trap again, it gives the other person permission to address your unpleasant behavior.

Second-Child Syndrome

It should be much easier to cope the second time around. After all, you've already made the transition from couple to family. You know what to expect and have less to fear. However, when I take a history of a couple's relationship, it is often the birth of the second child that's been the point at which things have started to unravel. Why should the arrival of a second baby be such a turning point?

First, every child is different. Donald Winnicott, the leading pediatrician and psychoanalyst who coined the term the *good enough mother*, wrote, "Almost from

> *When I take a history of a couple's relationship, it is often the birth of the second child that's been the point at which things have started to unravel.*

the start, the new baby has his [or her] own ideas, and if you have ten children you will not find two alike, although they all grow up in the same house—your household. Ten children will see ten different mothers in you." Sometimes you can be lucky the first time around and have a child who complements your personal strengths, but you may find your second one to be more of a challenge because he or she shares some of the character traits you dislike in yourself.

"Our daughter needs a lot more of my wife's attention," said Owen, thirty-six. "Although she's three, she's still sleeping in the bed with us rather than in her own room because otherwise there are tears and tantrums. I worry about my son, who's six: he knows that she sleeps with us. We can't hide it from him. What incentive is there for him to grow up when his younger sister gets all the special treatment?"

A second baby means significantly less couple time, and transporting two small children can be a nightmare. If you decide to go somewhere without them, it is harder to find someone to care for two children than for one. "When our first child was born, we'd just put him in a carrier and take him with us," said Jessica, twenty-seven. "He'd normally be sleeping, and it was never a problem, even if we were going to a restaurant. With two children, the amount of paraphernalia is extraordinary. You can see our childless friends raising their eyebrows as we cart more and more stuff through their doors. One of our children is on solids, and they both have to eat early. Who wants Sunday lunch at midday? My mother is happy to look after them, but since the younger one started crawling, my stepfather has been making noises about us 'expecting too much.' So I don't like to leave them there for too long. Slowly but surely, we're losing touch with anybody who isn't firmly immersed in baby world."

Your love life takes more of a hit after the second child, especially if you've decided that your family is complete. That's because it takes a woman's hormones about eighteen months to return to normal after giving birth.

Oxytocin, the bonding chemical that helps us feel close to our partners and in touch with our sensual feelings, is diverted into the bond between mother and baby. It doesn't mean that a woman won't be sexually responsive, but she won't be spontaneously horny.

Unfortunately, eighteen months is also the amount of time most couples leave before trying for another child, and the whole process starts again. "One of the main reasons that I agreed to try for a second child is at least I'd get plenty of sex," explained Jake, thirty-eight, "but my wife got pregnant almost right away, so I felt really cheated, and since we can't afford a third child, I sometimes worry that I'll never have sex again. Okay, I know that's an exaggeration, but when will I have *carefree* sex again, without my wife having one ear on the baby monitor?" (There is more on this topic in Chapter 7.)

The second child can also be the point at which a woman decides that working full-time is too stressful or decides to give up working outside the home altogether. "It wasn't just that I had no time to do anything," said Sandra, forty-three, "or that when I was at work, I was thinking about home, and when I was at home, I'd be thinking about work. I also seemed to be such a one-dimensional person. I hadn't read a book from one year to the next. When we went to a dinner party, people would be talking about a film or something in the news, and I wouldn't have the first idea how to join the conversation, because I was so out of touch. Finally, when I did the calculations, I found I was almost working just to pay for child care. It seemed like a no-brainer."

However, there is a much deeper reason why having two children can be problematic, and it goes right back to your own childhood again. "My earliest memory is waking up on Christmas morning and wondering why my mother wasn't there when I opened my stocking," explained Anthony, thirty-seven. "My father reminded me, 'She's gone to the hospital to get your baby sister.' I still remember the new play garage I got and, just as clearly, thinking, 'I don't want a sister.' When my mother did return—and I'm a bit hazy about how long afterward—she was really tired, and all she wanted to do was sleep. Fast-forward a few months, and I remember coming back from somewhere and seeing that my sister had piled one brick on top of another, and my mother and father were really excited. So what? Anybody could have done that, I thought, but there was also this dawning realization: I've got competition now."

Anthony had scarcely thought of these events until his wife gave birth to his daughter, and all the old feelings came flooding back. "I don't know whether I was jealous on behalf of my son or it was about me, but I felt angry for no reason at all." Like many clients in a similar situation, Anthony found it hard to accept the link between how he felt as a small child and how he felt today. "It doesn't seem to make sense that something so small, like seeing my sister playing with my bricks, would have such a big impact." I know it does not make *logical* sense, but we're dealing with emotions from when we were small, and these are beyond reason.

In effect, having a second child creates the family constellation that many of us were brought up in: a mother, a father, a sibling, and me—four of us. This gives us a chance to replay all the old dynamics, and unfortunately some people end up feeling defeated, excluded, and blamed all over again. Moreover, if your parents favored your brother or sister, if there was a crisis that consumed their attention, or if they simply ran out of energy by the time you were born, it can seem that love is finite rather than something that expands to include however many people there are in the family.

Under these circumstances, love will appear rationed, and your deepest and darkest fear will be that once you have a baby (and especially two babies), your partner will have less love available for you. "I've never really thought of it," Anthony explained, "but I suppose when it was just my wife, my son, and me, it was an even competition [for my wife's attention], but once we had our daughter, it was two against one. No wonder I've been feeling down, bordering on depression."

Although I've outlined the possible pitfalls, it is important to stress that they won't necessarily happen to you—especially if you are aware of the problems and take the precautionary steps that I outline below.

How to Put Your Partner First

It takes time to fit into the role of being a mother or a father and being parents together. In essence, there is *her* journey, *his* journey, and the relationship's journey, and the adjustments won't necessarily happen all at the same time. A woman has nine months to turn into a mother, and playing with dolls as a child prepared her for it. In contrast, a man turns into a father all at once. Everything is made doubly difficult for him if the new baby brings up old feelings from his childhood and he worries that there is not enough love to go around. If his wife is enveloped in the dreamy symbiotic world of mother and child, and all the other aspects of herself have been subsumed into this one identity, it can be a recipe for disaster.

Of course, it is hard to put your partner first, especially if you are a new mother. After all, how can you prioritize the needs of a big lump of a man over a tiny helpless baby? Don't worry, I'm not going to ask for much. In fact, it is more symbolic than anything else. I

> *Of course, it is hard to put your partner first, especially if you are a new mother. After all, how can you prioritize the needs of a big lump of a man over a tiny helpless baby?*

want you to go out as a couple and leave the baby or children behind and do something entirely devoted to adult pleasures. Even if you can't do it often, make a point of reserving a date on the calendar and making it a firm commitment. I'd also like you to make an effort to dress up and look nice for each other. In effect, I want you to say, by your actions, "I care about you, and we're not just mother and father, but a loving couple, too."

Isabel, twenty-nine, loved being a mother and was so wrapped up in her second baby that she joked she never wanted her children to leave home—or at the very least, they should buy the house next door! However, after a little persuading, she did agree to visit the local wine bar with her husband, Terry, while her mother babysat. "If there was a problem or we decided that it was not a good idea, I could be there in less than five minutes," Isabel explained, "and I agreed to go for one hour only."

It was really hard, and for the first fifteen minutes Isabel had to fight the urge to flee. "I kept thinking of that lovely milky smell of freshly bathed, fed, and sleeping baby, and I wanted to rush home and take a deep breath. Why did I want to be anywhere else than with my baby? But I told myself, 'Don't be stupid. It's only an hour, and if it gets to be too much, Terry will understand. It's not like you're addicted to your baby!' Although for a moment, that's how it felt. I had this ache, this need to hold her. Fortunately, it soon passed." Isabel discovered that it was really nice to be alone with Terry again. "In many ways, it was like old times, when we were first courting. In fact, we stayed out for an hour and a half and agreed that we would do it again sometime."

Ultimately, it doesn't matter what you and your partner talk about—although I'd prefer it not be about the baby—as long as you have some couple time in the first three months after the baby's arrival. If this is not possible, please tell each other, "I love you, and although I love our baby, I do miss time alone together, and I want to make it a priority that we have some couple time—and really soon." In this way, you're letting the other person know that he or she *is* important to each of you, rather than expecting him or her to know, and giving permission for the topic to be discussed (rather than swept under the carpet).

That request is often harder for women, and the next one can be harder for men. With your mother and father returning to center stage, you need to prioritize your partner over your parents.

Nigel, thirty-six, had a three-year-old son and a six-month-old daughter, and his mother would look after them from time to time. On one occasion, Kim, his thirty-four-year-old wife, went to pick up the children. The boy started acting up, and Nigel's mother admonished him, "Why did you have to start misbehaving when Mommy arrived? You've been such a good boy."

In the couple's next counseling session, Kim was furious. "What was she trying to say? That I'm a disruptive influence on my own son?"

"Not at all," Nigel said, trying to soothe her, "it's just that they were excited about you coming back and she was trying to calm them down."

"That's right," Kim snapped, "take her side, like you always do."

"She does a lot for us, and we should be grateful," Nigel defended himself.

It was clear that Kim believed Nigel was prioritizing his mother's feelings over hers. Nigel, of course, denied it.

"What would happen if you spoke to your mother?" I asked Nigel.

He looked doubtful, and I could understand his reticence.

Mothers are powerful people in their sons' lives, so when a man sees his mother interacting with his own children, it is bound to bring back unconscious memories. It is easy to be robbed of adult skills (negotiating or compromising) and return to being a child (people pleasing or sulking). Meanwhile, the man thinks his wife "knows I love her and will do anything for her," so he imagines that their relationship is protected and that he can therefore momentarily forget about her needs and concentrate on appeasing his mother. Unfortunately, his wife is feeling vulnerable, unsure of herself, and easily undermined. In her mind, his behavior is an act of betrayal.

After a long discussion, Nigel did decide to talk to his mother and tell her that Kim was upset about her comments. He would explain that they understood that she might need to reprimand their son when she looked after him. However, when their son was misbehaving and they were around, they would deal with it themselves.

If you've just had a baby, your priority should be putting a boundary around your new family unit. Obviously, it shouldn't be so high that no outside influences or advice can penetrate, but it also shouldn't be so low that anyone can wander in and make supposedly helpful comments.

Whether it is your parents or your partner's parents who are causing the rift, it is important to work as a team. You can achieve this goal by doing the following:

- **Discuss what you both agree on.** This shows that you're both on the same side.
- **Ask your partner how he or she is feeling at the moment.** This demonstrates that you're interested in your partner's emotions and accept that he or she might have cause to be upset.
- **Give your partner a chance to explain why he or she feels this way.** You might also learn something new about him or her.
- **Communicate your thoughts about the situation.** Although it might be helpful, in the long run, to see things from either your parents' or your in-laws' perspective, leave it until everybody is feeling calmer.
- **Give yourself time to reflect.** Then you are both ready to process any advice and decide whether to reject the outside influence or take part in it.

Summary

Children turn your life upside down and, no matter how much you try to prepare, there will be shocks and setbacks. If you're not careful, instead of supporting each other you can end up feeling alone or, worse still, blaming each other. So instead of coming down hard on yourself or your partner for any perceived shortcomings, accept that you will both occasionally get things wrong. Parenting ability emerges over time, through tackling challenges and overcoming difficulties. When you're feeling tired and stressed, it is important to tell yourself that this phase won't last forever and to be kind to each other.

Unfortunately, having children brings back problems from your own childhood that you thought had long since been buried, and this forces you to focus on your current relationship with your parents. Fortunately, there is also the potential to heal old wounds and right old wrongs.

4

What Children Need

Babies are small and helpless, and sometimes it feels like their needs are endless. They have to be fed, burped, diapered, held, and rocked to sleep. There's so much paraphernalia that has to be bought, from diapers, baby wipes, and changing tables to folding baby carriages and car seats. And that's just the beginning. Soon they will be crawling and then toddling off and exploring the world. It's not just their physical needs but their emotional welfare, too, that you need to consider. You want them to be happy, mix well with other children, and succeed at school.

In fact, if you have a quiet moment with your baby in your arms, it's easy to be overwhelmed by all the responsibilities and how much this tiny creature relies on you. You want to do your very best for your son or daughter (and possibly be the sort of parent you wished your parents could have been). But where do you start? What makes a good parent? How do you know if you're doing okay? There are so many components to the job of parenting and so many competing definitions of what being a successful parent means that I've decided to condense what babies and children need to its essence. In this way, you can decide what is truly important and not be distracted by the peripheral parts of parenting.

Your Children's Emotional Needs

Have you ever seen small children running down the street full of joy and the excitement of being alive? They're probably two or three and going faster than their little legs will carry them. It's almost inevitable that they'll fall down and start to cry. Perhaps they skin their knees or the damage is only to their pride, or maybe it's out of simple frustration, but they burst into tears. Their parents, who are watching, pick them up and soothe them. In a couple of minutes, the children are laughing again and either walking beside their parents or running off again—but probably a little slower.

This small drama is good parenting in a nutshell because it demonstrates the two key elements: helping your children regulate their emotions and fostering their independence. The first is important because young children don't have the ability (knowledge, experience, and a developed-enough brain) to soothe themselves. The second is vital because as much as we love our children, we bring them up to leave us. We don't want them still sleeping on our sofas at age forty!

Unfortunately, this simple scenario of children falling down and being picked up is harder than it seems. Many parents are tired and stressed, and instead of lovingly rescuing their children, they are annoyed and say things like "I told you to look where you were going, but did you listen to me?" or "That will teach you!" They might even give them a smack for being disobedient. Others will pick their children up but tell them not to make a fuss out of nothing: "Big boys don't cry" or "It's only a scrape. Look, there's nothing there." Instead of helping their children regulate their emotions, these parents are effectively saying, "Don't feel."

Occasionally, I see parents who try the philosophical approach and tell their children, "Crying won't make it better" (basically encouraging their children to rationalize away their feelings). Other parents are too busy talking to a friend on the phone or catching up on some work. Their children burst into tears and get no reaction, so they have to exaggerate their upset feelings and start to wail before getting any attention (and are therefore encouraged to set their internal "upset thermostat" so high that they need lots of soothing before they can feel safe again).

Not only is it important for parents to pick up their children when they fall, they also need to let them run off in the first place. From the moment babies can crawl and toddlers can walk, they want to test their independence and explore the world. However, they also need to feel safe. So a small child running down the street is probably looking back over his or her shoulder to check that Mom and Dad are still there.

> *Not only is it important for parents to pick up their children when they fall, they also need to let them run off in the first place.*

Unfortunately, it is hard to let our children make mistakes. We want to run after them and grab their hands before they fall over or keep such a tight watch on them that they don't escape in the first place. After all, it's a dangerous world, with speeding cars, aggressive dogs, and sharp objects. Obviously, we have to look out for our children's safety, because just as they can't regulate their feelings, they also can't judge risk. But it is equally important that we don't pass on our anxieties, either. (The speeding cars are on the other side of the park railing, the dogs are more interested in chasing sticks, and it's highly unlikely that our children will trip and hit their heads on the bench.)

When children run down the street and are lovingly picked up after falling, their parents have offered them everything they need. First, they have had the chance to test their independence and learn an important lesson for the future: I go faster running downhill, and therefore I'm more likely to fall down. (The experience will stick much better than merely being told, "Be careful!") Second, when things have gone wrong, their parents have kissed it better, rubbed it better, or given their kids a hug. (They've learned it's okay to express their distress, and someone will attend to their needs and help them regulate their feelings.)

Don't worry if once or twice you've been slow to pick up your child; you can't have eyes in the back of your head. What matters is not one particular occasion but the pattern. If you're concerned that you might not have been helping your children regulate their emotions or develop age-appropriate levels of independence, it's never too late to change, and when they're young, small adjustments in your behavior will reap big dividends.

So let's look at the key stages—baby, toddler, child, and teenager—and see how to regulate emotions and encourage independence.

Babies

There are hundreds of ways of successfully caring for a baby that cross many different cultures and eras. Ultimately, it doesn't really matter if you breast-feed or not, return to work or stay at home, or any of the other current controversies. What counts is that your baby feels safe and the care is reliable, predictable, and available.

John Bowlby (1907–1990) was a British psychologist famous for his pioneering work on child development and in particular the importance of parents in

> *Ultimately, it doesn't really matter if you breast-feed or not, return to work or stay at home, or any of the other current controversies. What counts is that your baby feels safe and the care is reliable, predictable, and available.*

providing a secure base for their baby: "These early attachment experiences then determine how one views the lovability and worthiness of the self, what it means to be cared for and care about others, what to pay attention to and what to forget, how to manage emotions and how to behave, what to expect from other people."

In many ways, looking after a baby is an interactive project. Your son or daughter arrives into the world with his or her unique store of genes that will be triggered and shaped by the world around him or her—which principally is you. Equally, you will be shaped by his or her needs and demands. Perhaps your baby is more sensitive and reacts more strongly to stimulation than others and therefore needs careful handling. Maybe your baby is calmer and more robust and you can pass him or her to almost anybody to hold. Slowly but surely you will get into the rhythm of each other and begin to "customize" each other.

Although you might think that experts hold all the answers—and certainly we can help by teaching skills and providing fresh insights—you and your partner are the real experts on your baby. After all, he or she is shaped by hours and hours of interaction with you, and his or her brain and emotions are being programmed by your personality and your family's way of doing things.

How to Help Regulate Emotions

Feelings in babies start in a very basic way. They are either content or distressed, comfortable or uncomfortable. Your job is to help your baby bring these intense emotions down to a more manageable level (so he or she can do it alone when older). The obvious ways of regulating your baby are touch and sound: holding, stroking, singing, cooing, playing, talking in a sweet, soft voice, and making eye contact. If you are calm and can tolerate his or her uncomfortable feelings, your baby will slowly synchronize with your relaxed, regular heartbeat and feel comfortable again. That's why it is particularly effective to hold your baby close to your chest.

However, if you are angry or hostile and pick up your baby abruptly or so tightly that it is stifling, his or her distress will be amplified by yours (and, potentially, yours by his or hers). Conversely, if you are insensitive to your baby's crying, you will upset the delicate programming that's starting in his or her brain. (These babies get no help bringing their distress down to a manageable level, beyond crying themselves to the point of exhaustion.)

Even from a very young age, babies are trying to make sense of the world around them and work out the difference between a smiling face and a cross face. If mothers and fathers act in predictable ways, babies begin to learn the pattern: If I cry, someone will pick me up gently. Their brains are being programmed with an important message: It's okay to have these horrible feelings, because they can be attended to and managed.

Equally important, babies learn that if they gurgle happily, other people will mirror those good emotions and support them. Slowly but surely, they are getting introduced into the human race and learning what to expect from other people.

How to Foster Independence

A baby is still very much part of the mother. She provides the milk to feed them and boost their immune protection. Her heart and blood pressure help regulate theirs. Her touch helps stimulate their muscles and encourage growth and, as I've already explained, disperse their stress hormones. So in many ways, it seems extraordinary to talk about fostering independence at this stage. Yet being a mother can become a form of slavery, in which you are not free to come and go. It is hard to be happy and contented if you can never step away, take a break, and mentally regroup (and since babies mirror their mothers, they won't be content, either).

So please, after the initial newborn stage, foster a little independence—which could be more your independence from your baby than vice versa—and allow other people to help out. Remember, what counts is that the care is reliable, predictable, and consistent. If you're a mother, that could come from your partner. If you're a father, step forward and become part of your baby's support team. If there are other people who are happy to assist, please welcome them with open arms.

To help your baby feel safe, even when you're in the next room, use your voice as a transitional object (something to take the place of the physical parent-child bond). I recommend singing or giving your baby a running commentary: "I'm just going into the next room to get some baby wipes to take all that goo off your face" or "Where are those wipes? Where are they hiding?" followed by "Guess who's coming back in a moment?" Make your tone of voice upbeat and exciting, as if this is the most thrilling news ever, because babies hear messages only as positive or negative and you don't want there to be any confusion.

Another idea is to play peek-a-boo with your baby. This is where you disappear out of his or her line of vision, like behind the stroller, for just a second and then pop back out again. You need to play it several times so your baby can predict the pattern. First you will disappear (potentially frightening), and then you will reappear (reassuring). Even at this early age, babies are learning to cope with separation, which will stand them in good stead when they are adults. What we fear (abandonment) can also be thrilling and have a positive side (independence).

How to Regulate Yourself

Understanding how your mood affects your baby can be a little unsettling. There's no problem when you're feeling relaxed and happy, but life isn't always like that. What about the times when your partner is yelling, "Where are the keys?," your toddler is scribbling over some important paperwork, and you've had only three hours of sleep? In fact, how can you regulate your baby's emotions when you're not quite certain how to regulate your own?

Don't worry, most people are equally shaky on this concept, but mastering it will not only help you raise a happy child but also improve your relationship with your partner and make you feel more grounded in your own skin. Here are some tips:

1. How do you currently soothe yourself or take the edge off your stress? Write down as many as possible ways on a piece of paper.

2. Divide them into positive ones (which not only work at the time but also have no long-term unwanted consequences) and negative ones (which temporarily make us feel better but often come back to bite us). For example, positive ways of soothing include taking a couple of deep breaths, counting to ten before speaking, soaking in a hot bath, making a cup of tea, having your hair done, or talking to a friend on the phone. Negative ones might be stuffing your face with chocolate, drinking a bottle of wine, shutting down (for example, ignoring your partner's request to help look for lost keys), or shouting at your partner, "How should I know where your damn keys are?" (which gets the anger out but makes matters worse).

3. How could you expand the positive ways of soothing and cut down on the negative ways?

4. Look at whether you are still expecting your partner to regulate your feelings—much as you were soothed by your parents when you were a child—and getting angry when he or she fails. (For example, the partner who has lost the keys wants the other one to find them and make him or her feel better.) Of course, our loved ones can help soothe us from time to time, especially in times of adversity, but ultimately we must take responsibility for regulating ourselves.

5. Offer yourself the same deal that you're going to offer your baby. You don't question whether your baby has the "right" to be distressed or happy, and I'd like you to accept and acknowledge your feelings too—especially the negative ones, which most people would rather ignore or suppress.

6. Identify the emotion and mentally tell yourself, *I'm feeling . . .* For example, *I'm feeling annoyed with my partner for demanding that I put down everything and find the keys.* You'll be surprised how difficult this can be—partly because we go to extraordinary lengths to avoid difficult feelings and partly because we seldom stop and think. However, it is useful to know if you are simply annoyed rather than angry, bitter, or boiling with rage.

7. Repeat the feelings to yourself. Just by naming them, you will begin to feel calmer.

8. Finally, you're ready to discover what your feelings are trying to tell you—because negative reactions are there for a reason— and start to act on them. Returning to our example, the couple with the lost keys could decide that mornings are too rushed and that it might be better to prepare as much as possible the night before.

Remember, it takes time and energy to become more in tune with yourself. However, you need to understand your own feelings to be able to read your baby's.

Toddlers

There is a massive amount of development in the brain between six and twelve months old. All the neurons, the nerve cells that communicate information, are present at birth, but it takes time and exposure to the world for them to begin to connect and to work. Around the age at which a child learns to walk, the frontal cortex begins to mature, and toddlers can register fear, sadness, shame, and guilt (which exist to help us control our behavior and fit into our families).

These are difficult and painful feelings, and toddlers need to learn to accept them, tolerate them, and discover that there are ways of dealing with them. (I will explain how in a moment.) It is not just negative emotions that toddlers need help dealing with; they also need help dealing with emotions at the other end of the spectrum, like joy and excitement.

Dr. Allan Schore, a leading researcher in neuropsychology at UCLA's Department of Psychiatry and Biobehavioral Sciences, has been studying how psychological and biological factors interact during the first two years of life. Much of his work deals not only with trauma and negativity but also the positive emotions of interest, excitement, and enjoyment. "Joy has something to do with the quality of life," he stated, "and the polar opposite of joy would be shame. The attachment to the mother is therefore not only minimizing negative states but also maximizing positive states."

Unfortunately, lots of parents are not comfortable with strong feelings themselves, whether positive or negative, and if you can't bear those feelings in yourself, you won't be able to bear them in your children. So these parents tell their offspring: "Shut up" or "Don't try it on me" or "There'll be tears before bedtime." In effect, the toddlers have to regulate their parents by being good little boys or girls (and not getting too excited or too upset). On the surface, these children seem calm and pliant, but their emotions are going through the roof. Since there is nobody to regulate them, they have no option but to shut down or dissociate from their feelings, which only creates problems for the future.

Another common pattern at this stage, with equally far-reaching consequences, is parents who are sometimes concerned and sometimes shut down. Their children are forced to register the state of their parents' minds. However, rather than suppress their feelings, they exaggerate them in an attempt to get their parents' attention. They end up becoming overly aware of their feelings and crying hysterically or throwing temper tantrums. This is horrible for the parents—who are equally ambivalent about sadness, shame, and guilt themselves—so rather than calmly helping their sons and daughters to regulate their emotions, they will try to suppress them (by blocking the upset feelings with sweets or some other treat, or else shouting at their children). The result is that the toddler's feelings are like a car speeding out of control when suddenly the brakes have been slammed on.

How to Help Regulate Emotions

Every toddler has tantrums. Sometimes they are frustrated that their arms can't reach something or they are tired, but more often than not, they are upset about something and don't have the words or skills yet to express themselves. So although it is tempting to try to discipline or reprimand them, you are wasting your energy (and probably just upsetting yourself, too, and because your toddler mirrors your mood, this only makes the situation worse). Think of your child's brain as being only partly wired, and the strong emotions have blown the fuse. The lights can't come back on until everything has calmed down. So how do you achieve that?

In many ways, the first step is the hardest: put your own stuff aside. I know that toddlers usually choose the worse place possible, like the middle of the supermarket, to throw a tantrum, and you're aware of all the other shoppers thinking, *He doesn't know how to control that kid*, or *Why does she have to bring that child to the grocery store?* It doesn't matter what they think (and you are probably projecting your own thoughts onto them, anyway). So stop looking at your watch frantically and wishing you were somewhere else. Use the tantrum as an opportunity to help your child's development.

Crouch down so you're at eye level with your child. Imagine what he or she is feeling and why, and put it into words: "You're angry because you wanted the sweets" or "You're upset because you want to go to the park." I call this technique *acknowledge and name*, because you acknowledge the feeling and name it. If you have no idea why your child is throwing a tantrum, just concentrate on identifying the emotion. Keep your voice calm, low, and soothing and repeat your sentence until you have your child's complete attention and his or her emotions have begun to return to normal. At this point, you can begin to reason or explain: "We'll have tea when we get home, and we're going to have sausages; you like that." Alternatively, you can distract—for example, let your child play with the little mirror in your handbag or play a game of I Spy.

A hug is also a good idea; it emotionally holds children and shows them that they are as acceptable when they're upset as when they're happy, and, even more important, that you care about their feelings (and not just the nice ones). In addition, you have also helped them begin to name, understand, and deal with difficult emotions.

How to Foster Independence

Toddlers need to explore, but they have no knowledge of the world and how dangerous it can be. So how do you balance their need to be free and discover things for themselves with your need to keep them safe? I know this is a controversial idea, but I'm a big fan of playpens, since they allow children independent play without us forever joining in and showing them how to put one brick on top of another or which shape goes through which hole. Lots of parents are uncomfortable with walking reins, tethers, and wrist links, but they give children a degree of autonomy and can prevent your whole communication from consisting of "Hold my hand," "Put that back," "Get away from there," and "Come over here."

You can help your toddlers begin to decide for themselves what is right or wrong by using *no* sparingly. (I'm sure you know lots of kids who think their names end in *no* (Jamie-No or Lucy-No!) If your toddler is about to do something that you want to stop—like reaching up to a coffee table to grab a glass of water—make a small *ahh* noise in the back of your throat. It acts as a mild corrective, and children have the option to decide to stop for themselves. You'll be surprised how often it works (please praise them when it does), and you can keep *no* for when you really need it.

In safe environments, like a park, let toddlers run off and decide for themselves what is an okay distance. If you're concerned that your children have gone too far, instead of running after them, try calling their names and getting their attention, and then pretend to run in the opposite direction. Guess what? Your children will turn round and chase you. It seems like a fun game, but you're also teaching them to watch you.

Improve Your
Toddler's Emotional Vocabulary

The more words your child knows, the better he or she will be able to express him- or herself. Unfortunately, even as adults, we are not always clear what is an emotion and what is a thought. Often in my counseling room, I ask people to name the feeling they are having, and they will say, "I feel he hasn't heard a word I've said" or "I feel she is shutting me out." I have to push to get them to name the feeling rather than explain the thought. For example, are they upset, angry, feeling misunderstood?

Look at the list below of common uncomfortable feelings and try to put them into your everyday vocabulary so they trickle down into your toddler's brain:

Afraid	Upset	Lonely
Anxious	Annoyed	Left out
Ashamed	Angry	Confused
Nervous	Frustrated	Disappointed
Sorry	Feeling misunderstood	Jealous
Unsure	Worried	Sad

Use these feeling words to discuss characters in the book you're reading to your child or the program that you're watching together on the TV. When your child is having a tantrum, don't worry whether he or she knows the word yet; it is a great opportunity to learn.

Children Older Than Three

Up to this point, children have principally seen the world through their parents' eyes. The family's way of doing things is the only way. (If they've been to a nursery or a day care center, this becomes an extension of their regular routine, and the people are like an extended family.) Even when your child has gone into unfamiliar surroundings, like a mother-and-toddler group or a playgroup, you or your partner has been there or has left the child for only a short while.

Around age three, your children begin to be exposed to the wider world and learn the rules (which could be different from yours). They will soon be going to school, making new friends, and discovering different ways of doing things. This age is a time of transition from babyhood (and complete dependence) to being a small child (and the beginning of independence), and children can swing wildly from one extreme to the other. This can be bewildering for parents, who never know quite what to expect, and it underlines the importance of regulating children.

How to Help Regulate Emotions

There is so much to discover and so much information to process that it can be overwhelming for a small brain. It helps to have a regular routine of what happens so that children know what is expected of them. In effect, there is a time to get up, to dress, to have breakfast, to brush their teeth, and so on. When everything goes in a predictable order, children can focus on the new and surprising aspects of life rather than encounter them with their brain already overloaded from making sense of how the regular things are being done today. A routine is safe and calming because children know where they are.

The best way for children to learn is through positive feedback. Unfortunately, we tend to take for granted what's going well and focus on what isn't. Recently I witnessed a mother having coffee in a café with her two daughters under five. She wanted to listen to the conversation between the woman behind the counter and another regular customer and then pitch in with an occasional comment herself. So when the children were eating their food and talking to each other, she ignored them. But when they started kicking each other or stealing each other's food, she gave them her undivided attention: "Sit up straight" and "Don't do that." In effect, she was rewarding their bad behavior, because children would rather have negative attention than none at all. It was not very long before both children were in tears and the mother was exasperated.

I wonder what would have happened if she had praised what she'd liked: "You're sitting up really nicely at the table" and "You're eating your own food; that's really polite." Not only would she have taught her children what was expected in these unfamiliar surroundings, but she would have also had the chance for a bit of uninterrupted adult conversation as well. In addition, her children would have had a clear sense of the rules and been able to regulate their own behavior rather than being forever corrected.

One of my key messages to clients in unhappy relationships is that carrots work better than sticks. It's even more important when dealing with children rather than adults. Try to make the feedback as detailed as possible so your children know exactly what they've done right and why you are pleased. For example, "You put on your own clothes this morning; that was really helpful" or "You hung your coat on the hook when you came home; that was really tidy." This technique is called *descriptive praise* because you describe the good behavior and thereby encourage your children to do it again rather than just giving empty compliments like "What a clever boy" or "You're a wonderful girl."

One of my key messages to clients in unhappy relationships is that carrots work better than sticks.

Stephen Grosz is a psychoanalyst and a lecturer at University College London. In his book *The Examined Life*, he quotes research by Carol Dweck (whom we met in the last chapter) on children's reactions to praise. One group was complimented for its hard work ("You did really well; you must have tried hard"), and the other was praised for its talent ("You did really well, you're so clever"). The children who were praised for being clever worried more about failure, took fewer risks, and experienced a drop in their self-esteem.

No wonder Grosz was anxious when he overheard a nursery assistant's empty praise for his daughter's drawing: "Wow, you're really an artist." He gave himself the task of solving the following problem: If praise alone doesn't build confidence, what does? He found the answer watching an eighty-year-old remedial teacher at work. When a four-year-old boy in her class stopped drawing a picture and looked up, Grosz thought he was looking for praise, but instead the teacher commented, "There's a lot of blue in your picture." It encouraged the boy to explain and draw more.

"Unhurried, she talked to the child," wrote Grosz, "but more important, she observed, she listened. She was present. Being present builds a child's confidence because it lets the child know that she is worth thinking about. Without this, a child might come to believe her activity is just a means to gain praise rather than an end in itself. How can we expect a child to be attentive, if we're not attentive to her?"

How to Foster Independence

Another way of building children's self-confidence is letting them do things for themselves. So although it is quicker, for example, to button up their coats yourself, it is better if you let them do it. Follow it up with a bit of descriptive praise: "You buttoned all your own buttons; you're becoming a big boy." Don't go overboard—for example, "You're so talented" or "You're the best girl in the world," because children know when praise is empty, and you'll have no superlatives left for something genuinely spectacular.

What tasks can your children perform? Even young ones can straighten up their blanket in the morning, dry themselves after a bath, put their toys away, or set the table for tea. Doing small jobs gives small children agency (having some control over their environment) and fosters independence. Once you've established a family routine, your children will start to adopt it as their own rather than forever having to be told, "Do this" or asked, "Why haven't you done that?"

You can encourage children's cooperation by helping them to think ahead. Adults usually have lists in their heads of tasks to complete: buy some milk, prepare tea, answer e-mails, and be ready to go out by seven. Children, however, live in the moment, which is one of their great charms, but it causes stress and arguments when they want to play and you need to rush them out the door. No wonder there are tears and tantrums and you lose your temper.

I witnessed a good example of how thinking ahead builds cooperation when traveling by train with my new puppy. Pumpkin was just a little more than a year old, cute enough to be a magnet to small children but steady enough for him to be safe. A three-year-old girl in our car was completely entranced, becoming more and more confident about stroking him and putting her arms round his neck as the journey progressed. Her mother was aware that her daughter wanted to continue playing with Pumpkin—and possibly take him home, too! There could have been an ugly scene.

However, she helped her daughter think ahead by saying, "It's our stop next and we'll have to get off, so give Pumpkin a last stroke." Children often get upset because our instructions come, for them, out of the blue, and they find it hard to switch from one activity to another. Fortunately, the mother had given her daughter enough time to prepare. A couple of minutes later, the mother explained what was going to be done next. "Let's get you into your stroller so we can get off the train easily." Rather than having to be lifted into the stroller, the child undid the straps and climbed in herself, without complaint, and was ready to leave when the train arrived at their station.

You can further help your children to "own" what comes next by asking them a question so they can think ahead for themselves rather than just being told. For example, you could say, "We're coming to our station. What do you do before we get off the train?"

Planning Realistically

This next idea comes from puppy training. This is not as strange as it might sound. One of the most important tasks is to get your puppy to heel without you having to pull on the leash. If you don't get it right, you'll spend the next twelve years or more being dragged behind an excited dog (something I know from experience). The dog-training book I bought advised that when my puppy pulled, I should stop immediately and wait until he sat down. When his bottom was on the pavement, I could start walking again. This advice was meant to let him discover the key to moving ahead for himself—rather than my saying, "Sit"—because this would make the lesson sink in faster and better. It's similar to asking your children questions ahead of time rather than always telling them what to do.

So far, so good, but the crucial advice that helped me crack the lesson to heel was "Never go anywhere with a puppy when you're in a hurry." With my previous dog, I'd be rushing to the post office before it closed and let him get away with pulling, not sitting, at the curb when I crossed the street or lunging at a passing leaf. The more I let him get away with things, the worse his heeling became and the more likely he was to pull next time we were out together. In effect, I had set myself up for a lifetime of pulling on the leash.

So here's my tip in a nutshell: "Never go anywhere with a small child when you're in a hurry." Children know when you're up against the clock.

They know you will buy them off with sweets. They know you will put up with bad or whiny behavior because you haven't got time to deal with it. (You're also too busy clock watching to help your child think ahead or praise any helpful behavior.)

Obviously, it is impossible to *never* go anywhere with a small child when you're in a hurry. However, you *can* plan realistically and not try to fit too much into your day. Remember, small children live in the moment; you don't need to stuff their day with exciting activities; they can learn so much from something simple, like going to the store, if you use your imagination. They're at their best when not harried and hurried, so do less and take longer to do it.

Children Six and Older

With better coordination, strength, and motor skills, children develop quickly, trying different sports and learning to read, write, and draw. They are also beginning to find their own interests and tastes (which might be different from yours) and make their own friends (rather than play with the children of your friends). Whereas previously their main focus might have been on how acceptable they were to their parents, siblings, and grandparents, now their attention switches to their peer group.

At this stage, children start to identify as boys or girls and develop strong loyalties to groups (like Brownies, Scouts, a soccer team, or a drama club), idols (music or TV stars), and, of course, their friends. This goes hand in hand with the development of a strong sense of fairness and the importance of following rules. However, if children have a falling out with their peer group, it can seem like the end of the world, and they need a lot of help and understanding from their parents to handle the difficult feelings. Ultimately, the most important lesson to learn at this age is that it's possible to have a disagreement with someone but still love that person.

How to Help Regulate Emotions

Parents need endless patience because small children are always asking difficult questions—like "Why is water wet?"—as they try to make sense of the wider world. Although these questions might test our knowledge of physics, history, or math, what is most unsettling is that they question our rules and test our boundaries. It might seem they are being difficult or rebellious, but they just need to understand before they can adopt the rules themselves. Children around age six are obsessed with fairness, and their standard answer to any request is often "Why?" or, more likely, "It's not fair."

Don't get drawn into a debate about the rights and wrongs, but ask, for example, why they think they should stay seated at the table while eating their food. If they refuse to answer or claim they don't know, ask them to guess. They will probably come quite close. For example, "I'll make a mess if I stand up" or "I'll get a stomachache if I run around." Praise what they get right and add any explanation of your own. Next, get them to repeat why they shouldn't get up from the table—for example, "I shouldn't get up from the table because I'll put sticky fingers everywhere." By repeating rules, children own them and begin to regulate themselves.

If your children refuse to answer or run away, let it drop until they are calmer and able to think straight. At this age, children will always need to ask something, so wait for your opportunity. Put down whatever you're doing, give them your full attention, and say, "I'd be happy to answer your question, but first, will you answer mine? Why shouldn't you get up from the table while you're still eating?"

Praise your children when they give the right answer, or even when just some element of the answer is correct, and ask them to repeat the reason again. Next time they stay at the table until given permission to leave, use descriptive praise to explain why you approve: "Well done for sitting still at the table; that was really polite."

Children of this age still need help processing difficult feelings and often end up acting out their distress. It is tempting to discipline them or give them a good talking-to for bad behavior—for example, shoving one of their teammates while playing soccer. Instead of concentrating on *what* they have done, spend a moment with them to look at *why*, and thereby acknowledge their upset feelings.

Perhaps they will be able to name the feelings for themselves, so ask, "What did you feel when you pushed your friend?" If they don't know or they give their thoughts rather than feelings ("He was calling me names"), ask them again to guess. Be aware that they are struggling with the most toxic of all human emotions: shame. This makes us feel that we are not good enough or are bad people, which is the opposite of feeling acceptable and loved. Although shame is a difficult feeling at any age, it is particularly hard between six and twelve, when we're desperately trying to fit in.

If your children can't name the feeling, provide the word for them: "You were angry" or "It felt unfair." Next, address the thoughts attached to the feelings: "Your friend seemed to get all the passes" or "Her dad has been giving her extra coaching."

My basic rule is to *accept the feelings* (we can't help how we feel) but *challenge the thoughts*. So instead of saying, "Don't be stupid" or "You shouldn't do that," be sympathetic and then help with the underlying problem. For example, you could ask, "How could you get more passes from your teammates?" or offer solutions, like "Your uncle's a good coach. Shall we get some advice from him?"

By following this pattern—identifying the feeling and then looking at the underlying causes—you will have helped your children learn perhaps the most important lesson of all. We should listen to our feelings rather than ignoring them, suppressing them, or distracting ourselves, because our feelings, especially the negative ones, are telling us something important.

> *We should listen to our feelings rather than ignoring them, suppressing them, or distracting ourselves, because our feelings, especially the negative ones, are telling us something important.*

Once you've learned anything from the event, that's the moment to make it right. So, for example, encourage your children to apologize to their friends, whatever the provocation, because they broke the rules (of the game or of friendship). Apologizing reinforces the idea that you can argue, make up, and still be friends.

While I'm on the subject, when you've done something wrong yourself, please apologize to your children. For example, "I'm sorry I shouted at you; that was wrong" or "I'm sorry I lost my temper and didn't listen properly to what you said." Not only are you modeling the behavior that you want from them, you're also showing them that you play by the rules yourself (rather than having one rule for yourself and one for everybody else). Ultimately, knowing that there are rules that everybody abides by makes children feel secure and less anxious.

How to Foster Independence

Although children want your physical presence less by the time they are six, they need more time alone with you to process their difficult emotions. That's why I recommend regular one-to-one time with each child—especially by the parent of the same sex—so your children can begin to learn what it means to be a boy or a girl and how men and women do things.

Whether you read a story each night or bathe your child, set aside ten minutes a day (at least five times a week) when you can be quiet together and your child has your undivided attention. (If you can do a longer activity together as well, that's great.) I know from my clients how busy families are and how much I'm asking—particularly of men, who often prioritize work. However, your children need regular time alone with you (rather than mediated through your wife), and that's much more important than all the gadgets, holidays, and bigger backyards that you're toiling so hard to buy.

Most days, these few minutes will be full of trivia. However, time alone keeps you informed about the minutiae of their lives (such as who's their best friend today and the name of their soccer coach) and provides the opportunity for important conversations and a safety net as they launch themselves into the wider world. There is a second advantage to time alone with you: fewer squabbles between siblings. This is because each child feels secure about your love and is therefore less likely to compete with a brother or a sister for your attention. It might be tempting to weigh in when your children argue with their friends or each other, but hold back on minor disputes; this will give them the opportunity to resolve things for themselves.

Finally, it is important to give your children enough space to develop interests for themselves. Erik Erikson (1902–1994), a German-born American developmental psychologist, coined the term *identity crisis*. His life's work was understanding how we develop an identity—possibly because he was born after his mother had an affair and his biological father's identity was kept a secret. In addition, Erikson was blond-haired and blue-eyed and Jewish. At Hebrew school the kids teased him for looking Nordic, and at public school he was mocked for being Jewish.

Erikson described the stage from ages five to twelve as the "age of competence," when children start recognizing their special abilities and pursuing particular interests. He warned that if they were not allowed to discover their own talents in their own time, they would lack motivation and develop low self-esteem and lethargy.

How to Deal with Your Frustration

Everybody gets frustrated with their children from time to time. The temptation is to beat yourself up—and maybe your partner, too—for not being patient enough. Or maybe you snap at the kids and are then doubly down on yourself. However, just as I asked you to help your children accept their difficult and uncomfortable feelings, I'd like you to extend the same courtesy to yourself (and your partner). When one or both of you are feeling frustrated, ask yourself: Why am I frustrated? What are my feelings trying to tell me? What do I need to do differently?

Here are some possible answers:

- You and your child have gotten out of sync with each other. Perhaps you're responding not to the needs of your child but to what you think those needs should be.
- You have not given enough descriptive praise, and your child is acting out in order to get your attention—even if it is crabby and distracted attention, because that is better than no attention at all.
- Your children are unclear about the rules and what you want from them. In your head, for example, it's obvious that they should put on their shoes and be ready for school; but have you told them, nagged them, and shouted at them rather than getting them to think ahead and own the routine for themselves?
- You have been thinking too far ahead yourself. Instead of focusing on the next step, are you worrying, for example, about taking the car in for service after lunch or how to pay the bills at the end of the month?

- You need to remove obstacles that make it harder for your children to cooperate. For example, they are less likely to be getting dressed if the TV is on. What could you do to make it easier for your children to succeed?
- You have been trying to fit too much into your day, and you're making yourself stressed and anxious.
- You need to look after yourself more. How can you attend to everybody else's needs and keep on giving when you're close to empty yourself?
- You find it hard to ask for what you need. Perhaps you're hoping that your partner will come and give you a kiss on your forehead and say, "You're doing so well" or "I love you." Instead of waiting, possibly forever, why not ask your partner, rather than expecting him or her to be a mind reader?

Teenagers

Whatever happened to that pleasant and cooperative child you once knew? It might seem that overnight your son or daughter has been replaced by a surly and dismissive stranger, but teenage rebellion is a vital part of growing up. Whereas the previous stages were all about belonging and fitting in, first with your family and then with the peer group, this stage is centered on asserting independence and becoming his or her own person. The easiest place to start is by saying, "I don't want to be anything like my parents." Obviously, it will feel incredibly rejecting to you.

However, please be reassured. It is only once your children have questioned or rejected everything that you stand for that they can begin to form their own identities. In the end, they will probably choose to adopt many aspects of your lifestyle, morals, and way of looking at the world. For example, my mother was a teacher (her mother and her grandmother were, too). The last thing I wanted to be as a teenager was a teacher, but here I am, forty years later, writing books and teaching about relationships! So although the teenage years are a difficult life stage and there will be times when you feel overwhelmed, I would be more concerned if your teenager was *not* rebelling.

> *Although the teenage years are a difficult life stage and there will be times when you feel overwhelmed, I would be more concerned if your teenager was not rebelling.*

Diana Baumrind is a developmental psychologist (born in 1927) who worked at the Institute for Human Development at the University of California at Berkeley and conducted a series of important studies on Western parenting in the 1960s. She is best known for classifying three types of parents: authoritarian (who expect high levels of conformity and compliance with little or no discussion of the rules), permissive (who are indulgent, lenient, and responsive but place few demands or controls on their children's behavior), and authoritative (who are demanding but also responsive to their children, so there is discussion and explanation about the rules). Although there are pros and cons for all three styles, during the teenage years, the first two can become problematic.

Small children respond well to rules; however, teenagers need the reasons for something explained (rather than being told, "Because I say so") and to believe that any punishment is both reasonable and fair. Therefore, authoritarian parents have to become more responsive to their children; otherwise, the children might have a spectacular teenage rebellion to try to make themselves heard and be taken seriously. With permissive parenting, children tend to be more impulsive, since they've had little external help to regulate themselves, and in their teenage years, they may engage in heavy drinking or experiment with drugs. It is often necessary for permissive parents to introduce a consistent set of rules so their children have something solid to rebel against.

Authoritative parents should find it easier to negotiate with their teenagers, because these parents are used to explaining rather than demanding. However, it is still hard for them to find a balance between disciplining their teens with restrictions and setting standards for socially acceptable behavior. There should be plenty of time to consider each decision without, on the one hand, simply giving in to your children's desires or, on the other hand, falling in with the group consensus of other parents.

Finally, whatever your parenting style, it is important to remember that teenagers are incredibly vulnerable because they are trying on new identities and experiencing everything, like attention from the opposite sex or falling in love, for the first time. It is easy to tease them or put them down, especially if you are not that comfortable in your own skin, but be aware that words at this age resonate stronger and last longer than you imagine.

> *Whatever your parenting style, it is important to remember that teenagers are incredibly vulnerable because they are trying on new identities and experiencing everything, like attention from the opposite sex or falling in love, for the first time.*

How to Help Regulate Emotions

The idea is to give your children a secure base to rebel against rather than making up the rules (or bending them) as you go along. It is particularly important that you and your partner present a united front, since children, and teenagers in particular, will do their best to divide and conquer.

So while you might have gotten away with different rules from each of you when they were younger, it is important now for you and your partner to agree on four central tenets:

- **Be consistent.** Otherwise, your children will spend their energy and exhaust your patience wheedling, testing your boundaries, and looking for loopholes. Remember, you hold all the main cards (like money and car keys), whereas your children's only power is to wear you down. If you give in because they're asking for the hundredth time, you've just trained them to pester for longer and longer. It might be hard to stand firm, but you will save yourself a lot of aggravation in the long run.
- **Don't argue about the children in front of them.** Otherwise, you're handing them ammunition to divide and conquer.
- **Don't make a policy on the spot.** Give yourself time to think through new requests and discuss the implications with your partner.
- **Back each other up even when you disagree.** This is perhaps the hardest part of parenting teenagers, since you're bound to have different opinions. I'll have more advice on being a team at the end of this section.

Ultimately, teenagers need time, attention, and to have their rebellion be center stage rather than in a dark corner because their parents are too busy working, fighting with each other, or struggling with their own issues. If it does not seem safe for your children to rebel, because they don't want to add stress to a chaotic household or are too busy supporting their parents and helping them through *their* distress, they will push their identity issues aside. On the surface, these teenagers will seem really "together," but in reality, their adult persona is flimsy, without the space to experiment or discover their true selves. What normally happens is that they put off having their rebellion until they are older—normally around forty, when they have a spectacular midlife crisis instead.

While some teenagers opt out of rebelling altogether, others find their rebellion ignored or noticed only when they go spectacularly off the rails (with alcohol, drugs, or teen pregnancy). I know this sounds really scary, but if you have been used to giving your children plenty of positive attention and praising their good behavior, you are unlikely to fall into the trap of giving them negative attention when they become teenagers.

How to Foster Independence

Although teenagers want your presence less, they need you more; this is in sharp contrast to babies and toddlers, who might want you more but actually need you less. Although any competent adult can change a diaper or make tea, you don't want to delegate the important teenage issues to someone else, like choosing exam options, monitoring whether your child has fallen in with the wrong crowd, and offering moral guidance.

Because parents still have better judgment about risks and the long-term implications of any behavior, it is really hard to strike the right balance between being in charge and allowing teenagers enough freedom to discover who they are and what is right for them. However, do give them room to develop their own cultural interests: being into punk, Goth, heavy metal, hip-hop, or whatever is the first draft of defining who they are. At this age, there is nothing more annoying than your parents muscling in on your music or television programs or, worse still, trying to be friends with your friends. If you're ever in doubt, think back to your own teenage years.

I would also choose your battles very carefully. Ultimately, we can't *make* anybody—our partners or our children—do anything, and we waste a lot of time and emotional energy in the process. We can, however, influence, encourage, teach, negotiate, or make a deal. If you find yourself trying to make a rule stick as a point of principle, please stop and think again.

Laura, forty-two, had a daughter of twelve and a son of fifteen, and she was fed up with them leaving the back door open. "The dog comes in from the garden with his muddy paws and goes straight up to my bedroom and climbs on to my white bedspread," she complained. "I've had to wash everything three times in the last week. How can I make them close the door?"

Although I expected Laura to be annoyed when I shrugged and explained that it was impossible to *make* anybody do anything, she seemed relieved instead. "I've tried nagging and shouting," she admitted, "and of course they don't work. And now I realize that I'd been setting myself up for failure." So we discussed the techniques for thinking ahead, and Laura decided to talk to her son and daughter when she was calm.

"Ask them what they should do when they come back into the house and why," I suggested. "When they can answer and repeat the policy back to you, they begin to own it."

Next, Laura began to come up with other ways to solve the problem, like closing her bedroom door and training the dog not to jump on the furniture, but she broke off halfway through. "It would be really nice if someone listened to something I said!" she exclaimed. The force of that statement almost took my breath away, so I stopped her and we looked deeper.

The back door had become a *point of principle* that was important to Laura but seemed totally random to her children, and her level of distress about it was out of all proportion to their crime.

"What would be a much more important battle to win?" I asked.

"My son tries to get away with the minimum amount of homework," she replied, "and as long as he scrapes through, that's good enough for him."

"So perhaps the 'something' he listens to should be homework, not shutting the back door," I proposed.

When Laura began to choose her battles, she reported back that she felt less out of control, and the atmosphere at home became calmer.

Defining Your Specific Parenting Differences

Creating a united front can be really difficult. Not only are teenagers experts at finding your weak points and exploiting them, but many of the dilemmas they pose need an answer one way or the other—for example, whether your daughter can go to the rock festival—so you and your partner can't agree to differ. Here are some guidelines for avoiding the worst pitfalls:

- Give each other your undivided attention. There's no point trying to talk while one person is cooking or is on the computer.
- Set a limit on how long you're going to discuss the issue. If you haven't come to a resolution by the end of the allotted time, it probably means you're going in circles. Stop and make an appointment to talk again.
- Stick to one topic at a time. Resist the temptation to throw in similar situations, even if they back up your case, because you're making it harder for yourselves.
- Start with what you agree on—for example, "We both want the best for our children" or "Schooling is a top priority."
- Avoid describing the problem (which can be heard as blaming); instead, focus on finding an answer.
- It is important that both of you try to find a solution so that both of you will have a stake in following it through.
- Never criticize your partner's ideas; even seemingly stupid ones can trigger better ideas.
- Give positive feedback to your partner during the discussion: "That's a good point" or "I agree with you on that." This will help build agreement.
- Remember, there is no right or wrong way to bring up children, just lots of different opinions that deserve to be listened to and taken seriously.

Why Couples Argue About Their Children

When an issue keeps coming back, it is nearly always about something deeper than, for example, what time children should go to bed or saying "please" and "thank you." In my opinion, the argument is probably only 20 percent about the topic under discussion and 80 percent about hidden subjects.

Sometimes one partner is afraid to talk about what's really driving his or her anger for fear of being rejected. For example, an argument about children's bedtimes could really be about sex, because one partner feels that unless the two of you have enough adult time together *and* get into bed at a decent time, then you will never have enough sex. It is hard to admit that you feel unloved; it's easier to try to tackle what you consider the cause of the problem than own up and discuss possible solutions to the underlying issue.

Perhaps one or both partners are not wholly aware of what's behind the argument; perhaps they have never stopped to think about it, or the roots are too far back in childhood. For example, whether the children say "please" and "thank you" could be important to the wife because her own father or mother was a dictator, and extreme politeness could sometimes tame the anger. To the husband, whose childhood did not make him feel anxious, this attitude makes no sense or, worse, seems over-the-top or stifling.

So if you're having repeated argument about something, look at the following issues, because these often lie at the bottom of most couples' hidden agendas.

Male Versus Female Parenting Energy

I'm going to state the obvious: A baby comes out of a woman. For the mother, the baby is part of her and is vulnerable in the big outside world. For the father, conversely, the baby is a separate and independent being.

Therefore, men and women can have fundamentally different approaches to caring for children and two different parenting energies. I label them *male* and *female*, although I have seen men radiate the female parenting energy style and women radiate the male parenting energy. Female parenting tends to focus on *accepting*, and male parenting tends to focus on *challenging*.

Trevor and Louise, thirty-one and thirty-two, respectively, would frequently argue about their two children's lunches. Trevor thought that their son, ten, and their daughter, eight, should be making their own sandwiches for school or for a family picnic.

"He'll get really angry if he finds out that I've done everything myself," explained Louise. "It can leave a horrible atmosphere over what should be relaxed family time. He'll open a sandwich and inspect it, trying to figure out whether the children cut the cheese and sliced the pickle. Why can't he just enjoy himself? I don't mind. It's quicker and easier. I know what we've got and where it is."

Trevor saw the issue differently. "It's teaching them to be independent, to stand on their own two feet, and not take stuff for granted. Why shouldn't they help out? It's not like any of our knives are sharp."

"Can't you let them just be children instead of making them think about whether we've got enough bread and putting it on the shopping list?" Louise asked. "What are you so keen to prepare them for? Running their own sandwich shop?"

"That's not such a bad idea," Trevor said sarcastically.

Louise believed that she was defending her children and accepting them as they were—especially since, as she saw it, her husband was critical of their efforts. Meanwhile, Trevor wanted to challenge and stretch them.

"These are really valuable life lessons that they don't really get taught at school," he said earnestly.

It is easy to get entrenched in your position, because from your perspective (informed by your parenting energy), you are right and your partner is wrong. However, children need to be both accepted (so they feel secure) *and* challenged (so they grow and develop). That's why it is important to value your partner's different parenting energy. And there's an added bonus: once you accept that your partner has a valid case and stop defending your own position so carefully, you will find a middle path, where your parenting energies are in harmony rather than in competition. In the case of Trevor and Louise, they agreed that he would organize the picnics in the future but with help from the children.

It's Not About the Children, It's About You

What upsets you about your children says more about you than it does about them. So before you try to change their behavior, it's important to look at yourself first.

> *What upsets you about your children says more about you than it does about them.*

For many mothers, their daughter's waist size can be a measure of whether they have been a success or a failure as a parent. "My daughter is really outgoing and popular, and is doing well at school," said Lizzy, forty, about her nine-year-old daughter. "It's probably only puppy fat, and I hate to admit it, but I would much prefer that she was slim." Unfortunately, these adult concerns trickle down to our children. A recent poll of 1,500 children revealed that 40 percent of those under ten years old worried about their weight, two-thirds of children ages seven to ten admitted weighing themselves, and nearly a quarter of the children ages seven to ten had been on a diet in the last year.

For fathers, their son's prowess at sports might be a measure of how "manly" he is. So if the son "throws like a girl," it is hard for the father not to feel like a failure. Even the son's team's success can become a measure of the father's own standing in the world.

"My father didn't say anything, but his silence said it all," said George, now thirty-eight, about trying out for his father's cricket team's junior squad when he was six or seven. "I desperately wanted his approval, to do well and fit in with the other boys, but even at that age, I knew I was different. Of course, I didn't have the words to explain what sort of different—that would come later—but I knew I was a disappointment, that I had let him down, and that we couldn't talk about it." George grew up to be gay and came out to his parents in his twenties, but his father remains uncomfortable about the subject.

Although I've given examples of mother and daughter and father and son, it's equally possible for characteristics from a child of the opposite sex to hold up a mirror that makes us question ourselves. Perhaps the child is shy or socially awkward or gets angry just the way we do. Conversely, your children may grow up to be different from you—for example, nonacademic while you're a professor, or a budding capitalist while you're a trade unionist—and that can be equally challenging.

With sensitive subjects, it is often difficult for your partner to step in. For example, Lizzy's husband, Patrick, left nutrition and portion control up to his wife. "She has really studied this subject," he said. "She has read everything that's been written on the subject, so I don't like to intervene."

This was the official story, but I discovered that Patrick would secretly subvert his daughter's diet plan. "If I take her out and we stop somewhere for lunch," he admitted, "I'll go somewhere like a Chinese restaurant, where the 'sensible eating' rules are not quite so clear, and we can relax and enjoy ourselves. I've also been known to buy ice cream."

George's mother guessed that her husband's relationship with their son was strained. "She would sort of overcompensate by making a fuss of me and letting me hang around the kitchen and help her," he explained. "I don't know if she would have voiced—even to herself—what was really going on. I don't think she would have wanted to look at why my father was so determined to 'make a man out of me' or what that said about him. So although she never said anything against his desire on summer vacations to get me to go rock climbing or, on one terrible occasion, bungee jumping, she would show me how to bake cookies or ice a cake."

I have two positive messages to share. First, if you don't make something an issue, it will not become one (and the reason it is an issue is nearly always about you). Second, there is nothing wrong with straightforward honesty with your children—for example, "I have a problem with my temper, but I'm trying to do something about it." What is damaging is saying nothing or pretending there isn't a problem, because the hidden subtext remains, and children are really tuned in to what their parents are thinking and feeling.

If the problems are yours, that's reasonably easy to fix. Start by recognizing that you are stressing yourself out, because making a conscious effort to be calmer will have a positive effect on your child. Next time you catch yourself slipping back into old behaviors, stop and apologize. Not only does an apology clear the air, it also gives your son or daughter permission to talk about what previously seemed unmentionable.

If you're concerned that your child's problematic behavior is being fed by your partner's own anxieties, that is harder to resolve. My advice would be to ask questions rather than give advice, because, however kindly it is meant, advice will be heard as criticism.

For example, Patrick could ask Lizzy, "How old were you when you first weighed yourself? What triggered your interest? How do you feel now, looking back? If you could give yourself some advice as a child, knowing what you know now, what would you change?"

During the conversation, make certain your partner feels heard by trying to identify the feelings (such as "You felt unwanted") and repeat back statements that seem particularly striking (such as "You were given a scale for your birthday").

Aim to ask at least four or five questions and for the conversation to last at least fifteen minutes, so your partner feels truly understood, before making the links between his or her behavior and your child's: "To what extent do you think our daughter has similar feelings?"

Once again, don't offer solutions, even if you think you've got the answer; ask more questions and listen to your partner's thoughts. Slowly but surely, a way forward will emerge.

Discipline

Discipline is a really difficult subject because on the one hand, we want a relaxed and joyful relationship with our children but on the other hand, we have a responsibility to make certain their behavior is not antisocial. What makes the subject particularly toxic is that our parents probably had different attitudes and methods from those of our partner's parents. Finding a compromise is always going to be difficult, especially if the partner who spends less time with the children does not want his or her few hours to be dominated by rules and regulations.

"My job can involve evenings and some weekends," explained Ethan, thirty-two, the father of two boys ages eleven and nine, "so when we have time together, I want it to be special. I know I bend the rules—like sweets before dinner—but it's not like it's very often, so I don't see the problem."

"But it's not just bending the rules, it's undermining them," his wife, Matilda, thirty-one, cut in. "There are times when I've sent our youngest to his room to cool down and reflect on his behavior, but you go in and have 'a little chat.'"

"He was genuinely sorry," Ethan said, "and I thought he'd been in there long enough."

"Sometimes it feels like I have three children, not two," Matilda said angrily. "Life can't be all putting on puppet shows and kicking a ball around the yard. The children need to do their homework, too, but do you ever insist on that?"

"I back you up," Ethan insisted.

"But it's *me* telling them to come in and start their schoolwork," Matilda pointed out. "Why should I always be the Wicked Witch of the West?"

Instead of focusing on disciplining your children, it is better to avoid the bad behavior in the first place. If you have been using descriptive praise and thinking ahead and have helped your children name and acknowledge feelings, they should be more cooperative and a pleasure to be around. If you understand that they act up because they are overwhelmed by difficult feelings (and don't have the ability to regulate themselves yet), tired, or fractious because their regular routine has been disrupted, then you will be able to look at their "naughtiness" in a different light.

What should you do, however, if they are truly behaving badly? I think it is up to you to decide how to discipline your children. After all, you know your children best and what motivates them. However, I have three general principles to share. First, it is better to offer incentives to good behavior rather than punishments for bad behavior. Second, I want you to model the behavior that you want your children to exhibit. (So please try not to lose your temper, and don't hit, slap, spank, or use any similar physical force, because you are just teaching your children to resort to similar means when they're annoyed or not getting their way with their friends or a younger sibling.) Third, always follow through: don't make idle threats that you're unlikely or unable to carry out. There is more about dealing with bad behavior and stopping dangerous behavior in Chapter 8.

Communicating Better (Again)

If you and your partner are still having problems agreeing on how to discipline, use the communication exercise from Chapter 2 to solve your dispute. I'm going to recap and add an extra element to contain your argument:

- **Flip a coin and decide who goes first.** The winner speaks without being interrupted.
- **This is the difference.** He or she can talk for only *three* minutes. Set an alarm on your phone or use a kitchen timer. (The advantage of the three-minute rule is that you deal with only one or two topics at a time. This will contain your argument, because discipline raises strong emotions.)
- **Summarize.** The listener doesn't think about how to respond or rehearse what he or she is going to say but gives the speaker undivided attention. At the end of three minutes, the listener repeats back the essence of what's been said (and nothing more).
- **Give feedback.** The speaker can give feedback about anything important that has been missed.
- **Switch roles.** The partner who was the listener becomes the speaker and sets out his or her case for *only* three minutes, without being interrupted. Afterward, the other partner summarizes what was said.
- **Repeat as many times as necessary.** When both parties feel heard, you are ready to find a solution.

Finally, try to aim for a middle way, rather than one partner just giving in. For a deal to stick, there has to be something for both parties. For example, Matilda decided to join in the game of soccer in the backyard for a couple of minutes so she could be perceived as fun, too. Ethan really liked the idea of all the family enjoying themselves together and agreed to call time after a couple of minutes and insist that the boys start their homework.

How to Put Your Partner First

There is a particularly nasty trap that lots of parents fall into, often unwittingly. They set up an alliance with one or more of their children and leave their partner feeling isolated and often angry.

> There is a particularly nasty trap that lots of parents fall into, often unwittingly. They set up an alliance with one or more of their children and leave their partner feeling isolated and often angry.

For example, when Matilda came into the yard to remind the boys about homework, Ethan rolled his eyes. In effect, he was saying to the kids, "Here comes nasty Mommy to spoil our fun." So instead of backing up his wife and acting as a team, he set up an alliance of "Dad and the boys versus Mom." Not only did he make his children more rebellious, because they knew they could exploit the differences between their parents; he was also sending a message to Matilda: "I care more about being popular with the boys than what you think of me." In effect, he was putting what he perceived as his sons' needs (for fun and bonding time with their dad) before his wife and her beliefs (that homework is important).

It is not just men who set up alliances with their children. George's mother had fallen into the same trap. Instead of being up front about giving her son baking lessons, she waited until his father was out of the house. Her unspoken message to George was "If you don't tell your father, I won't." Sometimes the criticism is more overt: "Your father is late *again*" or even "Don't take any notice of Daddy; he's just being silly."

If you and your partner are going through a tough patch, it is very easy to lean on one of more of your children, especially since many small children will want to try to "make it better." For example, when George was about nine, he would sit on the landing listening to his mother crying in the bathroom after an argument with his father and would push drawings he'd made under the door. Obviously George's mother must have been touched by this loving gesture. However, she was getting a child, who doesn't have the emotional maturity to understand, involved with adult problems.

My golden rules for avoiding alliances are as follows:

- Don't discuss or comment on issues between you and your partner with the children. If they ask about something, don't lie, but tell them as little as possible: "Yes, we had a disagreement, but we're working on resolving it."
- Don't use children as go-betweens.
- Don't go behind your partner's back. Tell him or her what you've been doing, even if he or she will disagree. It is better to have these issues out in the open where they can be discussed rather than hidden like a festering sore.
- Don't discuss issues about the children in front of them. If something comes up, make an appointment with your partner to speak about it when they are out of earshot.
- It's fine to argue about issues that are not child related when the children are around—for example, "What have you done to the computer?" or "Did you move my papers?" If you can argue constructively—by which I mean sticking to the point, not dragging in other examples, listening to each other, negotiating, and finding a compromise—you will have taught your children an important lesson about relationships: it is possible to hold different opinions, argue, and make up, and still love each other.

Summary

Once you have children, everybody seems to have advice—much of it contradictory. However, there are some core ideas that run through all the research. If you can stay calm, your baby will relax, and the positive mutual feedback between the two of you will increase. Conversely, if you are stressed and annoyed, your baby will be stressed and fractious, too.

Babies and toddlers have strong feelings that they do not understand. Your job is to help them cope with the highs and lows and also provide enough space to discover the world and their place in it. Don't worry if you and your partner have a different take on how to achieve this goal. By capitalizing on the strengths of both of you, you can find a middle way and a balance that's best for your children.

5

Housework and the Responsibility Gap

A lthough most modern couples believe that a relationship is an equal partnership, the day-to-day reality can end up looking very different, especially after the children arrive. On a typical day, 66 percent of men reported to the Bureau of Labor Statistics that they perform some sort of household activity, women still dominate in food preparation and cleanup (69 percent of women and 39 percent of men), and the statistics are even more sobering for general housework (51 percent of women and 20 percent of men). This is despite the number of stay-at-home dads doubling in the last ten years, according to the Census Bureau. Of course, men today are more hands-on in the home than their fathers were, but it is often at the fun end of parenting, whereas the mothers are

> *Of course, men today are more hands-on in the home than their fathers were, but it is often at the fun end of parenting, whereas the mothers are still running round in circles doing all the hard work behind the scenes.*

still running round in circles doing all the hard work behind the scenes.

"Julian is a great dad and the kids love him, so I'm not complaining," said Daisy, thirty-two—and then, like a lot of mothers, she proceeded to do just that. These women often seem too frightened to complain, for fear of a backlash from their husbands, but in my counseling room or in a group of other mothers, it is just too tempting to resist. After all, they have a lot of pent-up feelings that need to be released.

"Take Halloween as a good example," Daisy continued. "Julian was happy to come home early and help the children carve the pumpkin and take them trick-or-treating around the neighborhood. At some houses, the moms would say [about my husband], 'Isn't he great?' And he is."

She took a deep breath. "But who bought the pumpkin and the bags of sweets for the children who came to our door? Who made the costumes? Who reminded him twice the week before that it was Halloween, so he wouldn't put anything in his work diary that might clash? And who makes the kids their dinner on the other 364 days a year? Of course, I want him to see the kids all dressed up—this year he helped paint their faces green—and it's great that they're spending quality time together, but I'm doing all the drudge work to make it happen."

What she's talking about is not just the hard physical work of cleaning, cooking, and looking after the children—these are beginning to be shared more—but the emotional housekeeping, too: remembering birthdays and medical appointments, sending thank-you cards, arranging playdates for the children, and checking if the babysitter is free. More often that not, this is still considered "women's work," and men get a free pass. No wonder many mothers are exhausted.

"I have to keep going even when I have the flu or my period cramps are so bad I just want to crawl into bed and curl up," said Sophia, twenty-nine. "That's partly because my husband is away a lot since his work involves travel, but, to be honest, he can't really be trusted. Okay, he can get the children up for school and give them breakfast—particularly if it's one of my working days and he's at home—but he'll send our daughter off to school in her hockey boots but forget to pack her ordinary shoes to change into after the game. He'll pack the lunch for our four-year-old for nursery school but forget to cut the grapes in half —they're a choking hazard—and I'll get a nasty note from the school. There are so many things to juggle, and I can't relax, because if *I* don't get it right, everything in the family will collapse."

When you are under such stress, it only takes one extra burden, like Sophia's mother being diagnosed with cancer, for the family to plunge into a crisis. The family had arrived in my counseling room complaining of bitter and destructive arguments. Sophia was feeling particularly unsupported. "I want a partner, not a third child to look after," she complained.

Daniel, her husband, felt criticized and devalued. "I'll do a hundred things right, but all she comments on are the few things I got wrong."

"But these are important things," Sophia protested. "What was our daughter going to do? Wear her hockey boots in the classroom?"

Why do so many women feel like the responsible adult with no backup in place? Why does the housework and responsibility gap seem to be widening, despite all the good intentions of men? Before we tackle these questions, it's important to understand their full effect and how they undermine relationships.

The Toxic Effect
of Unequal Parenting

Many partners feel embarrassed about discussing hockey boots, grapes, and Halloween pumpkins in my counseling room, as though they should be dealing with more serious topics. But if you can't sort out these everyday problems, there is a danger you could fall into one of the traps described below.

Resentment

Resentment normally starts over small things but is a bit like a snowball rolling down a hill: it increases in size and momentum and risks crushing everything in its path. Natalie, thirty-eight, found that although her division of labor with her husband Frank made logical sense, she was growing more and more resentful.

"When it came to finding a playgroup for our son," she said, "I had the time and the local contacts, so I was happy to do the footwork. I whittled it down to three possibilities and explained all the pros and cons to Frank. He came to see the first one and said, 'That's fine' and 'Whatever you think best,' but he couldn't get time off to see the next two. I have to admit, I felt resentment. It was as though he were saying, 'I've better things to do,' but what could be more important than our son's future?"

With the playgroup being a sensitive subject, Frank didn't risk asking much beyond "How did it go?," and Natalie didn't tell him the ins and outs of the playgroup activities or the personalities and politics of what happened there. "I didn't think he was interested," she admitted. "He certainly didn't care enough to come and see it for himself."

No wonder they began to drift apart, with such a large topic becoming increasingly toxic. It didn't take much probing, however, for a much bigger resentment to come out in therapy.

"My life has been turned upside down [since having children]," said Natalie, "but for Frank, things have hardly changed at all."

Unfortunately, this resentment is so big it hardly ever gets spoken. Although we love our children, we can sometimes resent the burdens and restrictions of being a parent. However, this is such a taboo topic that it is easier to just resent our partners instead.

Report your feelings rather than acting them out. Instead of expressing your resentment, anger, or disappointment through your body language (rolling your eyes, sighing heavily, and slamming the cupboard door) or as a tirade of criticism, tell your partner how you are feeling and then explain why. For example, "I'm upset because you didn't notice that I . . ." or "I'm frustrated because you didn't listen when . . ." Reporting your feelings is important because it stops your partner from imagining that something worse is going one. By explaining why you're feeling this way, you can stop your partner jumping to the wrong conclusion and limit the upset feeling to this particular event.

Nagging

You've tried asking nicely. You've tried reminding when nothing happens. So the only way to get anything done is to drop pointed hints, criticize, or lose your temper. Especially when you're feeling a lot of righteous anger, fueled by all your justified resentments, nagging seems like the only way to get things done. Even if you don't particularly like yourself afterward, it does get results—eventually. Unfortunately, nagging also poisons a relationship and sucks all the fun out of your day-to-day life.

Although nagging is seen as something women do, I find it to be an equal-opportunity trap. Adam, forty, had always been a stickler for good food hygiene and would wash bananas before eating them and garlic cloves before frying them. He would often "remind" his partner, Miranda, thirty-eight, to wash her hands—for example, after she touched the lid of the kitchen garbage can to throw something away. After they had a baby, it became more of an issue.

"It seems like he's always asking me, 'Have you washed your hands?'" Miranda reported. "I know hygiene is important, but it feels like I'm being nagged *all the time.* I used to like it when we prepared Sunday lunch together. We'd have a glass of wine and chat about the week, but now it is too stressful for both of us to be in the kitchen at the same time, especially if our daughter is going to have a few vegetables or some meat from the meal. I'd much rather I cooked alone or that Adam did."

Although nagging might take the edge off our resentment, it doesn't solve anything. If it isn't working, you'd think we'd stop and try something else. Unfortunately, we think that if we say it one more time or shout louder or really shame our partner, he or she will change. Yet all we achieve is digging a deeper hole of resentment, for both the person who nags and the person who is nagged (and it is not uncommon for both partners to nag on different topics).

Apologize and aim to build cooperation and teamwork instead. This chapter and the next are full of alternatives that work much better than nagging, but first, it is important to stop the old, unhelpful behavior. You have probably said you're sorry a million times, but it often doesn't register because either you don't really mean it (you're just trying to keep the peace) or it doesn't properly register with your partner. Instead, try a sincere apology (see Chapter 3).

Let me recap: identify the behavior that you regret: "I'm sorry I have been nagging you about getting home after the children go to bed." Next, identify how it must have affected your partner: "It must have made you feel unwelcome when you did arrive." Please do *not* add an explanation: "I think it's really important that the children see more of you"; this weakens the power of the apology because it can be heard as justification for your nagging. (Your partner probably already knows why you want him or her to do something, because you've already told him or her a million times. If you've realized something new, you can always explain on another occasion.) Finally, make your apology.

Passive-Aggressive Behavior

Passive-aggressive behavior occurs when someone agrees to do something to your face but then goes ahead and does the opposite. For example, a husband might say, "Yes, I'll be home by five-thirty to take care of the kids so you can go to your meeting," but then he forgets ("I was caught up in something else"), deliberately misunderstands ("Oh, did you mean *today*?"), makes excuses at the last minute ("I've suddenly remembered I have to go to a meeting"), or deliberately sabotages (shows up on time but lets the children stay up too late, so they're fractious and running around the house when you get back, or they're finger-painting on your new sofa). Any of these behaviors will make the wife decide it's just not worth the hassle the next time around.

It's impossible to challenge someone who is passive-aggressive because he or she "wants" to help, it's just that _____ (fill in the excuse), or he or she will get around to it "in a moment" (but that moment is not going to arrive anytime soon). This is one of the reasons that passive-aggressive behavior and nagging go hand in hand, because when something doesn't happen as promised, the other partner has to bring it up again and again, or it will just be forgotten.

Passive-aggressive behavior is triggered by a feeling of powerlessness. Christopher, thirty-eight, did not agree with his wife, Melanie, about enrolling their eight-year-old son as an actor for TV commercials.

"The casting calls are like cattle markets, and it involves a lot of rejection," Christopher explained. "I don't really think it's right for him. My wife thinks he wants to do it, but I believe he only does it to keep her happy."

"Have you told her how you feel?" I asked.

"I've sort of said it."

"But not in so many words," I suggested.

"She pulls rank. She knows *her* son best. She spends the most time with him. And what have I done for him? I want to take him to my tennis club because they have a class for young kids, but it clashes with acting lessons."

Not only had Christopher failed to state his opinion strongly enough, so his wife took his silence for agreement; he had also become a second-class parent whose opinions did not count. This problem was reinforced because Christopher did not prioritize his son's acting career. In his mind, it wasn't important, so he failed to collect glossy promotion prints from the studio close to his office, and he wouldn't take time off work to take his son to an audition. So it seemed to Melanie that she was always nagging him to get these things done.

There was a similar problem with their love life, but this time the roles were reversed. Christopher would drop repeated hints and nag that he "hardly ever got sex." Meanwhile, Melanie would be passive-aggressive. She would tell him that she enjoyed making love and that she was still attracted to him. However, she just never seemed to be in the mood.

"To be honest," she said, "there's nothing less sexy than being pestered to do something. Not only do I close up inside, I feel resentful and angry." The result was that Melanie "gave in" often enough to keep the peace and keep the lid on the problem, but it only increased the level of resentment for both her and Christopher.

Take the opportunity to practice your assertiveness skills and give your partner permission to say no. People behave in a passive-aggressive manner because they want to keep the peace. It causes arguments and upset feelings in the long run, but at the time, it keeps everything nice with an "Of course, darling." So next time you get an agreement that's too easy, double-check that your partner really means it by saying, "Are you sure?" or "I'd much rather know how you really feel."

If the answer to the first question is no, you can change the request, negotiate something your partner will accept doing, or arrange for someone else to do it. At least you know where you stand. If you're the partner using the passive-aggressive behavior, give yourself time to think, rather than being caught off guard or agreeing out of habit. Choose a quieter time and discuss your reservations with your partner. He or she might be annoyed, but that will pass. In contrast, the resentment that is created by agreeing to something and then not doing it will only build and fester.

Pleasure in Your Partner's Downfall

Each consequence of unequal parenting compounds the others. In the worst cases, resentment will breed nagging by the parent "in charge" and passive-aggressive behavior by the "second-class" parent. Fortunately, most couples don't reach the fourth trap, in which the "in charge" parent secretly wants the other to fail.

"I wanted my husband to experience just how hard it was looking after our daughter," explained Tanya. "So I almost willed her to puke and scream when he was in charge of her. When it did happen, I would look on coldly and offer no advice or support. If things went from bad to worse, I would criticize from the sidelines and then take over and show him how to do it."

Although deep down Tanya wanted help, support, and some acknowledgment that her life had been turned upside down by having a child, she kept discouraging her husband and casting him forever in the support role. I've had male clients who were simply incapable of looking after their small children on their own, because they had no idea about feeding routines or how to get them in and out of car seats, so if they're wives were away, the men had to get their mothers or sisters to help.

If you've reached the point of wanting your partner to fail just to "show him," it is a clear wake-up call that something has to change. Although you are unhappy and desperate for help, you are going about getting it in

> *If you've reached the point of wanting your partner to fail just to "show him," it is a clear wake-up call that something has to change.*

the worst way possible. So step back and think about what would help. If you can make the solution something concrete—for example, time to yourself to go to the hairdresser—that's even better. Review the section on being assertive in Chapter 2. If you ask for something clearly in an open and straightforward manner—rather than hoping that he will guess or getting angry and driving him away—you will be much more likely to succeed.

How to Ask for What You Need

One of the most important relationship skills—which will help you be a good partner and a good parent and also feel good about yourself—is to be able to ask for what you need in a simple, direct, and honest way. Unfortunately, many of us have been brought up with the idea that it's wrong to simply ask for what we want, and, all too often, we're frightened to ask for fear of being turned down. Somehow, we believe it is better to hint, because the rejection does not feel quite so devastating. However, not asking leaves your partner guessing (probably wrongly) or maybe even oblivious to your needs, which leaves you wondering why he or she doesn't care. Here are the alternatives:

- Skip the preambles, like "I don't often ask, but . . ." or "I know you're busy, but . . ." The danger is that your partner will have turned off before the request, having heard the preamble as an attack or having been unwittingly handed an excuse for not cooperating.

- Skip the explanations, like "I haven't asked for much before . . ." or "I'm really short of time . . ." It is almost as if you're saying you don't deserve to ask beyond exceptional circumstances, which is not going to be good for your self-esteem. The other problem with explanations is that they invite a debate—for example, about who is more tired or busier—and you get distracted from asking.
- Keep it simple: "Please, could you . . . ?" or "Can you . . . ?"
- Once you've asked for what you need, make certain that you listen to your partner, rather than jumping to conclusions about his or her response. If you think the answer is a "maybe" or a "yes, but . . . ," get clarification or ask another question. This could be the time to explain why you're asking.
- If you need emotional support, ask for something specific and concrete (like a hug) so your partner does not get confused. If you ask for something general (like "more help"), your partner could interpret that in a million different ways, some of them more irritating than helpful.
- Don't underestimate how hard it is to ask in a clear and direct manner, especially if you have always dropped hints or thought your partner should "just know." Practice asking your friends or colleagues for something. If you find that hard, practice what you're going to say in your head first. Slowly but surely, it will become second nature.
- If you just need to talk, explain what sort of reaction would be helpful. Are you looking for your partner's opinion? Do you need advice? Do you want reassurance or just someone to listen?

Why Do Parents End Up on Different Sides of the Responsibility Gap?

It is easy to lay all the blame on men. I've heard it many times in my counseling room. They're lazy, self-centered, and, well, they're *men*, so what can you expect? There is a similar dialogue in the media and on social networks, too. Although there are occasional "great dads" who are singled out for praise, the majority of fathers are simply written off. I think the selfish man and the superwoman are really unhelpful stereotypes, because the real picture is more complex, and labeling men as the problem just puts them on the defensive and makes them opt out. Instead of complaining, ask the following question: *Why* aren't men doing more?

Men Can Feel Excluded

Right from the beginning, a mother and her child are wrapped in a cocoon of care that is sometimes difficult for fathers to penetrate. The vast majority of men, after watching their wives giving birth, are shown the door. There are simply no birthing facilities—short of a home birth—in which the whole family can stay together for the first crucial hours. If the baby wakes up in the middle of the night or needs something, he or she is, at best, sleeping on a cot next to the mother's hospital bed or the baby may be in a nursery down the hall while the father is phoning relatives, buying diapers, or celebrating with friends. Right from the beginning, she is "in charge" and he's off running errands. In addition, breast-feeding tethers the child to the mother, and all the follow-up services are naturally designed to check the health of mother and child. Even fathers who are determined to be hands-on feel uncomfortable going to the clinic with their wives and newborn babies.

"I was the only man in the waiting room, and I didn't know quite what to do with myself," explained William, twenty-three, after the birth of his daughter. "So I buried myself in the information leaflets on the coffee tables. But they were all aimed at mothers and babies, and the only reference to men was a poster on the wall for a domestic violence phone line. I did ask one of the nurses if she had anything for new dads, and she dug around and found one leaflet." Needless to say, he did not go back. "I felt like a spare part, and who wants that?"

The sheer amount of contact time is important for bonding between father and child, according to research at the University of Calgary on what happens to the brains of male mice after the birth of their offspring. The scientists discovered that the male mice grew new cells in the region of the brain connected with smell and memory to help recognize the scent of their pups. However, it happened only when the father mice were snuggled up to their offspring in the nest. If they were separated by a mesh screen, the cells did not grow.

Men Have Their Own Problems

Although there are low expectations of men as their children's caregivers, there are high expectations of them as breadwinners. It is not surprising, therefore, that they put more effort into the latter than the former. In many cases, fathers are left trying to keep everybody happy and finding it increasingly difficult to reconcile the demands at work and at home.

"My manager was reasonably sympathetic to me taking time off after the birth of both my son and my daughter," stated Charles, thirty-five, who works for a large firm of auditors. "However, it was made very clear that I shouldn't take more than a few days, even though the statutory parental leave was up to two weeks. I was told that my team was counting on me and that clients like continuity."

Eventually, Charles's wife returned to work three days a week, and occasionally she would have a child-care crisis and ask him to take time off.

"Nothing can be put on an official basis because it might set a precedent," he noted. "It's really stressful because I never know what answer I'll get, and my wife doesn't really understand the culture at my work. If I say it's not a good time to ask or I get resistance from my manager, she acts as though I don't think her job is important, I don't care about the children, or I'm just plain difficult. But the company is always looking for cost savings. There's a real attendance culture, in which your bottom being on the seat is more important than what you do, and I don't want to be thought of as a lightweight."

Other men will agree to something that makes sense for the rest of the family but that has a huge effect on their lives. Sebastian, a forty-eight-year-old lawyer, bowed to pressure and bought a house in the countryside that involved a two-and-a-quarter-hour commute to his office in the city. "We didn't want the children growing up in a city, and the schools are better here, but I'm often up at five-thirty for an early train. My work involves a lot of socializing, so sometimes I'm on the last train home and get less than five hours' sleep. I can easily fall asleep on the sofa in the evening, but then I'm considered to be boring or accused of avoiding family life. It's getting harder and harder to exist on so little sleep, especially as I get older. We've discussed moving to a local firm, but we would never be able to have the lifestyle that working in the city gives us."

These men would claim that they take their share of the responsibility, but unlike putting hot meals on the table and picking up the children from school, their contributions are not so clearly visible.

Men Get Demoralized

Most men measure how much they're doing around the house and the amount of effort they're putting into raising a family against their fathers' contributions to their own childhood. Research from the Fatherhood Institute, an organization that lobbies on men's behalf, reported that in 1997, men spent eight times longer with babies and young children than they did twenty years earlier. Today's fathers believe they are doing their part, but they often don't feel appreciated. The message they give me, time and again, is "I'm doing all this, and it's *still* not enough." Although their wives hope that pointing out the responsibility deficit will make their partners see the light

> *Most men measure how much they're doing around the house and the amount of effort they're putting into raising a family against their fathers' contributions to their own childhood.*

and offer more, it often has the opposite effect. "What's the point?" these men say to themselves as they withdraw and do just enough to keep the peace but not enough to solve the problem.

Men are particularly likely to be demoralized if their partners are asking for help but then refuse to cede control and therefore feel free to tell the men what to do and how to do it—to oversupervise and criticize. The problem is compounded if their wives use their "expert" status to overrule them.

Returning to Natalie and Frank, whom we met earlier in this chapter: He would offer an opinion but found it was often ignored. "At the first playgroup," he said, "I really liked the relaxed atmosphere, but Natalie didn't think our son would be challenged enough, so that was the end of the discussion. It's pointless explaining that he's only four, because although it's not explicitly said but certainly implied, she knows him better."

Meanwhile, Natalie, who had given up a high-powered career, believed that raising their son was her domain. "Sometimes it feels like he's stepping on my toes," she said. "I've read all about how to stimulate children and how they learn best, and he comes crashing in at the last minute into my project."

"It's like you want me to rubber-stamp your choices," Frank retorted.

They were stuck in a trap that I see quite often. On one hand, Natalie was complaining that Frank was not involved enough, but then that he was interfering on the other.

Oliver, forty-two, was trying to save his marriage. In the middle of an argument in which he had threatened to seek custody of their sons, ages eleven and eight, his wife, Rosemary, spat back that they were "her" children.

Obviously, she felt hurt and rejected and simply lashed out, but it made her husband feel completely demoralized. "Didn't my efforts, all the hours at work to support the family, count for anything?" asked Oliver plaintively.

Women's Expectations of Themselves

There is something about being human that makes us competitive. Men compete over who earns the most, who's the best at sports, and who has the most beautiful woman on his arm. When women compare themselves to other women, it is more likely to be about their looks, how well their children are doing, and what kind of homes they live in. Their identities can also be tied up with their work, too, of course, but normally this is not to the same extent as men. (I used to lead focus groups of male and female consumers talking about products for a market research company. When the men introduced themselves to the other participants, they would always mention their jobs but sometimes had to be prompted about their marital status and whether they had children. Conversely, the women always started with how many children they had, followed by whether they were married, divorced, or a single mom, but sometimes they had to be prompted about their work.)

With so much of a woman's identity tied up with being a great mom and having a beautiful home, it is not surprising that many women have higher standards and expectations of themselves.

"My home isn't just somewhere I live but an expression of who I am," explained Cristabel, twenty-nine and the mother of two boys ages eight and five. "So if the place is a mess, I also feel all over the place and can't relax until order is reinstated. I'm horrified when Toby invites someone over and the place looks like a bomb has hit it. What must they think?"

"They're dads, too," Toby countered. "They know what family life is like. They're more than used to stepping over toys."

"I'd never invite another mother around without running the vacuum cleaner first," Cristabel protested. "Same if there are other children coming around for tea; I don't want them taking back stories that our house is a mess."

"That's fine, we have different standards," Toby conceded, "but what makes me angry is that you expect me to care as much as you do if there's a coffee-cup ring on the table or the baseboards are a bit dusty. It's important to you. I get it. It reflects on you. But it's dominating our lives. What about having some fun instead?"

In effect, some men aren't "pulling their weight" not because they don't believe in doing their share but because their partner has different standards and expectations.

Toby summed up a lot of these men's attitudes when he said, "I thought, if Cristabel wants to run herself ragged, that's a shame, but don't expect me to do half. So I stepped back and let her do it."

When I explore the wife's notion of high standards, I often find something else that is particularly unsettling. Fortunately, by this stage in Cristabel and Toby's counseling, I had built up a strong relationship with Cristabel and could probe deeply.

"So if things are not perfect, how do you feel?" I asked her.

"That the whole edifice I've built around myself will be destroyed, and they'll see who I really am," she answered.

"What's that?" I pressed on, holding my breath.

"Worthless," she replied. "I'm not acceptable, and worse still, they might have a point. There is something wrong with me."

"There is nothing between perfect and worthless?" I inquired.

> *There is one final problem with having sky-high expectations of yourself: It allows you to ask something similar of other people. And when they fail—for example, to clean the sink in the "perfect" manner—you're likely to brand them as worthless, too.*

Cristabel shook her head. No wonder the stakes were so high.

Time and again, I find perfectionism is a defense against shame—possibly the most destructive emotion, because it attacks not just our behavior but our whole being.

There is one final problem with having sky-high expectations of yourself: It allows you to ask something similar of other people. And when they fail—for example, to clean the sink in the "perfect" manner—you're likely to brand them as worthless, too.

Social Changes

Both fathers and mothers are interacting with their children more than ever before. When the Centre for Time Use Research in Oxford, England, asked parents to keep a diary of activities and compared them to a generation ago, the contact time had tripled. Previously, children would have gone out to the street or the park to play, but today there is much more adult-supervised play. Even if this is not always being led by mothers or fathers, the parents still have to drive their sons and daughters to the activities and pick them up. Children are also spending more time in adult-oriented places like restaurants.

Meanwhile, despite the extra time pressures, we still cling to all the activities that our parents did with us when we were kids.

"I never feel so right as a mother as when I'm doing things that my mother did with me," explained Jocelyn, thirty-three. "So I love baking cakes and making jam—giving my daughter the spoon to lick and helping her write the labels for what fruit and what year." Jocelyn's mother, however, had not worked three days a week, and she had let Jocelyn and her sister wander in and out of their friends' houses on their street.

"Around here, it's very different from where I grew up," she noted. "It's mostly younger couples without children and older couples." So even though she had more responsibility outside the house and less shared child care with other local moms, Jocelyn still felt compelled to replicate her mother's mothering—despite the fact that before having children, she had baked maybe one cake and had never made jam.

There are two other social changes that are putting immense strain on parents. On the one hand, we're getting married later—around thirty—and having our children around ten years later than people did in the 1950s. On the other hand, the peak career years, in terms of advancement and promotion, are occurring earlier. We used to spread our peak career and child-rearing years across three decades, so the responsibilities could be staggered, but now it's condensed into one.

It's Hard for Women to Step into Their Partners' Shoes

For many women, running a home is more than a practical necessity; it's also an expression of their nurturing and love for their partners and their children. So if they perceive that they aren't getting any help or appreciation, it can feel like an insult or a rejection. Meanwhile, for men, chores are chores are chores. Doing the weekly grocery shopping is something functional—nothing more, nothing less. Chores have low status for a man, and he would much rather hire a housecleaning service or get the groceries delivered. He shows his love by providing and is puzzled when all his hard work is not enough.

In terms of child care, men really do want to be involved with their children, but they define the concept differently. They rate having a good emotional relationship and being able to talk to their sons and daughters over seeing them often. Women, conversely, value the sheer volume of time spent, since they believe that closeness and connection comes from doing small tasks together—even something like supervising brushing teeth—because you cannot schedule intimacy.

When both partners work outside the home and share the load in child care and chores, there is generally a good understanding of each other's burdens, but when the workload is split into homemaker and breadwinner, it can be hard to step into each other's shoes—even though the sex differences regarding these roles have lessened in the last fifty years. Men no longer go straight from living with their mothers to living with their wives. They've had to cook and clean, and maybe even iron their own shirts for ten years or more. Similarly, women don't go from their fathers' houses to their husbands' houses anymore but spend time living on their own and earning their own money. They know the problems of keeping a balance in the bank account and the fears that the restructuring at work could spell redundancy and financial disaster. However, the arrival of children changes everything, and a little knowledge of the other's stresses can be misleading.

"I don't think Nicholas understands the sheer volume of washing that three children and two adults generate," said Naomi, thirty-eight, "or what it's like to cook two meals, one for the kids at six and one for us at eight. Everything has to be washed up and cleared away, and all while you're being asked a million and one questions by the kids and juggling playdates to fill a gap in child care and wondering who will come in and feed the dog while we're out on Sunday afternoon. Perhaps I'm being a bit harsh. He does have *some* idea, but when the going gets tough, he can opt out. He'll say, 'I've got an important presentation in the morning, so I'll go downstairs and sleep on the sofa so I can get at least six hours' sleep.' That's fine. But I've also got a big day and lots to do, and I can't just bow out."

It is not surprising that Nicholas, a company representative, saw the situation differently. "I don't think Naomi understands what it's like to do a job that you don't really like," he said. "She always did fulfilling and creative work, in TV production. If she didn't like a particular contract, we'd talk it through and maybe she'd wait for something better, since we could rely on my steady income. When there was a huge decrease in work about five years ago, and she was getting bored, I was happy for her to opt out and become a full-time mom. We agreed it was best for our children. However, I think she sees work through rose-tinted glasses; it's all people in sharp suits being dynamic and having interesting conversations. She forgets the tedium of interminable meetings, office politics, and the daily slog. The new technology means my supervisor has a log of every call I make and can track everywhere I've been in the car. There are times when I dream of just throwing in the towel, retraining, and doing something interesting—but who would pay for it? We're only ever two or three paychecks away from disaster."

It is always easier to see your own position in the responsibility gap than to try to understand your partner's, but in addition, the media and online communities that each partner consumes can act as an echo chamber, making your complaints seem even more right and your partner's failings starker.

> *It is always easier to see your own position in the responsibility gap than to try to understand your partner's.*

Building Bridges

It's hard to step into your partner's shoes if you're feeling angry, resentful, or unappreciated. So to get an idea of the state of the situation, I ask couples to do an audit of their positive and negative interactions in a good week and then in a bad one. Here are some examples of the differences:

Positive Interactions	Negative Interactions
Smiles	Nagging
Thank-yous	Ignoring
Eye contact	Averted eyes
Greetings	Sarcastic comments
Laughter	Coldness
Listening	Interrupting
Sharing personal information	Holding back personal information
Casual touches	Turning your back
Hugs	Shrugs
Kisses	Walking away
Small presents (chocolate)	Complaints
Making a cup of tea	Holding grudges
Doing something for the other person	Long silences
Compliments	Criticism
Pet names	Name-calling

Write down how the contact between you is in a good week, a bad week, and perhaps the last seven days. Ask your partner to do the same and share the results.

Interpreting Your Balance

When researchers at Washington University in St. Louis, Missouri, looked at the balance between positive and negative interactions, they found that couples heading for divorce were reporting an even split. Those who were in conflict but were maintaining their relationships had five positives for every negative. However, for a good relationship, the researchers recommended twenty positives for every negative.

Improving the Ratio

Think about how you could be more positive. Partners often have warm or loving thoughts—for example, looking forward to getting home or being pleasantly surprised at some help they were offered—but instead of saying something, they keep it to themselves. Look at the list of possible positives and think about what you would like to offer your partner. It is not an exhaustive list, so perhaps you can think of other ideas, too—for example, sending a nice text message ("Can't wait to see you") or making your gratitude explicit ("Thank you for your help yesterday when we were expecting guests and I panicked"). Make a commitment to perform at least one item on your list every day. At the end of the week, write down your ratios of positive to negative and share the results with each other.

How to Put Your Partner First

One of my golden rules is this: *If it's good enough for your kids, it's good enough for your partner, too.* It's not only children who thrive on praise; adults need it as well. That's why successful companies review their employees on a regular basis and give positive feedback.

However, when it comes to our home lives, we are slow to give compliments (and sometimes even a thank-you). In fact, I would be a rich man if I had been given a bonus every time I heard the words "I shouldn't have to thank my husband for [emptying the dishwasher, looking after his own kids, coming home when he said he would]" (or put in your own example) or "I shouldn't have to thank my wife for [cuddling on the sofa, letting me go fishing, keeping the children quiet while I'm busy]" (or put in your own example).

Imagine for a moment how you would feel if, in your view, you have put yourself out to do something, and not only was there no recognition but there was also a slight overtone of "About time, too!" or "Is that all?" My guess is that you wouldn't be rushing to repeat the activity again. It's like a company telling its employees, "At last, you've made your target." How motivated would that workforce be?

One of the best ways of motivating your children is descriptive praise: praising what is right rather criticizing what is wrong. Here's how you can use this idea with your partner:

- We are often too busy going through our mental to-do list to register what our partners have done that is helpful or to give positive feedback. So make a conscious effort to slow down or stop. It takes only a few seconds to offer descriptive praise.
- Instead of general comments, such as "That was a great day out," pick a particular aspect and talk about that. You can never be too specific. (This is why the technique is called *descriptive* praise.) For example, "You really handled our son well when he had a tantrum about the ice cream."

- If you can't find anything recent to praise, look for something in the past that you'd like to happen again. Choose a quiet moment, like on a long car journey, and reminisce. For example, say, "It was really nice when you came home half an hour early and we were able to have a cup of tea and talk over the day before I went out" or "I still remember that time you looked after the children for the weekend and I went off with my sister to a spa."

- In the same way that I've asked you to avoid superlatives with your children, I'd like you to do the same with your partner. So drop "You're the most wonderful mother" or "You're the best dad" and concentrate on the details. Remember the appraisal you get at work: your boss spells out what you're doing well to encourage more of the same.

- Look for any small step in the right direction and praise that. For example, if you need your partner back at a certain time and he or she is running late again but does at least call with an update, instead of biting his or her head off, say, "Thank you, it's helpful to know." For looking after the children, even if it was done grudgingly, say, "It was so nice to come home to a quiet house and find you'd put them all to bed."

- Explain *why* a particular behavior was helpful—for example, "It gave me a chance to alter my plans slightly" or "It was really nice to have some time alone together." After all, your partner is not a mind reader.

- Don't take change for granted. Notice and comment on improvements: "You've made a real effort to _____ [fill in the blank], and I wanted to let you know how much I appreciate it" will encourage your partner to continue and offer more.

- If you think that you don't get enough descriptive praise yourself, use descriptive praise to remedy the situation. For example, think back to a time when you were motivated by positive feedback and tell your partner, "When you noticed that I had cleaned the bathroom, I thought, 'You *do* appreciate my efforts.'" In this way, you are modeling the behavior that you'd like to see.

Summary

When you're trapped in a dispute about who does what around the house, it is easy to take your partner's behavior personally or make blanket statements about men or women. However, parents are under more pressure than ever before—from society and from each other's expectations. Deep down, both men and women can feel a sense of injustice and easily lose their motivation. That's why it is important to praise rather than criticize. The issue is often not just how the responsibilities for running the house, raising the children, and earning money are divided, but whether you feel you're taking on too much of the burden. There is more in the next chapter about closing the responsibility gap and finding a middle way that will work for both of you.

6

Parenting as
a Team

I hope that by exploring the pressures on parenting from society, ourselves, and each other, I have made you feel more understood and less overwhelmed. It's only once you've been heard that you can begin to listen to your partner and the two of you can work as a team. Time and again, I have found that parents get trapped on either side of the housework and responsibility gap because they have rushed to find a solution before each partner feels truly understood.

There are three steps to resolving a problem together (rather than one person imposing a solution): explore, understand, and act. You can't get to the last without going through the first two. If your negotiations hit an obstacle, my advice is always to go back to the beginning and explore again by asking the following questions: Why is this issue so difficult? What is stopping you from making progress? Why are you both upset?

Since the last chapter was devoted to exploring and understanding the responsibility gap, we are ready to move to acting and find ways of resolving the issue.

Drop the Word *Should*

At the heart of most arguments over child care and how best to bring up children, there is one small word that causes a lot of misery: *should*. John and Marie, both in their early thirties, came into counseling because he had fallen out of love with her, but I suspected that at the heart of their problems were parenting issues. They had two children ages seven and three. Marie was a stay-at-home mom, and John spent a lot of time traveling because of his job. Although they claimed that they never argued, and only occasionally had arguments about whether they argued, it did not take long to remember a squabble from the past few days. As I suspected, it was about parenting.

> *At the heart of most arguments over child care and how best to bring up children, there is one small word that causes a lot of misery: should.*

"We've decided that I'll get out more when John's home and can look after the kids," explained Marie. "But if I was going to go to the gym, I had to go right that very minute."

"So I told you to get ready and I'd give them their snack," said John.

"When I came down, the kids were eating and he was on his laptop," Marie noted, "which just drives me wild."

"They were happy, involved doing something, so I just took a sneak look," John stated.

"But they hardly see you," Marie protested. "I think when you're with the kids you *should* give them your undivided attention."

I was not surprised that Marie didn't say anything at the time, because she had to go to the gym. However, she didn't say anything when she returned home or at any point in the next few days. With no argument, there was no opportunity either for Marie to let off steam or for John to challenge the idea that he *should* give his children his undivided attention. So I asked John to address Marie's statement.

"I suppose Marie has a point," he admitted. "I don't see them very often. Okay, I won't do it again."

If John wasn't going to challenge the *should*, I needed to give him a nudge.

"What were you doing on the computer?" I asked.

"I just had a couple of e-mails to check," he replied. "It only took a second."

"But you *should* have waited until the children were in bed," Marie insisted. There was that word again.

"We don't spend much time together, either," John explained, "and I wanted to have all my work finished so we could watch a movie together or something when you got back."

"But it meant that you didn't put the children to bed properly," Marie declared. "When I came back, Charlie [their three-year-old son] got out of bed and was complaining that he hadn't had his story."

"We did a jigsaw puzzle together," John informed her. "I thought that would be enough to settle him down."

"I have this tried-and-true way of getting them off to sleep, and I think you *should* stick with the plan." Marie tried to soften this *should* with "I think you should," which is better than just a plain *should*, but she was still laying down the law.

John just sat there looking miserable.

At this point, I remembered one of my own mother's sayings, which I suspect had been handed down from her mother, too. Sometimes, I just go with my instincts and state them. "There's more than one way to skin a rabbit," I interjected.

John seemed energized. "They seemed happy enough eating while I replied to my e-mails. I got them washed, their teeth brushed, and our daughter in her pajamas. It all went very smoothly."

Marie seemed to have softened, too: "I had to go away for the weekend, and I sort of dreaded coming back because Gracie's [their seven-year-old] teacher had left one of those 'parent' homework projects. Gracie had to build Dracula's castle, and I had left everything for John, but I sort of expected to come back, find the house in chaos, and have to make the castle last thing on Sunday night."

"I did things my way, but everything ran really smoothly," John pointed out.

"To your credit, you built the Dracula castle," Marie admitted, adding, "not the way I would have done it, but you fulfilled the task."

I found the idea amusing that there was possibly a right and a wrong way to build a castle for a class project, but I let the subject drop.

It's not just *should* that drives arguments and undermines team work but also *must*, *always*, and *never*. These words, however well meant, come across as domineering and shut down conversations.

Ask *Why* Rather than Focusing on *What* (and Assuming Why)

Lots of couples worry that these arguments seem petty and spoil the atmosphere, so the partners swallow their differences, and the "helper" parent bows to the "in charge" parent's wishes. But what happens when these parenting squabbles don't get expressed? There are two possibilities: nothing gets solved or, even worse, the unexpressed feelings behind the squabble pollute the way you see your partner. In effect, you start concentrating on *what* your partner has done, either without thinking about *why* or coming up with your own *why* (often something incredibly negative), and, over time, this solidifies from your opinion into a "fact." Let's return to John and Marie's argument to see these two problems in action.

"When I'm tired or stressed, all these resentments come pouring out," Marie explained.

"Normally, when we're in bed and about to switch the lights out," John interjected, "I'm tired and want to go to sleep, so I suppose I have 'argument deficit disorder.' I can be quite rational and calm for about five minutes, but then I want to be done with it. So I'll say something like 'Got it.'"

"And that really upsets me," Marie declared.

Hence the argument about arguments. In effect, if you don't resolve the squabbles, they'll erupt as major conflicts. Indeed, John and Marie had described their week as very up and down.

Moving on to the second problem, *what* had John done that night that Marie could have been storing away for a future fight?

"He had been too busy on that laptop to look after his children and he hadn't put them to bed properly and left me to fix everything when I got home," she explained. "No wonder I sometimes think it's too much hassle to go to the gym."

It was a pretty damning list, especially when you consider it was just one evening's worth of disagreements. Even so, it was difficult to resolve the major conflict when it finally erupted, especially late at night.

"*Why* did you think John behaved this way?" I asked Marie.

"Because he doesn't love me or the children enough to put himself out," she replied, without hesitation.

This is an incredibly negative *why* and one not really supported by the evidence. For example, in the counseling session, she had learned that he checked his e-mails so he could give her his undivided attention when she returned home. He substituted a jigsaw puzzle for a story because he thought that would be a nice way to get their son to relax. (Marie had not known about the jigsaw puzzle until John told her about it during our dissection of the issues.) In other words, John's *why* had been reasonably benign. However, concentrating on *what* he had done made Marie take her negative interpretation, treat it as the gospel truth, and overlook hundreds of other explanations for John's behavior.

If you're ever in any doubt about *why* your partner did something, don't assume; stop and ask him or her.

Resolving Squabbles

Ultimately, there is no right or wrong way to give children their snack or put them to bed. In some cultures, children are fed separately from adults, and in others, they eat with their parents and just have smaller portions. Some cultures have separate bedrooms, and in others, everybody sleeps in the same bed. Despite living in hundreds of different environments and eating a variety of diets, humans continue to thrive. There is no *should* for bringing up children. However, the benefits of dropping *should* are wider than just making child rearing less contentious and the source of a million and one squabbles. It gets around the trap of one partner (usually the mother) being in charge and the other (usually the father) feeling devalued and relegated to assistant.

In the case of John and Marie, she was indeed an expert, being the eldest of five children and having helped her mother bring up her younger siblings.

"When I was sixteen," Marie recalled, "my parents went away for the weekend and left me in sole charge of a child of four and a baby of eighteen months old. So when it came to bringing up our own children, I knew what to do. In fact, John has never been woken in the night by a baby crying because I had it all taken care of."

"She's right," John conceded, "but the downside was that I felt that my opinions didn't count, or not as much as hers—and her mother's. In fact, I not only wasn't Marie's assistant, I was second assistant, after her mother."

Fortunately, John was gaining in confidence and started to give his opinion, whether or not it was asked for. In a subsequent counseling session, he reported that "Marie was arguing with Gracie about bringing her math book home. Gracie was being awkward and coming up with a reason she couldn't do first one and then another thing."

"One of my younger brothers was just the same," Marie stated, "and Mom and I would try to solve the problem for him."

"But you were getting more and more upset," John pointed out, "and Gracie was enjoying the sport. I thought, 'Just tell her she needs to bring her math book home tonight.' She's seven and old enough to figure it out for herself."

"I realized that he was right," Marie concluded. "She was deliberately upsetting me. So I listened and stepped back, and Gracie brought the book home without her and me having an argument about it."

In effect, they had begun to turn into a team in which each partner was allowed to give the other feedback—to the benefit of the smooth running of the household and the upbringing of their children. When you're deciding together as a team, the tyranny of *should* is no longer an issue because you've discovered there truly are endless ways to skin a rabbit.

Resetting the Default

If there is a housework or responsibility gap in your relationship, instead of always scrapping over particular tasks or having to ask for help, what would happen if you looked at how tasks are allocated and found a fairer formula? In this way, your partner could take on responsibility for something as a matter of course rather than always having to be asked, reminded, or nagged. In my experience, the division works best when there are clear boundaries.

For example, I had a couple in therapy in which the woman was responsible for taking the children to the doctor and the man was responsible for the dentist appointments. What works worst is a situation in which everything is left vague. For example, she does the laundry, but if he sees that the laundry basket or the dryer is full, he is "expected" to load the washing machine or empty the dryer. With this kind of arrangement, the person who cares most about there being enough clean clothes—normally the wife—is *de facto* in charge, and the other is being nagged to "help out."

Here are some suggestions for resetting the default mode in your relationship:

- Choose a good time—when you're getting along well, not right after an argument.
- Tell your partner what you appreciate him or her doing. If you can't think of anything around the house, talk about how hard he or she works to pay the bills or maintain the car. If your partner feels appreciated, he or she will not be so defensive and will be ready to listen.
- Talk about how you've been feeling. You are the expert on your feelings, so there cannot be a dispute about them. For example, "I've been feeling really tired and irritable lately."
- You might like to consider making a sincere apology, as discussed earlier, because admitting your mistakes will really get your partner's attention. This is especially important if you've tried to have the same conversation before but it ended up in an argument in which one of you was blaming and the other one was getting defensive.

- From this point on, ask questions rather than making statements or offering solutions, because questions build teamwork. For example, instead of saying, "It's not fair" or "You could do the ironing," say, "Could we look at how we divide the tasks around the house?," "What could you take over?," or "How would that work?" In contrast, making statements can easily descend into describing the problem (which will be heard by your partner as more examples of what a poor parent he or she is) or offering solutions (before each party has had his or her say), and this can lead to a power struggle.

- Look for specific jobs to divide ("If you cook, I'll clean up afterward") or volunteer to take on ("I'll bathe the children in the evening and be responsible for keeping the bathroom clean").

- An agreement sticks when there is something in it for both parties, so ask you partner what he or she would like from you in return. In most cases, in my experience, the "helper" partner does not ask to be relieved of a particular task. Normally he or she will just ask, "Can I have half an hour to unwind when I get home without being asked to do something?" or say, "I'd like to go on the computer after ten without being made to feel guilty."

- Once your partner is in charge of a task, it is up to him or her to do it in his or her way and time frame. Please don't interfere; otherwise it perpetuates the "in charge" and "helping out" roles—or even worse "master" and "servant." If, after a few weeks, the situation is not going well—for example, the ironing pile has reached the ceiling—you can have a review. Once again, ask questions rather than making statements: "How do you think the arrangement has been going?" or "How could we make things better?'"

Becoming a Team

Time and again, female guilt and male stubbornness turn dividing the responsibilities for running a house and raising the children into a minefield that threatens to destroy the relationship. However, when a couple becomes a team, the man finds the rewards of a closer relationship with his children and the woman is free to think about her own needs more. So how do you reach this goal?

Stop What Doesn't Work

If you're in a hole, the first thing to do is stop digging. It seems like such sensible advice that you'd think I wouldn't even need to mention it. However, I find couples using the same failed strategies over and over. Somehow they imagine that if they shout louder, pour out more feelings, or make nastier personal comments, there will be a breakthrough. The other partner will see reason, be shocked into changing, or admit, "You're right and I'm wrong." The problem is that they've tried this behavior a thousand times before, and there is no reason to believe that using it once more will achieve anything except to make the situation worse. So look at the following list of potential failing strategies and make a commitment to change. If changing the habit of a lifetime proves too difficult, monitor what happens and whether the hole does indeed get deeper. Here are some failing strategies:

- **Festering in silence.** This just builds resentment, provokes sarcastic comments, and makes noncooperation the norm in your relationship.
- **Saying, "It's not fair."** This invites a long academic discussion or the "Suffering Olympics," in which each partner goes for the gold in being more misunderstood.

- **Nagging.** This provokes your partner's defensiveness and makes him or her believe that he or she is "put upon" and that therefore his or her intransigence is justified.
- **Sulking.** This builds a wall between you and your partner.
- **Walking away.** This freezes the problem, especially if this discussion is shelved rather than continued when both parties are calmer. It also makes your partner anxious and more likely to use a failing strategy in return.
- **Criticizing.** This also provokes your partner's defensiveness.
- **Judging.** This puts you in the "expert" position and your partner in the "servant" position.
- **Hovering.** This poisons the atmosphere in the house.
- **Losing your temper.** This just puts you in the wrong and makes it easier for your partner to label you as the problem.
- **Pouring out your feelings.** Usually so much material comes out that your partner is overwhelmed by the avalanche and cannot properly respond to any one item.
- **Making life unpleasant.** Your partner is unclear about what in particular is wrong and is left guessing or else turns off and doesn't care.

Instead of having arguments that can potentially sabotage your relationship at any moment, start a weekly planning meeting. This allows you to raise any upcoming issues (and head them off before they become a problem) and calmly discuss any differences of opinion from the past few days. I find that these planning meetings lower the emotional temperature, because the partner who is aggrieved can let something drop during the week, knowing that there is a forum in which to discuss it. Choose a good time (like Sunday evening) and a fixed length of time (such as half an hour) and try to stick to it.

Even if you think there is nothing on the agenda, get together in order to double-check with each other that there are no issues stored up, then get out your calendars to go through your upcoming commitments together. If something comes up for the scheduled time, such as you know your parents will be coming over on Sunday evening, shift the planning meeting to another day or time—but *don't* skip it.

Stop Defending Your Position

When we are not appreciated or we feel misunderstood, the temptation is to stop listening to our partners and just repeat our position over and over. I ask my clients to imagine sitting on a seesaw. The more you push down on your side, the higher your partner will pop up on his or her side. Then your partner pushes down on his or her side, and it's your turn to fly up into the air. The only way to stop seesawing up and down is for you both to move into a more central position.

Josie and Howard, both in their early forties, were arguing about planning their New Year's holiday for themselves and their daughter. It had been Josie's responsibility, along with the other mothers in their circle of friends, to find a cottage. Unfortunately, one family hadn't been included, and there had been a socially embarrassing conversation. Later, when Josie and Howard were alone, it turned into a nasty argument. Josie finally stormed off after swearing at Howard, and the argument had not been referred to again. The issue was still alive forty-eight hours later, when they arrived in my counseling office, and replaying it took up half the session.

"Josie tried to smooth it over by making some polite but empty comment like 'I'm sure there would still be room somewhere close by,' and I joked that was typical girl behavior," explained Howard, "because boys would have just been more direct and explained that there weren't enough bedrooms."

"I don't like my behavior being dismissed as girly, especially after I've done all the hard work organizing the holiday," replied Josie.

"I can't even make a harmless joke without getting my head bitten off," Howard retorted. "Aren't I allowed an opinion?"

"Can't you see that my opinion's being discarded because I'm a woman is insulting?" Josie shot back. "What's the point? You'll never understand."

As Howard and Josie took turns pushing down on their respective ends of the seesaw, gathering more evidence from other arguments to reinforce their points of view, the higher the other one went—along with the stakes. Finally I was able to intervene and ask them to imagine sitting on the other end of the seesaw.

"It can't be particularly nice," Howard conceded.

"I've been tense all day worrying about how this session would go," Josie offered.

"I didn't realize it affected you so badly," he admitted.

"I know it's stupid that I should let something like that get to me, but it does," she said.

Finally, they were beginning to come toward a middle position, where Howard would try to offend less and Josie would try to be offended less.

Ask yourself the following question: How much of the problem is me? It is easy to see your partner's failings but harder to spot your own. After almost thirty years of listening to couples' arguments, I believe that problems are usually six of one partner and half a dozen of the other. If your contribution to a fight is hard to spot—perhaps you were quietly doing something and were ambushed—widen the time frame. What if you look back over the past twenty-four hours? From your partner's perspective, does this fall into a pattern (and therefore you might need to think even further back)?

> *Ask yourself the following question: How much of the problem is me? It is easy to see your partner's failings but harder to spot your own.*

If you still can't see your contribution, perhaps you need to look deeper. Even though you *do* want your partner to take a fairer share of the burden, if you were truly honest with yourself, perhaps you *like*, for example, playing the martyr. It could make you feel important, or maybe your mother played the martyr, and although the role is unpleasant, it's at least familiar. Once you're aware of your part in the problem, think about what you could do differently. We like to imagine that everything would be better if only our partner did _____ (fill in the gap with your particular wish), but we can't *make* our partner do anything. The only behavior we can change directly is our own. So what would you like to do differently?

Stop Turning Your Partner into a Caricature

When we are angry, stressed, or tired, it is easy to see everything in very black-and-white terms. This is particularly the case with our partners' behavior or motivations. Instead of seeing them as complex and rounded people, we turn them into cartoon characters with one defining feature. For example, Wile E. Coyote is hungry (and therefore wants to catch the Road Runner), Pepe Le Pew is amorous, and Donald Duck has a short temper. Once we've exaggerated a particular characteristic out of all proportion, we get angry with our partners for behaving like that. It's as though we're both prosecutor and judge.

Ryan and Anna, both in their early thirties, had been married for ten years and had two young children. Ryan had been reluctant to start a family because he still wanted to travel and see the world (and believed that children would make this harder). One Sunday, he had been surfing the Internet and come across a blog from a couple who had sold up everything and planned to visit every country in Europe in a camper van over the next two years.

"I just said something like 'Wouldn't that be fun?' and I really got my head bitten off," said Ryan. "I was told that I wasn't pulling my weight and that I was thoughtless and irresponsible, but all I was doing was trying to read Anna a funny snippet from a blog!"

"It's like he's got gypsy blood in him, and nothing will please him but the open road," Anna retorted, "and somehow the kids and I are holding him back."

"What makes you think I didn't want to take you and the children with me?" Ryan asked. "I never said I wanted to sell everything. I was thinking about taking a couple of weeks off, maybe three, and renting a camper van—perhaps traveling through France and Spain that way."

"Okay, that's different," Anna admitted, "but you'd really like to pack up everything. What about the children's education? I don't want our daughters to be running around campsites with twigs in their hair in dirty vests."

"It's just a fantasy," Ryan said, "and I did say the people writing the blog were probably in their sixties—their children had grown up, and they had no responsibilities."

Meanwhile, Ryan had created a caricature of Anna as obsessed with order and cleanliness and moving up in the world. There was more than a kernel of truth in that. She did want a promotion at the bank where she worked. She did value tidiness and being able to find things. She did want the children to wash their hands before meals. However, there was more to Anna than being sensible and responsible. In the same way, Ryan was not just about fun and freedom.

Once again, start with what you agree on, not what you disagree about. For example, Ryan and Anna could have talked about how they both wanted their children to experience different cultures and understand different ways of life. They both wanted their children to know and enjoy nature, not just watch it on TV. They both wanted their daughters to do well at school so they would have more choices in the future. By focusing on their agreement, they were less likely to caricature each other and more likely to build further agreement. In most circumstances, the middle way is always the best. Their daughters needed to be able to enjoy themselves *and* to work hard at school.

Recruit Others

The more adults who are regularly involved in your children's lives, the better, because children thrive on adult attention. Look beyond the obvious members of the family, like grandparents, and ask brothers and sisters without children to do some babysitting. I have several clients who have confirmed their own desire to start a family after having looked after their nieces and nephews for a weekend while the parents had some time alone together. Other possible recruits for child care are godparents and close friends.

Unfortunately, most people feel uncomfortable asking childless siblings or friends, for fear of imposing. Meanwhile, most childless adults never think of offering. On the rare occasions that I have looked after my nieces and nephews—because I've either offered or been asked—I've really enjoyed myself. It was great to see the world through a child's eyes and connect back to that sense of wonder, possibility, and freshness that children have (and to be able to give these qualities back). For parents, it's great to have extended time together without your children (and to be reunited with them afterward). It's a win-win situation.

The other pool of untapped energy that could fill the household chores gap is staring you straight in the eye: your children. According to an article in the *Canadian Globe and Mail,* only 39 percent of teenagers in Canada do daily chores, and even those who are pitching in are doing five minutes or less a day. However, children as young as two can pick up their toys, and a three-year-old can set the table.

Parents of boys have a particular responsibility to make certain they do their fair share of chores, partly because their future daughters-in-law will thank them, but mainly because it's in their sons' interest not to be helpless and hopeless. I left home at eighteen having never used a washing machine or an iron and unable to cook anything beyond a hard-boiled egg and beans on toast. I still can't sew on a button. (There's advice on asking your children to take on chores in Chapter 8.)

If you find the idea of asking for something from your parents, siblings, or friends difficult, ask yourself why. Did nobody listen when you were a child, so you don't expect anyone to now? Were you encouraged to suppress your needs or told, "Can't you see I'm busy?" Remember our discussion on being assertive (see Chapter 2). It's okay for you to ask, and it's okay for the other person to say no. So choose someone who knows you well and whom you feel safe asking. Be direct and get to the point rather than dropping hints. Listen carefully to the response rather than jumping to a conclusion. If the person says, "I'd love to, but I can't this time," it's fine to ask again, but after that I would take a second refusal as a polite way of saying no.

Aim to Be Good Enough

When I challenge perfectionists, they seem to think the alternative is chaos. It's either sparkling clean surfaces or rats and disease. However, there is a middle way. We're back to *good enough*.

> *When I challenge perfectionists, they seem to think the alternative is chaos. It's either sparkling clean surfaces or rats and disease.*

"I have a guilty secret," admitted Jane, forty-two, "but I doubt I'm the only working mother who thinks this way. I always talk about being organized, but to be honest, I have to let things slide or I'd go mad. My husband doesn't mind a bit of mess, and the children create most of it. Nobody cares if you lower your standards except you."

Jane had had her epiphany when she was remembering her grandmother's house. "She lived in a terraced house that opened straight onto the street. She had a donkey stone [a scouring block used to clean stone steps] that she used to rub on the front step. It would clean and color at the same time—not that the effect would last long—and all the women on the street would be on their hands and knees scrubbing every week, too. It was supposed to be a sign that you ran a clean and respectable home. By the late 1960s, when I was a girl, it was dying out. Nobody does it now. I doubt you could even buy a donkey stone today. I stood in my kitchen thinking about all the energy my grandmother put into cleaning her front doorstep, and suddenly it hit me. One day, society will be laughing at some of the things *we* think are essential."

Housework is not the only area where you need to question whether you are aiming too high. Sometimes it's a good idea to lower our standards for our children as well as for ourselves.

Marie, whom we met earlier, wanted her daughter to be a high achiever, even though she was only seven. So when it came to dance lessons, instead of letting her daughter just prance around, Marie insisted that she learn a routine, and she made her practice it until it was drilled into the child's memory.

"It was a lot of hard work, but she was thrilled about getting a distinction and thanked me afterward," said Marie.

"But you put both yourself and your daughter under a lot of extra pressure," I pointed out.

Her husband, John, added, "You were really crabby and short-tempered with us and complaining that I wasn't pulling my weight."

"What would have happened if she had just pranced around and passed the course?" I asked. "I doubt that she wants to be a professional dancer."

Marie smiled. "It wouldn't have been the end of the world, and of course she has no idea what she wants to be when she's older."

In effect, once she had stepped back and considered the bigger picture, Marie realized that she could aim to just be good enough for herself and her daughter.

Good enough looks different on the opposite side of the responsibility gap. If you're the partner who is holding more responsibility, it might feel frightening to relax your control—either because you're worried that your partner will not pick up the slack (and, for example, there will be no food in the house) or because your self-image is so tied up in the house or in being "in charge." If this is the case, experiment for a week or a month. What would happen if you left something to your partner and he or she did it "well enough"? What would happen if you lowered your standards and, for example, left the same sheets on the bed for a couple of extra days? Remember, it is an experiment, not a commitment from now to eternity.

If you're the partner who is normally on the supporter side of the responsibility gap (perhaps you work full-time), it can seem daunting to fill the chores and child-care deficit. Lots of men in this position get depressed as they stare into the void and either become defensive ("I already do so much") or give up ("What's the point? She'll never be satisfied"). Instead, experiment with good enough. By this I mean, make a contribution toward closing the gap by taking on something, such as the laundry or Saturday child care. It might be only a gesture, but it shows a willingness.

Your deficit can also be made up in a different sphere, such as romance. Time and again, when I counsel couples with a wide responsibility gap, the wives are asking for a little more help, but what they really want is to feel loved and cherished. So although, for example, your being responsible for the children on Saturday or doing the laundry is a help, it will seem like something you're doing for the children or the household rather than for her.

However, bringing home some flowers (for no reason whatsoever), giving her a hug (other than when you want sex), making an effort to notice when she has bought something new (and complimenting her), or using your imagination to plan a date together (rather than doing the same old dinner-and-a-movie routine) will make her feel appreciated and desirable. (There will be more on this subject in the next chapter.)

King or Queen for a Day

This exercise gets around the "He just doesn't get it" and "She's turned into a control freak" trap. You take turns being in charge for one day, and, like royal proclamations, your wishes are granted. Here's how it works:

- On your day, you choose all the activities for the family. Don't choose anything that would terrify your partner or cause a major argument.
- You are in charge not only of *what* happens but *how* and *when*—starting with getting the children up and ending with putting them to bed.
- Your partner complies with good grace and follows, without question, your suggestions, requests, and even instructions about managing the children.
- Don't talk about how things are going during the day, make snide remarks like "See, it works better like this" (which could start an uprising from your "subjects"), or criticize from the wings (an "I told you so" could get you sent to the darkest dungeon!).
- Enjoy yourselves and be playful.
- Afterward, when you've had time to digest, talk about what you've both learned from the day.
- On another occasion, perhaps the next day or the next weekend, the rules are reversed and the king or queen becomes the loyal subject.
- The same rules apply, along with a discussion at the end of the day.
- Look at what you've both learned and what could be incorporated into your regular life together.

Let's look at this exercise in action. Rachel and David, whom we met in Chapter 1, should have been cooperating. She wanted more help, and he wanted to be more involved, but weekends were a battle zone.

"If I don't do it exactly as she says and when, she criticizes," David complained.

"He has no idea how much work is involved in caring for a baby 24/7," replied Rachel.

So I started them with David being king for the day: in complete charge and with everything he said treated as law. Rachel could choose to be around but taking the backseat, or she could go off and pamper herself.

"I had to bite my tongue because I would have done things differently, but I helped out when asked," she reported. "We went out for lunch in the restaurant in the park, fed the ducks, and played on the swings, and instead of micromanaging every moment, I could relax—and David seemed to bond better with our daughter."

David admitted, "I never actually realized how much concentration caring for a child took, because I would sort of zone out before."

When it was Rachel's turn to be queen for a day, David learned a lot, too. "Rather than resenting her systems and getting moody, I went along with what she said, and a lot of her ideas made sense."

When the Gap Narrows

The more partners can step into each other's shoes and understand the particular problems of running a home, managing child care, and being responsible for paying the bills, the less likely their relationship is to be undermined by having children. There are also individual benefits to being creative about how you divide up the responsibilities. Men who are fully involved with their children, who prioritize the whole family's happiness rather than their professional status, don't miss out on the closeness that comes from casual everyday intimacy with their children. Women who keep at least one foot in the world of work and share the economic burden of running a family don't miss out on the intellectual stimulation and financial security of having a life beyond the children.

In the thirty years that I've been counseling couples, there have been huge changes to the way we work. More people are their own bosses and can choose their working hours. Technology has allowed us to have an office at home, and our twenty-four-hour society has meant less nine-to-five, Monday-to-Friday working, and this has brought more opportunities for parents to share child care.

Jeremy, twenty-seven, had always paid lip service to being a hands-on dad for his daughter, age six, and his son, age three.

"I worked hard, and I didn't really see why I should keep working when I came home, so I would often pretend that I had lots of e-mails that had to be answered when there was really only one, and I'd relax by playing computer games," he confessed.

However, his work patterns changed. His job in the leisure industry meant that he might be away on the weekend but home on Monday and Tuesday. Meanwhile, his wife returned to work as a teaching assistant three days a week.

"I had the chance to do things with my son that I'd never done before, and the more you do, the more you see needs to be done. I did the weekly grocery shopping, and afterward, I felt like having a sit-down, so I had a coffee and my son had a cake and I told him we were going to have a 'man talk.' Previously, I would have just let him prattle on, but I thought I'd give him my full attention, and I discovered he's really funny. Now he often asks me, 'When are we going to have another man talk?'"

On another occasion, his son brought him a broken toy.

"Previously I would have just said, 'What a pity' but done nothing about it," Jeremy explained. "However, this time I asked, 'Do you want me to fix it?' He did, so I got out my toolbox, and it only took about ten minutes. He ran around the house shouting, 'I've got the best dad in the world!' It was like a bolt of electricity going through my whole body. The more I put in, the more I get back."

Ellie and Clive are both forty-one and have two sons who are five and three. Ellie originally returned to her job as an IT consultant for sixteen hours a week after her maternity leave ended.

"I wasn't getting the juicy or difficult projects," she said. "I wasn't feeling effective and thought my career had stalled. Meanwhile, Clive was seeing our children only on weekends and thought he was missing out."

Clive worked as a physiotherapist and struck a deal with his employers to work two and a half days, and Ellie went up to four short days a week.

"If I saw anymore of my children," Ellie confessed, "I'd strangle them, because they can be really demanding—always saying, 'Do this with me.' I find that work helps me relax and unwind because I like getting engrossed in problem solving. The result is that I'm a better parent because when it's my turn, I'm refreshed and ready to see them. I'm also 100 percent confident in Clive's ability to give the kids a really great time. I came home yesterday and found them all wriggling on the floor and pretending to be sardines, which really made me laugh. It takes so much pressure off me, knowing that they're getting quality input from their dad."

She also thinks the job sharing has helped their relationship, since there is no unspoken resentment. "We have insight into the each other's lives, and we're a team, not two isolated individuals. However, we do wish we had more time together. Sometimes we'll have a passing hug in the kitchen and say, 'See you tomorrow.'"

How to Put Your Partner First

Bringing up children, providing a roof over their head, and running a home is a serious business. If you're not careful, all the fun and pleasure can drain out of your relationship, and before long, it seems that the two of you are just paychecks, child minders, and housekeepers. On the surface, your relationship might be fine, and beyond a few arguments about who does what (or, more likely, who has not done something), everything seems okay.

However, your lives are a long way from what brought you together in the first place: you had fun in each other's company and you enjoyed doing things together. Although you might have fun with the children, either individually or together, it is easy for your relationship as partners

> *Although you might have fun with the children, either individually or together, it is easy for your relationship as partners to become all about chores and responsibilities.*

to become all about chores and responsibilities. And here's the catch, which most couples don't understand: A happy relationship is defined not just by an absence of serious problems but by sharing a life together that is exciting and in which you feel connected to each other.

At this point, in my therapy office, couples will either start to roll their eyes (when are they going to have time for fun?) or they'll sigh and think I'm talking about date nights (which require a lot of organizing, and that's another chore to add to the list). So here's what I mean by having fun and enjoying each other's company:

- Smiling and laughing.
- Using pet names.
- Having inside jokes and shared catchphrases (for example, references to your favorite sitcoms or films).

- Saving up and sharing jokes you hear at work or funny things the children say.
- Sending a nice text message in the middle of the day.
- Forwarding a link to a comedy sketch on YouTube.
- Engaging in general silliness and mess around together.
- Leaving small presents (like chocolate on your partner's pillow) or a note on the dashboard of the car.

As you can see, my ideas of fun don't require a lot of time or money but are more about how you interact on a daily basis. However, these gestures show that you're thinking about your partner and that he or she is more than a coworker on the project of raising a family. Of course, there will be times when you need to talk, plan, or have a business meeting, but have some team-building time too.

While I'm talking about fun and being silly, I think it is important to make one thing clear. Something is fun only if both of you enjoy it. So if your partner does not like being teased, that does not fit my definition of fun. For me, fun is anything that builds a connection. So even chores, like writing the Christmas cards, can be fun if they are done together.

Let's return to Blake and Emily from Chapter 2, who have two children under three, and reflect on the need for a rock-solid relationship. Both of them had demanding and absorbing jobs and little time for fun.

"We try to do nice things and make life easier for each other," said Emily, "so the other morning, I said I'd take our elder child to day care while Blake got the younger one ready for the babysitter. In that way, he'd be able to start work a bit earlier."

"I like to get up earlier and take my time," said Blake, "so I can, for example, play a little game with my daughter as she brushes her teeth, whereas Emily prefers to stay in bed longer and be more efficient with her time when she gets up."

"It works well," Emily agreed, "because Blake can have the bathroom first, and then it's free for me to blitz through later."

I was aware that they worked very well as a team but on separate tracks. Where was the connection? Where was the fun? The next week, they decided to work together rather than split the tasks.

"We decided to clean together," said Blake, "rather than me taking the kitchen and Emily doing the bathroom." They were also able to enjoy his idea of fun. "I put on some music I've been enjoying and wanted to introduce to Emily, and we talked about what we'd been doing over the week." They also played a game in which they had to come up with as many recording artists for different letters of the alphabet as possible.

In effect, they had made their connection with each other a priority rather than just accomplishing a list of jobs.

Summary

You cannot find a solution until you have fully explored the problem and understood each other's feelings and thoughts. When you have explored and understood, you can act. In most cases, the resolution is not so much to aim for a fifty-fifty split as to understand each other's contribution to the family and making certain you both feel loved rather than just viewed as service providers. That's why fun and silliness are not just things for your children; they are part of your everyday relationship with each other, too. In fact, this idea is so important that it straddles two of my golden rules, as we will see at the end of the book.

7

Being Mom and Dad and Lovers, Too

E very couple expects babies to have an effect on their sex life. The later stages of pregnancy can make lovemaking uncomfortable, and it takes a mother time to recover from the pain and sometimes physical trauma of giving birth. Add the sleepless nights and the relentless demands of a newborn, and it's not surprising that parents' love lives are disrupted. However, there is a guilty secret that many couples do not tell anyone—not even their friends, their doctors, or even their marriage counselors. Furthermore, the partners are unlikely to discuss it with each other. So what is this secret?

Although most couples resume making love again within the first few months after giving birth, the frequency of sex drops dramatically, and for many, it can happen fewer than ten times a year, which sex therapists categorize as a low-sex relationship. If this is the couple's first child, there is normally a boost to lovemaking as soon as the couple tries for a second baby, but once that is achieved, it is not uncommon for the couple's sex life to diminish drastically. In the worst cases, I have counseled couples who have been in sexless marriages for years—beyond once or twice when they have made a special effort—even though their children were old enough to be in elementary school. Fortunately, the vast majority of couples do not fall into this category, but most parents with two children under five have issues about the frequency and the quality of their lovemaking.

The Effect of Hormones on Your Sex Life

Advances in neuroscience have given us better information about the biology of desire. When a woman gives birth, she produces more oxytocin, a hormone designed to encourage bonding, nurturing, and nursing her child. This increased level of oxytocin will last for about two years, then it will start to wane and she will become more sexual again. In this manner, evolution has encouraged women to want a child about every two years. Dr. Glyn Hudson-Allez, a psychosexual therapist and the author of *Sex and Sexuality*, a training guide for counselors, believes that once women have had as many children as they want, their overall sexual desire drops. "Instead of being spontaneously horny, as they might have been before they had children," Hudson-Allez wrote, "they become sexually responsive. In effect, their partner has to push the right buttons for them to be sexual. They are less likely be rushing around feeling up for it." I know this sounds depressing, but I have plenty of advice to overcome this problem.

Unfortunately, the man whose body and lifestyle has not been through the same seismic shift can begin to think his wife is not attracted to him anymore. If he is unsure how to woo her from the everyday world of diapers, feeding routines, and cleaning up after babies into the sensual world of making love, he can become angry and resentful. Naturally, this is a turnoff for most women, and the chance of sex drops even lower.

"I love my youngest daughter, but I really resent that she came along so quickly," said Robert, thirty-nine. He already had a son, eighteen, from a previous marriage and a daughter, five, with his current partner. "I agreed to a second child, even though I was happy with our family at the size it was, because I thought I'd get lots of sex, but she became pregnant almost immediately."

"I'm sorry, but I just don't need to make love," Claire, thirty, responded to Robert. "I have two small children hanging on me half the day, and I don't need to be groped by you, too."

Although I needed to look at how Robert initiated sex—which was clearly part of the problem—it seemed that the physical demands of child care provided plenty of skin-to-skin closeness that satisfied most of Claire's needs for intimacy. Robert, who was out at work all day, did not get this.

Dr. Hudson-Allez sees another difference between men and women: "When men have sex with a long-term partner, it is part of showing their love. So when women say, 'I don't want it,' men feel personally rejected because it is their love that has been turned down." This is possibly because, as scientists have discovered, ejaculation is the only time men produce oxytocin. "For women," Hudson-Allez added, "sex becomes an optional extra as they are showing their love with all the other things they're doing in the relationship."

Whether you have two children under five (and your hormone levels had only just returned to normal before the next child came along) or your children are older (but your love life has still not recovered) or you just want to improve the frequency or quality of your sex life (so it is a resource to keep you lovers rather than just parents), it is important to understand what promotes desire and what kills it.

Three Barriers to Desire

In my experience, turnoffs have their roots in our attitudes, the things we have done and the things we have left undone. The three most common reasons for couples falling into the low-sex or no-sex trap are unrealistic expectations, pestering, and resentment.

> *The three most common reasons for couples falling into the low-sex or no-sex trap are unrealistic expectations, pestering, and resentment.*

Unrealistic Expectations

If I could change just one preconception about relationships, it would be that *Love happens naturally*, because that does more damage than anything else. With this myth, what matters is the feeling of connection, because the strength of the chemistry between two people will overcome all obstacles. With this expectation, you think you don't need to feed your relationship or prioritize each other because your partner loves you and your relationship is naturally self-sustaining. So once you are married, the work of courting and seducing each other is complete, and you can relax and put your feet up. Worse still, the preconception that love happens naturally easily leads to *Sex happens naturally* and that somehow good lovemaking should happen spontaneously.

"I don't want to plan to have sex," Claire objected. "What if I'm not in the mood? It all seems a bit calculating and . . ." Her voice trailed off.

Dirty? I wanted to add, but I kept quiet and instead asked about her sex education. I wasn't surprised to discover that her mother had very puritanical views.

"She warned me that 'boys are only after one thing' and that they can't be trusted. If there was any of what she called 'lovey-dovey' on the television, she would start bristling or get very quiet, and sometimes it was easier and less embarrassing to change channels."

"It sounds like sex is okay as long as you're carried away by a wave of passion," I said, "but to actually ask for it makes you into what?"

Claire thought for a second. "Not a nice girl?"

"And probably a whole lot worse."

She nodded.

"No wonder you believe in spontaneous sex," I continued. "But what about when you were trying for a baby? I bet you took your temperature to know when you were ovulating and counted how many days from your last period to maximize your chances of conceiving."

Claire laughed. "I suppose I would say that's different."

Of course, there is nothing wrong with spontaneous sex; I'm all for it. However, in my experience, the only occasions on which parents have enough time to unwind from everyday responsibilities and are in each other's company enough to synchronize their desire is when they are on vacation, and that's not enough to sustain a good sex life.

A related unrealistic expectation that harms our sex lives is *My partner should fill the gaps in me and fulfill me.* You only have to listen to popular music to realize how deeply this idea is ingrained in us. Whether it's "You lift me up," "I believe I can fly," or "lost without your love," the message is that love will transform or rescue you. This expectation is also at the heart of at least one of the most popular fairy tales, *Cinderella.* This structure has been used a million times in movies and books like *Pretty Woman, Cocktail* (*Cinderella* in reverse, with a man being saved by a woman) and *Jane Eyre* (in which they save each other). Of course, love does feel good, and someone finding us attractive does make us feel worthwhile. However, it is a big jump from this to making your partner responsible for your well-being.

During counseling, Robert had complained about his job as a salesman and how hard he found it to stay positive. "There is a lot of rejection," he noted. "You have to pick yourself up after a potential customer has said no. Of course, it's the product that they're not buying, but it's easy to take it personally. However, if I've had sex with Claire, that buoys me up. I have a spring in my step. I feel funnier, nicer, a better man. I can shrug off any setbacks. But if I haven't had sex and I fail to get the order, I can really plummet."

Claire was also expecting Robert to fill the gaps in her life. "Sometimes I'm almost counting the minutes until Robert arrives home. It gets really boring being home alone all day and starved of adult company. However, he can be stressed and want to unwind, and I want to unload everything that's happened."

Of course, your partner should be kind and offer help, but he or she is *not* responsible for your happiness and self-esteem or for making sense of your life. If Claire and Robert had taken charge of their own lives, rather than expecting each other to fill the gaps, she could have arranged to meet other mothers during the day (so she was not starved of adult conversation), and he could have asked his boss to send him to a sales course (so he had new selling techniques). In that way, when Claire offered sex or Robert provided a listening ear immediately after arriving home, it would be as a gift, not a duty.

The most dangerous expectation is that *A couple does not need to have sex but can still have a good marriage.* Traditionally, it has been women who have bought into the myth that if their husbands love them and the children, this will be enough. However, I have counseled lots of relationships in which men have a low libido and the women feel unwanted. Whichever way it occurs, it is equally harmful for the relationship. Of course, nobody should be forced to have unwanted sex. However, it's just as true that nobody should have to go without the sex that he or she *does* want.

> Of course, nobody should be forced to have unwanted sex. However, it's just as true that nobody should have to go without the sex that he or she does want.

When a couple cannot talk about something, each partner's expectations of the other remain unspoken and therefore unchallenged. Unfortunately, sex is notoriously difficult to discuss. If you said to your partner, "Can we talk about our summer vacation?," you'd order brochures or do an Internet search about possible destinations. If you said to your partner, "Can we talk about our sex life?," he or she would probably reply, "What's wrong with it?" or worse, "Are you having an affair?" How can you bring up the subject without one or both of you becoming defensive?

I recommend using *appreciative inquiry*, a concept from management consultancy. Traditionally, workers identified a problem, tried to understand what went wrong, and then looked for a solution. However, they would usually just defend their respective turfs, opt out, and not bring any creativity or imagination to finding a solution. So they turned the process on its head, focused instead on what *was* working, and asked, "How can we build on that?"

There are four stages to appreciative inquiry: discover what works, dream, design, and deliver. So start by discussing the good times: "When do we have good sex?" and "What do you enjoy?" Remember a particularly good occasion and try to give as much detail as possible. Not only will this make your partner feel appreciated, it will also provide material for the next stages. Next, dream about how you would both like things to be: "What sort of sex would you like?" Then, in design, you work together to make your dream into a reality: "How could we make this happen?" and "What would each of us have to do differently?" Finally, to deliver, you discuss how to sustain the changes.

Pestering

There are many different styles of pestering for sex. There is dropping hints—usually incredibly unsubtle ones, like reminding your partner how long it has been since you last made love—and making double entendres or sarcastic comments. There's also sulking and being in a bad mood that is lightened only when you're given sex.

People who nag know it doesn't work; it just builds resentment, undermines the relationship, and gets only partial results. Similarly, deep down, people who pester for sex know it is destructive. Just like nagging, pestering is an equal-opportunity failing—although there tend to be more men pestering for sex and more women nagging for help with the chores. Both naggers and pesterers find it hard to stop, because they can't think of any other strategy.

"I don't like to keep asking," said Timothy, a forty-one-year-old father of two teenagers, "but if I didn't push for it, we'd never have sex."

"How do you know you'd *never* have sex?" I asked. "*Never* is a long time."

"Okay, I *fear* we'd never have sex."

"I don't mind you asking," explained his partner, Charlotte, thirty-eight. "It's what happens if I'm not in the mood. You let out a deep sigh or get angry or turn your back on me. I feel horrible. If I try to reach out to you, you inch farther away. It takes ages before I can fall asleep."

"It's not great for me either," replied Timothy.

The situation had gotten so bad that Charlotte was going to bed early so she would be asleep by the time Timothy came up. She had also started to avoid all casual physical contact. "I don't come and sit with him on the sofa when we're watching TV in case I send out the wrong signals."

Not only did pestering put up a wall between Timothy and Charlotte, making it harder for him to initiate sex and increasing the chances of being rejected; when they did have sex, it was not particularly satisfying.

"It feels like her heart isn't in it," Timothy revealed, "like she's just going through the motions." So although I've had an orgasm, it's frustrating because the gap between us is wider than ever."

"Have you ever thought about why that might be?" Charlotte asked him.

Timothy was beginning to doubt whether Charlotte found him attractive. And that brings me to the biggest problem with pestering: Your partner is responding to your desire rather than feeling sexual and initiating sex him- or herself.

Alan Riley is a professor of sexual health at the University of Lancashire in Britain, and he's been tracking a large number of people and their levels of desire. He has plotted graphs of those with the lowest levels of arousal to those with the highest. The majority of us lie somewhere in the middle. However, Riley has found that, in general, women tend to fall somewhere on the lower end of the scale and men on the higher. Therefore, a typical woman in a relationship with a typical man will want to have sex less often than he does. If he pressures her and she gives in to keep him quiet, there is a danger that she will never feel totally aroused, and sex becomes something for him rather than a shared pleasure.

If you're worried that if you don't pester for sex you'll never, or hardly ever, have sex, the solution might be hard to accept: Wait for your partner to initiate. It will probably take a while. Your partner will need to let go of some of his or her resentment and begin to feel in the mood again, but, trust me, he or she will want sex, and probably much sooner than you expect. Even better, if your partner initiates, you will feel desired rather than placated. When Timothy agreed to wait for Charlotte to approach him, it took about twelve days, whereas normally they had had sex about once a week, but afterward they lay in each other's arms and felt truly close for the first time in years.

It is important to stress that this strategy has to be set up properly, rather than just saying nothing and waiting. First, you need to make a sincere apology, as we discussed earlier, in which you take responsibility for your share of what's gone wrong and identify the effect on your partner—for example, "I'm sorry I've pestered you for sex, it must have made you feel pressured and fed up." Second, make a commitment to change: "I'm going to wait until you feel ready and ask me."

Finally, discuss casual touching and whether it has become a minefield (because your partner is worried that "one thing will lead to another"). If this is the case, recommit to waiting for your partner to initiate, so in the meantime, a cuddle can be just a cuddle rather than an overture for sex and the two of you can experience the joy of stress-free intimacy. It will be hard to hold back; keep the touching sensual rather than sexual until your partner either gives the green light for sex or decides to cuddle. However, the effort and self-control will be repaid by a dramatic increase in your loving connection to each other.

Resentment

I have placed this chapter about sex after the ones on chores and child care because there is often a link. It happens in two ways. First, if the person who is responsible for running the house and managing the children's lives feels unappreciated and resentful, it often seeps out somewhere else—most frequently in the bedroom. Second, it is much harder for this partner to switch off (because what needs to done is right under his or her eyes) than for the partner who is the principal breadwinner (who can at least close the door to the office and go home).

If your mind is forever running down a to-do list or you cannot relax until all the chores are complete, it is going to be hard to find enough psychological space to feel sexual. So one of the first tasks for improving a couple's sex life is to find a more equitable split over chores and child care, because this will have an immediate effect in the bedroom. Similarly, the goodwill created by a happier sex life makes it easier to close the responsibility gap in the rest of a couple's life.

Timothy used to really enjoy sex in the morning, but his wife would often have to get up early and take his eighteen-year-old son off to catch the bus to college. "There's no reason you can't come back to bed afterward and have a nice long cuddle before it's time for us to get up," he would object.

"But once I've dressed and put my makeup on, I don't really want to," Charlotte would reply.

With the link between child-care responsibilities and the lack of opportunity to make love presented so starkly, it was really easy to persuade Timothy to experiment with making a change. The next week, he reported back on the arrangement.

"If I get up and take my son to the bus, it's a real win-win situation," he stated. "We get a chance to have a chat together, and on the way back, I'm looking forward to slipping into a warm bed and cuddling up to Charlotte."

"I've really enjoyed the occasional lying around in bed," Charlotte commented, and then teasingly added, "I don't even mind your cold feet."

I was not surprised to discover that they often ended up having sex, too.

> *Pestering for sex can lead to resentment, and so can annoying habits that make one partner feel unappreciated or second-class; for example, forever checking your e-mail or not keeping a promise.*

The chores and child-care gap is, of course, not the only source of resentment. Pestering for sex can lead to resentment, and so can annoying habits that make one partner feel unappreciated or second-class; for example, forever checking your e-mail or not keeping a promise.

Don't ignore your resentment, irritation, or outright anger, because it will either seep out through your body language and snide comments or explode in an argument. Fortunately, there is a middle way. I call it *reporting your feelings*, and it works best when you use this formula: "I feel ... when you ... because ..."

If you name your feeling, it removes any possibility of a misunderstanding (such as your partner thinking you are angry when you're only frustrated) and releases a small part of the pent-up feelings. If you qualify the specifics—with the "when you"—your partner is reminded that you're not permanently frustrated but only under specific circumstances. Finally, with the "because," you are explaining the reasons and stopping your partner from jumping to the wrong conclusions.

Here's an example: "*I feel* lonely *when you* are working late *because* I want some time alone with you."

Myths About Sex

Look at the following list of statements and decide which are true and which are false. (The answers follow.) When you've finished and checked your answers, go back through the list and identify the myths that you believed, or would probably have believed, before reading this book, or still half believe. What effect have these myths had on your relationship? In light of these myths being exploded (or half exploded), what would you like to change about your behavior? If you're working through this book with your partner, compare your answers and discuss the implications for your sex life.

1. The sexual revolution of the 1960s and 1970s threw off our Victorian inhibitions about sex and our prudishness.

2. All touching is sexual or should lead to sex.

3. A man can have an orgasm even if he doesn't have an erection.

4. Nice girls are not as interested in sex as men are.

5. It's a man's job to make the earth move for his partner, or, at the very least, leave her begging for more.

6. Sex should involve intercourse, and anything else is preparation for the main course.

7. Women with better bodies enjoy sex more.

8. Good sex involves being selfish sometimes and concentrating on your own sensations.

9. If someone wants to use sex toys, it means they're dissatisfied with his or her love life.

10. Men who use pornography are comparing the models to their wives.

11. There's something wrong with a woman if she can't reach orgasm through intercourse.

12. A man has to have an erection for sex to take place.

13. Women don't enjoy pornography.

14. Men should know all about sex.

15. Sex should be spontaneous, without planning or talking about it.

16. A woman has a G-spot that will make her multiorgasmic if her partner finds it.

17. If you do not feel turned on, there's no point even starting to have sex.

18. You cannot teach an old dog new tricks.

19. My partner ought to know what I like without me explaining.

20. Sex should finish with an orgasm for both people.

Answers

1. **False.** We have made great strides, but most people are still uncomfortable talking about sex, even with their partners—especially their partners! When I'm interviewed on the radio or writing articles for daily newspapers about sex, I'm often asked to avoid using the words *penis*, *vagina*, or *intercourse*, and for some reason, any discussion about masturbation (beyond euphemistic references) is banned.

2. **False.** It is important that couples connect physically on a daily basis—as he guides her through a doorway or she strokes his neck while he's watching TV—so they do not fall into the all-or-nothing trap of having sex or sleeping on separate sides of the bed.

3. **True.** A flaccid penis is still sensitive, and it is possible for a man to masturbate and ejaculate without having an erection.

4. **False.** Although in high school, the girls who were interested in sex or had experimented with several boys were called sluts, in the adult world, a woman who is interested in sex is a real asset for keeping a couple's love life passionate and plentiful.

5. **False.** A good sex life is a shared responsibility, and each partner has to speak up and explain what makes him or her feel good.

6. **False.** There are lots of ways to have sex besides intercourse. If you're talking sexy to each other on the phone or Skyping and masturbating at the same time, you don't even have to be in the same country.

7. **False.** Ultimately, what counts is feeling comfortable in your own skin and accepting yourself as you are rather than yearning for some mythical point in the future when you've lost weight or had a surgical procedure.

8. **True.** Although good sex is about communication and sharing pleasure, there are times—especially when heading toward orgasm—when it is necessary to focus on receiving rather than giving.

9. **False.** Sex toys provide variety and opportunities for creative play together; they are not a replacement for a partner.

10. **False.** Men use pornography to escape from their everyday lives and to unwind.

11. **False.** Whereas men are more likely to reach orgasm when sex includes vaginal intercourse, women are more likely to reach orgasm when a variety of acts like masturbation and oral sex are included. The clitoris has more nerve endings than any other part of the human body, but it rarely gets stimulated through intercourse. Sometimes the penis entering and withdrawing from the vagina pulls on the hood of the clitoris and indirectly stimulates it. Sometimes rubbing against a man's pelvis can provide an orgasm, but the woman needs to be on top and leaning forward enough, which makes it hard to maintain the right degree of contact.

12. **False.** Men also have a tongue and fingers, and for many women, this is a surer way of providing an orgasm. In addition, erections come and go, even for young men, so if a man concentrates on giving pleasure rather than worrying about how turned on he is, his erection will probably return.

13. **False.** I have counseled women who enjoy a wide range of pornography. Meanwhile, some agencies who help people whose porn use has gotten out of control report that as many as one-third of their clients are women.

14. **False.** This myth causes a lot of unhappiness, and I regularly get letters from men who are virgins, terrified of being found out and of their first partners discovering that they lack some "essential knowledge" about how to satisfy a woman.

15. **False.** If parents did not arrange quality time together or for the children to be out of the way, they would seldom (if ever) have sex, and how can this be arranged without planning and discussing?

16. **Neither true nor false.** Certainly there are some parts of the vagina that are more responsive, but experts are divided on whether the G-spot is a true separate anatomical structure like the clitoris or a nipple.

17. **False.** You could easily get into the mood, and the sensual pleasure of being touched can be transformed into a desire for sex.

18. **False.** It is never too late to learn new skills or brush up on forgotten ones, but it is often easier to believe this myth and avoid the anxiety induced by trying something different.

19. **False.** You're changing all the time, and even though your partner might know what turned you on when you first met, are you still the same person? In addition, explaining your desires to your partner will help you become more aware of them.

20. **False.** This myth stops us from starting to have sex if we're frightened of not delivering, but it's fine to be in the mood just to be held and help your partner to orgasm through masturbation or for both of you to just drift off to sleep in each other's arms without either of you climaxing. Sex is what you want it to be and therefore does not always have to involve an orgasm.

Three Bridges to Desire

When two people are first dating, and limerence has crystallized, they don't have to think about how to cross over from the everyday world to the sensual world. They are spending as much time together as possible; if they are apart, they're texting, leaving funny voice mail messages, or sighing and thinking about each other, and when they're finally reunited, lust means they can't keep their hands off each other. With sex at the beginning being so easy, few couples are aware of what builds or sustains desire.

However, if you have been together for years and have children together, you cannot rely on lust alone, and you've got lots of other things on your mind beyond how cute he looks in a pair of jeans or how her face lights up when she smiles. Therefore, once I have removed the barriers to desire, I help couples find alternative bridges from their everyday reality to being sexual together. There are three bridges that parents find particularly useful: play, romance, and flirting.

Play

When we were children, play was at the center of our lives. It is how we learned to interact with our siblings and our friends, try out new skills, and develop our imaginations. It was also a way of releasing excess energy or motivating us when we were feeling sluggish or bored, and therefore it provided us with the first clues about how to regulate our emotions for ourselves. Most important, play was fun.

However, somewhere around puberty, a lot of children put play behind them. Although some teenagers continue to play sports, play a musical instrument, or perform in a school play, most people give up these activities by the time they leave college or full-time education. Certainly by the time we are adults and committed to the serious business of raising a family, play has been relegated to something we used to do or is a guilty pleasure (e.g., a round of golf on a Sunday afternoon). Of course we play with our children or as a personal hobby, but we seldom or never play with our partners. No wonder our partners think that we put them last.

Of course we play with our children or as a personal hobby, but we seldom or never play with our partners. No wonder our partners think that we put them last.

Why It Is Important

Play is anything that has no purpose beyond giving pleasure and having fun. It is about throwing off constraints, experiencing novelty, being open to new ideas, living in the moment (rather than planning for the future or worrying about the past), and building bonds—exactly what you need to keep your sex life passionate and interesting.

Why We Find It So Hard

Many people received mixed messages as children. We watched our parents work all hours and learned that work is a virtue and the ultimate validation. Some parents even explicitly tell their children that play is a waste of time, that winning or excelling is everything, or that they are clumsy, have two left feet, or are not as talented as their brother or sister is. As adults, we are frightened of making mistakes (even though that's part of the learning process) or looking silly (because we have low self-esteem and would not survive the shame). Some partners are also competitive or see the world through the lens of right and wrong. With this mind-set, you *shouldn't* need to play dress up (for example, in lingerie) to feel desire, or you *shouldn't* behave "like children" in public and push each other on the swing in the park.

Turning It Around

Think about what activities you have previously enjoyed together that provided fun, positive feelings and a sense of connection. To what extent do you do any of those things now? What new activities or interactions have you tried lately?

How to Play

The activities in this exercise are for just the two of you—adult play—rather than something child-friendly and therefore family play. Look at this list of the types of play and think which ones you would enjoy:

- **Cultural play.** Be a tourist in your own area or go to a comedy performance, the theater, a concert, or a lecture.
- **Entertainment play.** Go out and sing karaoke together, go dancing, visit an antiques or craft fair, go bowling, or watch a sporting event together (not one in which your children are playing).
- **Great outdoors.** Go to the seaside and skim stones over the waves, go for a long stroll, go canoeing or bicycling, play tennis, go bird-watching, or spend a weekend in a tent together.
- **Learning something new together.** Take a stand-up comedy class; try snowboarding, mountain climbing, scuba diving, or wind surfing; or enroll your dog in an agility class.

Make up a list of three things that you would like to do—perhaps from the list or ideas of your own—and ask your partner to choose one. Look at his or her list and chose one that you'd like to do. Just as with fun, the activity is play only if both partners are getting pleasure from it.

Romance

When we are dating, we are naturally romantic. We lean across the table, we show enthusiasm for each other's interests, we make good eye contact, and we find lots of little ways to say, "You're special." Unfortunately, when we have won our beloved's affection and finally feel sure of his or her love, we think we can relax and forget romance.

Why It Is Important

Some men are confused about how to be romantic. They know it involves flowers, chocolates, and candlelit dinners, but what else? So let me explain. Romance is anything above and beyond the everyday routine that shows your partner that you appreciate him or her. Picking up your beloved from the train station is part of what it means to be partners. However, if you have a bottle of champagne in a bucket of ice in the back of the car and a card that says "I love you," that's romantic.

Cooking your partner his or her supper is not romantic, because it's a regular event and we need to eat, but if you make a special trip to the butcher for steak or cook a complex recipe and dress up to serve it, that goes beyond the utilitarian and demonstrates that you have really thought about your beloved. Raking the leaves when your partner asks is a kind gesture, but it is not romantic. Going for a walk in the woods, holding hands, and kicking leaves together is romantic because you're not just getting from one place to another, you're also enjoying each other's company and indulging your senses.

Although I have stressed the importance of romance for romance's sake, it does have a purpose. Romance helps build sexual energy, and the planning involved shows that your partner is on your mind, even when you're apart. So when one of you decides to initiate lovemaking, romance has already got the engine running rather than you having to start from cold.

Why We Find It So Hard

Romance has been turned into big business, and we've been sold the idea that it involves large and expensive gestures. So now it is a Mediterranean cruise, a trip on the Orient Express, or a box seat at the opera. No wonder couples tell me they don't have the time or money for romance. Of course, these big surprises are great, but it costs next to nothing to leave a trail of Post-it notes around the house giving clues to where you've hidden a bar of choco-late. When it comes to showing you care, twelve individual roses on twelve separate occasions is more powerful than having a dozen delivered at once.

Sometimes men complain, "I'm not the romantic type." If I question them further, they can't see the point. So I try to repackage romance by explaining that even in action-adventure movies (think *James Bond* or *Spider-man*), the hero scales burning buildings not to serve his country or to save the world but to win the girl. Romance is just one of the tools in a bigger adven-ture: keeping your sex life passionate and plentiful. It is about being chivalrous, ide-alizing your beloved, and love being not just about sex but strong affection, too.

> *Romance is just one of the tools in a bigger adventure: keeping your sex life passionate and plentiful. It is about being chivalrous, idealizing your beloved, and love being not just about sex but strong affection, too.*

The final reason men find romance difficult is that it's seen as something for women. When a man says something along these lines, I always ask him, "Don't you want to feel special and desired?" Obviously the answer is yes, because everybody wants to be appreciated.

Turning It Around

Doing things in threes emphasizes just how much you care. Use the power of three to translate romantic energy into sexual connection. For example: First, don't share the bathroom while you're getting ready to go out; then there will be an element of surprise, because you don't know what each other will be wearing. Second, warm the car up so it's not freezing when your beloved steps inside. Third, drive past your usual place because you've booked a reservation at someplace special.

Here's another example of the power of three to change kind but normal gestures into something romantic: First, wrap a birthday present inside progressively larger boxes, to build intrigue and excitement as your partner goes through layer after layer. Second, stick the birthday card to the steering wheel of the car. Third, get flowers delivered to your partner's workplace.

Another tip is to store away small bits of information about your partner and look for ways to translate them into romantic gestures. If he likes the music of a particular rock star, you could buy the new biography that you saw reviewed in the paper. If she has fond memories of being taken as a child to see *The Nutcracker Suite* at Christmas, you can book tickets when it's staged in your town. Ultimately, what will turn your partner on is the amount of thought put into something—as much as the act itself.

How to Be Romantic

Romance is about showing your partner that you care, but its power is increased by novelty, so it's forever being performed in different ways and therefore has an element of surprise. Look through this list for new ideas:

- **Be sensual.** Take a bath together, wash each other's hair, give each other a massage, build a campfire and stare into the flames, light a scented candle, or read a poem out loud.

- **Add a new dimension to the ordinary.** Take your partner out for breakfast, meet for lunch, leave a chocolate on your partner's pillow, or dress up and look nice even though you're staying in.
- **Bring back memories.** Watch a romantic movie that you both enjoyed when first dating, look at your wedding photos or video together, put on a favorite song and dance in the living room, or go somewhere that has a special association.
- **Give small presents.** Buy flowers, a novelty gift (like a cuddly toy), a piece of jewelry, or music you know your partner will enjoy. Express gratitude for something that could easily be taken for granted.

Flirting

When I talk to couples about the bridge from the everyday world of raising children to the sensual world of making love, it's always a relief when I find that partners are still flirting with each other. It normally means that their sex life is alive and well. Unfortunately, this is another activity that is standard when we are dating but is either forgotten or considered unnecessary once we're married. Only 20 percent of the couples that I counsel are still flirting. Think back: When was the last time you flirted?

> *Only 20 percent of the couples that I counsel are still flirting. Think back: When was the last time you flirted?*

Why It Is Important

Flirting is giving your partner a bundle of sexual energy and seeing if he or she sends it back—with interest. It says, "I'm still attracted to you," reveals something about your heart, builds romance, and boosts your partner's self-esteem. However, I want to stress that flirting is playful and fun rather than a demand for sex.

Why We Find It So Hard

Flirting is not just in your intent but also in how your partner receives it. For example, a husband might think surprising his wife by coming up behind her and fondling her breasts is fun and demonstrates his desire for her. However, if she interprets it as pressure for sex or a form of harassment, then it's not flirting. Many couples find flirting to be such a minefield that it seems safer to step around the area altogether. Unfortunately, these partners are likely to slip into the role of coparents, friends, or brother and sister rather than staying lovers. If you find the idea of flirting difficult, don't despair. Your skills might be rusty, but there's nothing stopping you from either brushing them up or relearning them.

Turning It Around

I have placed flirting as the last bridge to desire because it can be difficult, especially if there is a wall of distrust or anger between you. However, if you can play and be romantic together, there will be a more positive atmosphere. So even if your flirting is too strong and you need to tone it down slightly, your partner will be able to tell you, and you should be able to take feedback as a gift to help you be better next time rather than as criticism (and therefore rejection). Start by taking a general audit of how you and your partner communicate. Are you in the same room, or do you shout up and down the stairs to save time? Do you put down what you're doing when your partner is talking? What is your eye contact like? (A lot of flirting is in the eyes.) Make a commitment to stop practices that almost guarantee misunderstanding and undermine connection.

How to Flirt

The secret of flirting is to start small, at the nonsexual end of the spectrum, and build slowly, checking out the reaction from your partner, then turn it into something a little more explicit and only later making sexually charged overtures. Here are some tips on how to flirt:

- **At a distance.** Leave a sweet message somewhere only he or she will find it, send a saucy text message, or tell your partner what you're going to do to him or her when he or she gets home.
- **Casual touch.** Rub your leg against his or hers in a restaurant, gently touch your partner's face, or stroke his or her hair.
- **Teasing.** Play peekaboo (i.e., look from behind the menu in a restaurant and then hide your eyes). Show him that you're wearing something sexy, like a garter, under your dress. Show her you've bought a small present, but don't let her open it until later. Tickle your partner.
- **Kisses.** Give an extra-long kiss when your partner comes home, kiss with your eyes open, kiss him or her somewhere unexpected on the body, or vary your kisses—try lots of light butterfly kisses on the neck followed by a raspberry on the stomach.

How to Have Better Sex

Although a lot of my work is in helping couples improve the frequency of lovemaking, it is equally important that when you do have sex, it is satisfying and anxiety-free (and therefore creates a cycle in which you want more sex and it becomes easier to initiate). Just as I have described three barriers to desire and three bridges to desire, I have three strategies for improving technique: slow down, be less penis focused, and make sex a shared responsibility.

Slow Down

In general, it takes the average woman longer to become turned on than it does the average man. Fortunately, most couples are aware of this discrepancy and make allowances. However, once a woman has children, she will also need to shift out of mother mode into sexual-woman mode. Unfortunately, once you have children, time is short. There's always the fear that the baby or the children will wake up. You're tired, there's another long day ahead tomorrow, and you want to go to sleep. All these factors make it more likely for partners to rush their lovemaking, just when they need to slow down more in order to ensure that the woman is fully engaged and ready for sex.

"I don't really feel that sexy," admitted Zoe, twenty-nine. "Since I had my daughter, I haven't been able to lose the weight I put on while pregnant."

"I'm still attracted to her, but she has a hard time believing it," said her husband, Ben.

"My mind is full of what needs to be done tomorrow, what I need to remember, and what I've forgotten," she explained.

"Sometimes it feels that you're not with me when we do make love," Ben confessed, "like you're mentally running down that list. It can feel very lonely."

"To be honest," Zoe declared, "sometimes I feel like 'Just get on with it'—which I know sounds cruel. But once I do get into the mood, I do enjoy myself."

"How long does that take?" I asked.

"I don't know," Zoe replied.

I sensed she was being diplomatic because the truth could hurt Ben. "Is it sometimes too late for you to get any real satisfaction out of your lovemaking?" I asked.

Zoe nodded.

Here's what I tell couples like Zoe and Ben. Extend your foreplay. Allow at least fifteen minutes for sensual touching, by which I mean stroking, fondling, and kissing each other but avoiding touching the breasts and the genitals. You can take turns pleasuring each other or do it simultaneously, but make certain that you explore every inch of each other's body (other than breasts and genitals).

Don't let each other know what's coming next. In this way, sex is not predictable and possibly boring. Change direction, speed, intensity of touch (lightly skimming to firm massage) and alternate between fingers and mouth. Look for new places that might be sensitive and elicit pleasure for your partner. Make certain that you communicate (let out a sigh if something feels good), listen to your partner's breathing (does it sound heavy and turned on?), and check that your partner is not tensing up (which suggests that you're doing something wrong).

After fifteen minutes of sensual touching, you can move on to exploring the breasts and genital areas with your fingers or tongue. Once again, vary your approach—stop, wait, start again—so that you keep an element of surprise. Allow at least ten minutes of this sexual touching, either taking turns or pleasuring each other simultaneously, before finally moving to intercourse (or deciding to make oral sex or masturbation the main course of your lovemaking).

Be Less Penis Focused

One of the most pernicious myths about sex, which I challenged earlier in this chapter, is that there has to be an erect penis for sex to take place. You might imagine that men are more concerned about the strength and sustainability of their erections, but it turns out that women are just as obsessed.

"I don't really like to say anything," said Zoe, glancing at Ben to check his reaction, "but if we want things to change, we've got to be honest."

"What she's trying to say is that sometimes I lose my erection," he explained.

"It's not that often, but . . ." Her voice trailed off.

"I *am* attracted to you," he tried to reassure her.

"You never used to go soft."

"So if he really was attracted to you, he'd have a rod of steel," I interjected, hoping to add a little humor into the situation and lighten the atmosphere. "The quality of a man's erection is not just about how turned on he feels. It's possible for men to have erections in the morning, when a full bladder is pressing on the prostate gland and they don't feel remotely sexy. Similarly, a man can be really excited but nervous or anxious, and that stops him from getting an erection. There is no straightforward connection between desire and erection."

"I do worry about being overheard or whether our daughter will wake up and want to come into our bedroom, so the slightest noise or click from the central heating can break the mood," said Ben.

"Men are not sex machines, we're fallible human beings," I pointed out, "but what happens if you're not giving Zoe a reassuring round of applause with your rampant penis?"

"I see the look on her face and I get angry with myself. The more I worry, the worse it gets."

"So you retreat to separate sides of the bed and lovemaking stops?" I asked.

They both nodded.

"And so when you do have an erection," I continued, "you want to—excuse me for being so direct—get on with it. So perhaps it's not surprising that Zoe hasn't had enough time to relax, unwind, and join in your lovemaking, because you're rushing toward the finishing line."

It had become a vicious cycle. Ben was focusing on his penis rather than communicating his love. Zoe was not fully engaged and therefore not giving him any sexual feedback or encouragement, so he was feeling less turned on and more likely to lose his erection and want to rush sex.

Erections come and go. Contrary to popular myth, even teenage boys don't walk around with constant erections. So instead of worrying, focus on something else. For example, the man could give the woman oral sex or masturbate her, or the couple could return to the sensual touching and cuddling part of foreplay. On most occasions, the man's erection will return. However, it could be that he's tired or has had too much to drink, and a cuddle is enough. Contrary to another common myth, sex does not have to end in an orgasm for both parties. What counts is that both parties feel close, sharing intimacy, and a sense of being connected. It's also fine for one partner to masturbate him- or herself while the other partner kisses him or her or whispers encouragement.

Having a variety of possible outcomes to sex helped to turn around Zoe and Ben's lovemaking. Instead of being focused on his penis, their lovemaking could consist of simple sensual touching, sexual gratification from masturbation (either by themselves or pleasuring each other), both of them climaxing from masturbation, oral sex, or intercourse.

Make Sex a Shared Responsibility

When a woman feels responsible for running the house and seeing to the children's welfare, she can easily feel unappreciated and resentful. Similarly, when a man feels responsible for initiating sex the vast majority of the time, he can easily worry that his wife isn't attracted to him, that she's only doing sex for him (which is a turnoff), and that there's no real sexual connection. In just the same way that I want to close the responsibility gap for housework and child care, I'd like to close the responsibility gap for sex.

In many cases, men are responsible not just for initiating sex but also for turning their partners on and giving them orgasms. (We're back to the myth about sex, stated earlier in this chapter, that it's a man's job to make the earth move for his partner.) With Zoe and Ben, it was Ben who was responsible for initiating sex.

"Except in the early days when we first got together," he recalled, "I suppose it must be 95 percent or more of the time that I make the first move.

"I've never really thought about it, but you're probably right," Zoe conceded. "Certainly you've kept track of how often we've made love, and once when we went through a dry spell, you told me that we hadn't had sex for five months. I'd been aware that it wasn't recently, but I didn't realize it had been that long!"

"Once he has initiated," I asked, "whose job is it to pull you out of mommy mode so you can feel truly sexual?"

Zoe looked puzzled for a moment. "I suppose I want him to seduce me," she replied.

"That's fine, and that's part of being a loving couple," I reassured her, "but what I'm asking is for you to take equal responsibility. After all, it's *you* that's going down your list of mommy jobs. Sure, he can take his time so you have a chance to close down that part of your brain. However, ultimately it's up to you to tell yourself, 'Enough of this mummy stuff. There's more to me than just being a mother. Let it go.' So you're *equally* responsible for turning yourself on."

Unfortunately, what can happen is that women—often unconsciously—give their husbands the responsibility for lovemaking and then become resentful when they fail to deliver, which makes sex harder to initiate and less satisfying for both partners.

However, men don't help themselves, either. In the same way that some women

> *In the same way that some women complain about carrying the burden of chores and child care (but hold on tightly to being in charge), men find it equally hard to share responsibility for sex.*

complain about carrying the burden of chores and child care (but hold on tightly to being in charge), men find it equally hard to share responsibility for sex.

"I get my pleasure from giving pleasure to Zoe," explained Ben.

"So how do you feel if Zoe pleasures herself to achieve an orgasm or if, for example, you try a position for intercourse in which she is on top and therefore determining the speed and depth of your penetration? If she's giving you pleasure rather than just receiving it?"

He looked uncomfortable for a moment, but finally he replied, very quietly and looking down at the floor, "That I'm somehow less of a man."

Deep down, men know this is nonsense. However, when partners don't talk about sex and confront the myths, they hold on to outdated ideas that spoil not only their own pleasure but that of their partner, too.

Negotiate when to have sex. Instead of sex being an unmentionable subject—so you send semaphore signals about your willingness or unwillingness to make love—I'd like you to be able to talk to each other. I know this sounds like a daunting task, but remember assertiveness. Say, "I have the right to ask [in this case, for sex], you have the right to say no, and then we can negotiate." This strategy works best if you have already extended your foreplay. In this way, the person who says no to sex can offer a cuddle and extended sensual touch as an alternative.

The other possibility would be to use another bridge to desire: planning. I'm particularly keen on planning because it makes initiating a shared responsibility. So for example, the person who says no could offer to make love the next day or on Saturday morning. This is followed by a discussion in which both partners decide whether this option is practical and how to turn it into a reality. Obviously, this is not an ironclad guarantee of sex. If one of you is ill, if your parents drop in unexpectedly, or if the boiler has broken down, you might need to negotiate a new time.

The Pros and Cons
of Shutting Down Sexually

Talking about sex, taking responsibility for your own pleasure, and dealing with your hang-ups is really hard. It is much easier to put the children first, reassure yourself that all parents' sex lives undergo a major change, and shut down sexually. So I wouldn't be surprised if you're thinking, *Yes, but—: Yes, I should do something about our sex life, but my husband loves me and the kids. Yes, I should bring up my unhappiness about our sex life, but my work is really stressful at the moment. Yes, but it'll be easier when the kids are older.* That's fine, but before you move on to the next chapter, I'd like you to complete this cost-benefit analysis of shutting down sexually:

Pros of Shutting Down	Cons of Shutting Down

If you're finding it difficult to come up with costs and benefits, I've gathered together some of the responses from my clients:

Pros of Shutting Down	Cons of Shutting Down
No anxiety about whether I please my partner	Missing out on the possibility of a better sex life
No embarrassing discussions about sex	Poor cooperation in other areas

I can hang on to my viewpoint and feel right	No romance and courting
I win an argument	Fewer orgasms
Sex is a bargaining tool for getting what I want	I don't feel close or connected
I don't have to confront a problem	More arguments
Revenge	Infidelity

How to Put Your Partner First

Every couple would agree that partners should be lovers as well as Mom and Dad. Unfortunately, they send out signals that say, "Our children's needs are more important than our couple needs," and sex drops down on their list of priorities.

Stella, forty-one, and Graham, forty, had two children, ten and eight. They both enjoyed sex, when it happened, but they found it difficult to find the time. Fortunately, they were comfortable with the idea of planning sex, so we were able to discuss when was the best time.

"Around about nine o'clock would be good for me," said Stella. "Any later and I'm too tired."

"Except that's around the time that we finish putting the children to bed," Graham pointed out. "If they go to bed too early, I don't see them when I come home, but they can dawdle getting to bed and want an extra story."

"Some nights we could be more focused and switch their lights off by eight-thirty and come to bed," Stella suggested.

"But then you've got to prepare for the next morning, sorting out their sports equipment and books," Graham reminded her, "so that's not always possible."

They sank into silence.

"Let me get this straight," I interjected. "Preparing your children for school the next day is more important than finding time to make love to each other—something you both enjoy. What message are you sending each other?"

They looked even more miserable.

"What would happen if the children prepared their own things for school?" I challenged them. "After all, they are ten and eight. The responsibility would be good for them."

"I never thought of that," said Stella. "We could introduce it for next semester."

Another example of this issue is provided by Julie and Max, both in their early fifties. I had given them homework, which involved setting aside half an hour to do sensual touch exercises. They had decided to have an early night together, but at the last minute their fourteen-year-old daughter announced she needed five pages of typing for her exam the next day. Max was angry, because instead of arriving in the bedroom relaxed and ready to be intimate, Julie was stressed and unreceptive. When I questioned her, she admitted that she found it almost impossible to say no to her child. Almost immediately, Max interrupted, "But she can say no to me."

One of the best ways of staying lovers, and sending a clear message that couple time is important, is to go on a date together from time to time. Unfortunately, this is another idea that couples might happily sign up for in theory but find difficult in practice. Here's what can go wrong:

- **Indecision leads to no decision.** The man does not take the lead, and the woman does not say what she would enjoy.

- **Planning becomes another wifely chore.** Basically, if a woman arranges everything, it's domestic; if a man does the planning, it's romantic. This also extends to planning child care. I can't tell you how often men tell me they don't know any babysitters and I ask, "Does your wife hide this information from you?"

- **Talking about your relationship.** This is supposed to be a chance to enjoy yourselves together. If something difficult comes up, make an appointment to discuss it at another time.

- **Mobile phones and social networking.** Turn off all electronic equipment. If you're taking messages from work or checking your Facebook page, you're saying, "You don't hold my attention" or "I'd rather be somewhere else."

- **Too much drinking.** This increases the chance of an argument or one partner thinking that the other has to be drunk to be sexual.

Now let's look at what makes a successful date:

- **Ask questions.** Admit that you don't know everything about your partner. Ask things like "What would you do if you won the lottery?," "If you could live anywhere in the world, where would you live?," and "What are your top ten favorite albums of all time?"

- **Share an activity together.** Instead of just talking over a meal, do something fun.

- **Be fully present.** Look into your partner's eyes, notice something attractive about him or her, and touch each other from time to time.

- **Make an effort.** We are committed to entertaining our children but not each other. Turn this around by storing up interesting stories, gossip or snippets from the news to share on your date.

There's more information about being lovers rather than parents in my book *Have the Sex You Want: A Couple's Guide to Getting Back the Spark.*

Summary

If you were to take only one idea from this chapter, it should be that sex does not have to be only spontaneous. After the birth of a baby, it takes longer for a woman to become physiologically turned on. Since you can no longer rely on lust to bridge from the everyday world into the sensual world, you need to find other ways, like having fun, being romantic, flirting, and playing together. In this way, sex becomes something to feed not just your relationship but yourself, too—so you do not become trapped in the role of parents (giving out energy) but are lovers (receiving energy), too. Whatever happens, it is important to talk about sex rather than just hoping things will improve at some unspecified time in the future.

8

Red-Carpet Kids

Throughout history, our ancestors have sought to improve the lot of their children, to give them the best possible start and watch them thrive. To our grandparents, almost any sacrifice was worthwhile to give their children (our parents) the opportunities they didn't have. In turn, our parents strived to pass on to us the advantages that they enjoyed. Now it's up to us to pass the baton on to the next generation.

Up to this point in the book, I've been stressing the importance of prioritizing your marriage—because unless you invest in your relationship, it will wither and die, and that's not good for your children—but now I'm going to shift my focus. I accept that everybody wants the best for their children (it's part of human nature), but I question whether making them the center of the universe is good for their welfare or prepares them properly for the world they will inherit. I'm concerned that we're creating a generation of "red-carpet kids."

What do I mean by this term? Basically, I've combined two very different ideas: ancient Buddhist teaching and the modern cult of celebrity. Buddha advised that if we have to walk across rough and thorny terrain, it's impossible to cover it in leather (or carpet), but we can cover our feet in shoes. In effect, he was saying that we can't change the world and eliminate unwelcome events, but we can change ourselves and our reactions to those events. Unfortunately, modern parents want to make everything safe and welcoming for their children, but sometimes it's like trying to flatten out the rough ground, uproot the thorns, and carpet the world.

> *Unfortunately, modern parents want to make everything safe and welcoming for their children, but sometimes it's like trying to flatten out the rough ground, uproot the thorns, and carpet the world.*

Meanwhile, the red carpet is the apex of the celebrity world; just walking down it triggers flashing cameras and fashion spreads in glossy magazines. Nobody remembers the film whose premiere these princes and princesses were attending, because the red carpet is the true event, and being on it has become an end in itself. Today's parents, wanting to boost their children's confidence, offer unquestioning adulation. In effect, they are forever rolling out the red carpet for their sons and daughters.

A lot of the ideas in this chapter will be challenging, but I think that's good. I hope I will make you think about some of the modern myths about parenthood and question not only whether they are good for your children but also whether some of the energy currently devoted to parenting would be better channeled elsewhere—like maintaining your marriage and your sexual connection with each other.

Why Are We Raising a Red-Carpet Generation?

Babies and toddlers need a lot done for them. They are small and vulnerable. So it's not surprising that we pour so much energy into looking after them. However, toddlers turn into children who need us less, but for some reason we find new ways to serve, even to the point of exhausting ourselves and our marriages. What makes us go over the top and risk spoiling our children? This section is devoted to examining those factors.

Smaller Families

My family is just one example of the trend of having smaller families. My grandfather was one of eight children, my mother was one of four children, and my sister has two children. How does this affect parenting? At the most basic level, if you have lots of children, it's impossible to roll out the red carpet for the older children because you're too busy breast-feeding the youngest and possibly still changing the diaper of the second-youngest. However, it goes deeper. If you have fewer children, each one becomes even more precious.

"I worry about my son going to day care and being out of my sight for four and a half, almost five hours a day," said Archana, who is thirty and has just one child. "What if another child wants a certain thing? He'll be one of the youngest. What if he gets bullied? He currently goes to a playgroup for two hours, but that just gives me enough time to come home and clean rather than fretting. What about when he goes to school?" In a bigger family, there is always safety in numbers, with older children looking out for the younger ones. Behind our modern tendency to be overprotective, there is an unspoken fear: our whole family could be wiped out by one fatal mistake. "My son is so precious and irreplaceable—and being an only child just emphasizes that," Archana added.

This trend is exacerbated if you wanted a larger family but had to settle for a smaller one. I did some research into family sizes with babycentre.co.uk and found that 38 percent of British mothers would like more children but were worried about the cost and whether they could give their existing children enough attention. Of these, 28 percent said they would like one more child, and 10 percent wanted two or more additional children. When these mothers were children themselves, only 4 percent dreamed of having just one baby, but this was the reality today for approximately one in three mothers in my survey. With all these missing babies that we wanted but did not have, it's not surprising that we make the children we do have the center of our lives.

We Want to Be Liked

At work, there are often flatter hierarchies, and many of us socialize with our supervisors and employers. We are less deferential to people who were previously treated as figures of authority—for example, we might use our doctor's or teacher's first name. We also have less respect for institutions like Congress, the news media, and even the presidency. No wonder we find it difficult to be authority figures to our children and would much prefer to be their "friends."

"I was very young when I had my daughter," said Katie, who is now forty and her daughter Nicole eighteen, "so we sort of grew up together. We are incredibly alike to the point of being telepathic, and I'd definitely say we were friends. Once when she was really upset about a boy, we talked for two hours over a whole bottle of Bailey's. We borrow each other's clothes, although she has a black skirt that she thinks is too tight on me and says that people stare if I wear it."

This kind of situation creates the risk of squabbling with your children, as though you were siblings, and losing your parental authority. "Generally we get on well," Katie continued, "but if I get irritated because she's not studying enough for her exams and I start shouting at her, I fear that I haven't acted as her friend. I've lit into her and told her she was useless. I panic and worry that our relationship will suffer because I got so heavy that she won't confide in me and I won't be there when she needs me. I'm so frightened of losing her friendship that I end up backtracking and giving in."

There will be more about Katie and Nicole later in this chapter.

It's Easier

When you're stressed and busy, it's much easier to give in to your children and let them have what they want. If your daughter is making a scene in the supermarket, you can avoid a prolonged tantrum by buying the chocolate cookies. If you're trying to get out the door in the morning, it's quicker to dress your six-year-old son and tie his shoelaces rather than insist that he does it himself. Parents think that giving in makes their children feel loved, but the children often get a different message.

> *When you're stressed and busy, it's much easier to give in to your children and let them have what they want.*

"I'm the youngest of five, and my eldest brother is twenty years older than I am," explained Keith, thirty-three. "By the time I came along, I think my mother was fed up with babies. She'd just started a business, and my stroller was parked at the back of the shop, where the staff used to take turns checking on me. Meanwhile, it was a family joke that our father missed out on our childhood because he traveled a lot for work and never came home before nine in the evening. They tried to compensate with the latest toys or gadgets—my brothers and sisters thought I was spoiled—but it felt like I could have anything except their attention.

"I went to a school where gold stars were a big thing. Once everybody in the class had one, we got an afternoon off. At that point in the term, everybody had one except me. In my hurry to finish my French homework and get my gold star, I wrote *le port* [for 'the bridge'] rather than *le pont*. Obviously, it was wrong and I was marked down, and, once again, I let the class down. So I went back to my desk and changed the *r* to an *n* and told the teacher that he had read it wrong. Obviously, he wasn't a fool, and he told me to sit down again. However, I reported him to my mother, who phoned the headmaster and got the teacher reprimanded. I was awarded the gold star, and the class got the afternoon off."

"Did you feel that she had attended to your needs?" I asked.

"Not at all."

"Why?" I inquired, slightly surprised. After all, he'd got what he wanted.

"She didn't stop and ask. Would an experienced teacher make such a mistake? She didn't take time to get to the bottom of the problem or ask why I felt compelled to cheat. No. She did the easy thing."

Guilt

There are hundreds of reasons for modern parents to feel guilty: not spending enough time with their children, not being able to afford everything their children want or need, losing their tempers, and feeling not good enough. Children have an unerring knack for sniffing out parental guilt and exploiting it, because when we feel guilty, we'll do almost anything to compensate.

Amanda, forty-one, from Chapter 1, believed that she let her daughter down by not providing her with a brother or sister. To assuage her guilt, she rolled out the red carpet. "If my husband and I are out and discussing whether we should go home and cook or go to a restaurant, we'll ask our daughter, even though she's three. Unless I accept that she's going to be an only child—and that it's not a bad thing—I'm at risk of turning her into a very unpleasant person, because she will expect to always be the center of attention."

Saying No to Your Children

Everybody likes to be liked, and saying yes is normally the quickest way to being popular. Of course, we know that we need to say no, too, and we say it reasonably regularly. But we don't want to upset our children, so we say no one minute and change our minds the next. How do you say no and mean it?

Audit Your *No* Record

Over the next few days, keep a mental record of how often you say no and the reaction of your children. Here are a couple of things, in particular, to keep an eye open for. Do you have to say no several times and possibly shout or lose your temper before your children listen? Are you training them to tune out because you'll get angry only when something is truly important? Do you follow through when you've said no, or do you back down, bribe them, or simply give in because they're making a scene? Could your children assume that you don't really mean no? Are you, in effect, training them to wheedle, manipulate, or throw a tantrum to get their own way?

For Future Events

Children have a habit of asking something when you're least able to think through the implications, such as when you're cooking or walking out of the door. They're not stupid; they know they're increasing their chances you'll say yes if they catch you off guard. However, you don't have to answer right away. It sounds obvious when I say it, but in the same way we've been trained to drop everything and answer the phone, we've also been trained to respond immediately to a question.

So don't fall into your children's trap. Buy yourself time. Say, "I will need to think about that" or even better, "I'll have to talk about that with your [mother or father]." Another good ploy would be to train your children to ask at a better time: "That's a good question. Ask me another time when I'm not so busy." When they ask a second time, reinforce the good behavior with some descriptive praise: "You've waited until I was sitting down and had time to think and answer questions; that's really thoughtful."

For Something Happening Now

Sometimes the children are asking to do something right away (like eat a cookie) or have already started to do something forbidden (like taking down your grandmother's ceramic animal figurines to play with) and are effectively asking retroactively. In these situations, it is necessary to say no immediately and mean it. If you're not in the same room, and your child's request is shouted up or down the stairs, go to your child rather than shouting back. Be calm and firm. Stay close rather than walking away; your presence will reinforce the required behavior. Use descriptive praise to recognize any step, however small, in the right direction—for example, "You've stopped playing with the ceramic dog, that shows you're listening." Keep praising good behavior rather than complaining about bad behavior. If necessary, give two acceptable options: "Shall I put the cookie tin back in the cupboard, or will you?" (This allows your child to feel that he or she still has a choice in how to behave.)

Acknowledge the Feelings

If your child is angry, upset, or frustrated when you've said no, rather than feeling guilty, reframe the event as a great opportunity to help him or her regulate his or her emotions. Start by acknowl-edging the feelings: "You're frustrated that you're not old enough to play safely with Grandma's ceramic animals" or "It's hard not being able to have your own way." Follow up with descriptive praise, if it is acknowledging the absence of something—for example, "You didn't roll your eyes at me; that's polite" or "You've stopped crying and you're listening."

Invite Them to Understand *No*

There is a good reason you've said no. Of course, once your child has calmed down, you could explain the reason. However, your child is more likely to accept your explanation and accept your rules and values if he or she says them out loud. So ask, "Why do you think you can't have a cookie?" If your child claims not to know or refuses to come up with an answer, ask him or her to guess. If the response is something rude ("Because you're mean" or "You never let me have anything"), don't react to it, just keep descriptively praising: "You're beginning to think about the reasons; that's good. Now guess again."

If your child is particularly stubborn and walks away, don't go after him or her. Wait until your child comes and asks for something or needs your help. "That's a good question and I'll answer it, but only after you tell me why we don't eat cookies between meals." In this way, you'll show that you will follow through, no matter what. When your child has identified the right answer, or something close enough, use descriptive praise again: "You've come up with the right answer; you've really thought this through."

Negotiate

Sometimes you say no because the issue is a cut-and-dried case—end of discussion. However, the situation is often more complex. For example, you don't think your children are old enough to go camping, but under different circumstances—such as putting up the tent in the back yard—you might say yes. In these cases, you can use the ABCs of communication: address the issue, bridge, and communicate. For instance, "You can't go to the music festival [addressing the issue], but [the bridge] I'm happy to drive you to a local concert and pick you up afterward [communication]."

Stick to Your Guns

Slowly but surely, your children will feel more comfortable when you say no—which is useful, because the larger world is full of *no*. Believe me, it will get easier. If you find yourself weakening, remind yourself of this: "If I say no and follow it with yes, I'm training my children to keep asking until they get the answer they want."

Give Yourself a Pat on the Back

You've taken your children's feelings seriously and taught them that it's okay to be disappointed, upset, or frustrated, that we have to tolerate these emotions and get over them. This is an important step toward helping your children to self-regulate.

The Effects of the Red Carpet on Children

Fortunes have been made peddling the idea of princesses to girls, and one of the latest fads for children's parties and high school proms is to have a red carpet outside and fake paparazzi taking photographs. Is this just harmless fun that makes our children feel special, or could it be dangerous? On a day-to-day level, is doing so much for your children and picking up after them a demonstration of your love, or do you risk becoming their unpaid servant? Let's look at some of the effects on your children of being the center of your world.

Stress

If you prioritize your children's soccer practice over anything else or spend the summer taking them to tennis competitions, you are going to be particularly invested in whether they win. If you do the vast majority of the chores around the house so your children can concentrate on doing their homework, you are sending the unconscious message that "your grades trump everything else." Under these circumstances, sports are not just a source of fun and exercise but are tied up with your children's self-esteem and identity. Meanwhile, passing exams and gaining qualifications become the key to a successful and fulfilled life (whereas it is only part of the picture). Even slipping behind in subjects your children don't like or have little aptitude for will feel like a disaster to them. No wonder today's young people are stressed and anxious.

Similarly, giving your children a pivotal role in the family can easily unbalance and stress them. By deferring to her three-year-old daughter over where to eat, Amanda was effectively making her the head of the household. I know I'm exaggerating, but from her daughter's viewpoint, that's precisely what they were doing. Unfortunately, at such a young age, her daughter could not possibly understand all the options and implications of her decision. No wonder she had problems fitting in with her peers and older friends. She would have been much happier knowing her true place in the family hierarchy and deferring to members who had the knowledge and ability to see the whole picture. In fact, Amanda admitted, "I scare myself when I think about how much power we've inadvertently handed over to our daughter."

Katie, who was introduced earlier in this chapter, also found that her daughter, Nicole, would overstep the mark. "If I don't tidy the kitchen, I'm told off for not putting things in the dishwasher. I find myself saying, 'Don't reprimand me as if you're an equal—I'm your mother.'" The constant switches in status, and not knowing where she stood, was a problem and a source of stress for Nicole as well.

"I get really cross when Mummy sides with Daddy, and I feel betrayed," she complained. "One moment we are really, really so close it's ridiculous, and the next she's my father's ally. I feel so alone. I have to realize that he's her husband and he's my father. I can't have all her attention. It's equally difficult when Mummy and I argue—it's like she's two different people. One of them I can talk to about anything, and the other's nagging me about my homework. I never know which one I'm going to get. For example, I came home once at four in the morning, after a party, and instead of her covering for me, both parents were waiting for me in their pajamas and summoned me into the living room."

Problems Growing Up

For previous generations, growing older meant gaining more privileges and more freedom. But what are the benefits to today's red-carpet children, who already have everything and expect all their needs to be met?

> For previous generations, growing older meant gaining more privileges and more freedom. But what are the benefits to today's red-carpet children, who already have everything and expect all their needs to be met?

Nicole, who is now a senior in high

school, is considering the next step in her education. "I want to commute to college, and although Mummy doesn't want me to, I really want to stay at home. People don't understand, and I've had arguments with my teachers. They say, 'Nicole, you've got to be independent.' I tell them I don't want to be independent yet—I'm okay at home."

No wonder there has been a growth in adults watching children's entertainment and reading books aimed at teenagers, creating the need for a booming "kidult" market. Retreating into childhood is so appealing.

Difficulty Regulating Themselves

When we are small, we need our parents to help us identify our feelings, deal with the painful ones, and soothe us. Slowly, as we get older, go to school, and spend more and more time apart from our parents, we take over this role and begin to regulate ourselves. However, what happens to red-carpet children who only have to snap their fingers and every whim is fulfilled?

Keith, whom we met earlier in this chapter, had no idea how to soothe himself. He would either expect his wife to make him feel better after an argument or self-medicate his unhappiness away through the attention of other women. He and his wife had come into counseling after she discovered a string of infidelities. One week, early in their work with me, they had an argument in the car on the way to my office. The atmosphere when they walked in was overpowering. Keith was like a cartoon character with a dark cloud hanging over his head. If I'd had to guess how old he felt inside, I would have said four.

So, like a parent with a small child, I used a lot of descriptive praise: "It's really good that you've still come; well done." (On a previous occasion when they'd had an argument in the car, they had turned around and gone home.) I also acknowledged his feelings: "It's really difficult when you've got so much pain inside." When he was calmer, I was able to find out exactly what had happened. His wife, Elizabeth, had stood up for herself in the argument rather than backing down and placating Keith. I finished the session by looking at ways that Keith could soothe himself rather than expecting others to do the job for him. It became a real turning point in his counseling.

The next week, a different Keith seemed to appear. What had happened?

"When we argued about something," he explained, "I decided to go for a run and sweat out my frustration and anger, whereas previously I would have boosted my self-esteem by flirting with other women. I've also been doing a lot of thinking. If there was a problem, it was always someone else's fault that I felt terrible, but now I've started to step into other people's shoes."

"Returning to your story about the French teacher [and the gold star], what must it have been like for him to be reprimanded by the headmaster and forced to give his class the afternoon off?" I asked.

"I've never really thought about it," Keith admitted. "I suppose if I had, I'd have said, 'It served him right for humiliating me.' In a way, I've been doing the same with Elizabeth. I told myself I 'deserved' those flings after what 'she'd done to me,' but of course, nobody 'deserves' to be lied to and cheated on."

Keith would never have reached this level of insight if he hadn't learned to tolerate being upset, self-soothe, and regulate his feelings. Finally, at thirty-three, he was acquiring the skills his parents should have taught him when he was a child.

A Need for Immediate Gratification

One of the most influential long-term studies on the effects of childhood behavior on people as adults was conducted in the late 1960s and the 1970s at the day care center of Stanford University in California. The researcher, Walter Mischel, sat some six-year-olds at a table, each with a marshmallow and a bell. He explained that he was going to leave the room, and if the children could wait until he returned, he would give them two marshmallows. If they couldn't wait, they could ring the bell and eat the marshmallow immediately.

About ten years later, he contacted the children's parents and asked them to score how well the children were doing both academically and socially. He returned to his subjects again when they were adults and looked at weight problems, drug issues, and divorce. He discovered that the children who were able to wait at age six (and had enjoyed two marshmallows each) had the best school marks as teenagers and were less likely to have weight, drug, or marital problems as adults.

Why should this be? The issue is *delayed* gratification. If you can wait in order to get an extra sweet at age six, you will also be able to balance the desire to go out and play with the need to study as a teenager, and when you're an adult, you'll be more likely to make better decisions about food, drugs, and relationships.

What does this have to do with red-carpet children? If we want to be friends with our children, take the easy option, or assuage our guilt when they are upset, we are more likely to buy them off or take away their negative feelings with a treat, thereby reinforcing their natural desire for immediate gratification rather than helping them develop the resources to delay gratification for a greater reward later.

The Effects of the Red Carpet on Your Relationship

If your children are the center of attention in your family, it is easy to overlook the state of your marriage and any individual problems with which you or your partner are struggling. Earlier we met Muriel and Neil, who were so focused on their three-year-old son that they drove halfway across London to buy a Thomas the Tank Engine costume before turning back.

"I'm worried because he seems more sensitive than other children his age," said Neil. "I've tried to toughen him up by taking away his ball and encouraging him to come and get it away from me."

"But that just makes him cry," insisted Muriel angrily. "He thinks Daddy is teasing him."

I wanted to reassure them that some children are just more sensitive than others and that it's better to acknowledge their emotions and find out what is behind them. However, my focus is my clients' relationships with themselves as individuals and with each other.

"Why is it is so important to 'toughen him up'?" I asked.

There was a long pause, and I could see that Neil was fighting back tears.

"I suppose that's what was done to me," he admitted. "I was a sensitive child, too." Neil's parents had divorced when he was a small boy, and he had been encouraged to "be a man," "look after his mother," and not just be less sensitive but also completely bury his emotions.

I turned to Muriel. "What about you?"

"My parents came from eastern Europe, where it is bitterly cold for half of the year and life can be extremely tough," she replied sadly. "You just have to put your head down and get on with it. Yes, I was a sensitive child, too, but my parents did their best to beat it out of me.

As you can imagine, Neil and Muriel's anxiety about their son, their different backgrounds, and their clashing opinions on how best to raise him had been causing arguments. Fortunately, they had enough insight to recognize that they had a marital problem and sought my advice. Understanding that their worries about their son being sensitive were really about them was a breakthrough in their counseling. As they worried less, got along better, and started to work as a team, their son began to thrive, too.

Unfortunately, a lot of people are so focused on their children that they are almost blind to everything else. So when their children start acting out any unhappiness—because they don't have the words to express it (or they do have the words but haven't been heard)—by misbehaving at school, developing an eating disorder, or experimenting with sex too young, they are rushed off to an expert. I work closely with a family therapist who treats such problems, and he is always amazed at how resistant parents are to looking at the whole family, how the general dynamic or their behavior might be contributing to the specific problem. They would much rather he concentrated on their children.

Unfortunately, a lot of people are so focused on their children that they are almost blind to everything else.

By raising red-carpet kids, we are so busy taking photographs and applauding as our children walk down the aisle that we not only forget about our own problems; if something goes wrong, it is easy to assume it's about the kids.

If any of this sounds familiar, I hope you're beginning to consider making some changes in the way your family is run. I expect you're also feeling a bit overwhelmed and don't know where to start. Don't worry, I'm going to break it down into small steps. The following exercise is the first step.

New Rules

I'm a great believer in change. Just because something has been done one way in the past doesn't mean that it has to always be done like that in the future. Children are always growing and have different needs at different life stages, and this makes new rules not only a natural part of parenting but also a very powerful tool. Here's how you set up change in your family:

1. **Discuss the issue with your partner.** It is important that you both agree on any new rule; otherwise, your children will divide and conquer. Take time to listen to any concerns from your partner, not just to humor him or her but because two heads are better than one in spotting potential pitfalls or inconsistencies. Keep talking until you have ironed out any problems and have both agreed to the rules.

2. **Admit your mistakes to your children.** If you haven't been doing something particularly well—perhaps you've been letting your children stay up too late—tell them about it: "Mommy and Daddy have been thinking about bedtime, and we think it's a mistake to let you stay up so late." First, nothing gets your children's attention better than admitting your mistakes, so you can be sure they will *really* be listening to what comes next. Second, you're modeling behavior you'd like from them and giving them permission not to be perfect (and thereby taking away a lot of unspoken pressure). After all, mistakes happen. They can be rectified and the world doesn't end, which is a valuable lesson for life.

3. **Set a starting date.** Change is easier when we have some time to mentally prepare. If we have something sprung on

us, especially retroactively, it seems unfair, and the world seems full of chaos, which is frightening. For example, you could prepare for the change by saying, "When you go back to school next week, we're going to have a new bedtime."

4. **Explain the rule.** Although this is the main part of the communication, it comes in the middle of your discussion. It takes time to set up a new rule and to make certain it sticks. If you have tried to make new rules in the past but failed, you probably skipped the preliminary or later stages. Do not justify the rule, just put it as simply as possible: "You will be going to bed half an hour earlier."

5. **Acknowledge and name your children's feelings.** Your children are unlikely to welcome the new rule with open arms. So acknowledge their reaction: "I can see that you're feeling [upset, angry, unloved]." Don't worry if you name the feeling wrong, because your children will correct you. The point is that you've shown you're interested in their feelings and that it's okay to be disappointed (or whatever negative feeling they are experiencing).

6. **Help them to own the rule.** Once again, instead of explaining why you've decided to make a new rule, ask *them* to think why and tell you. If they come up with something negative ("You're horrible"), don't get defensive or angry; praise them for starting to think, but ask them to look again for a positive reason, such as "You love me and want the best for me," "You want me to be properly rested so I'm ready for school in the morning," "I've been cranky in the evening, and you hate to end the day with an argument," or "It will make it easier for me to get up in the morning." If you're asking them to do

more chores, the reasons for change could be "to make us more self-reliant," "We're becoming older and can take on more responsibility," or "Everybody does his or her fair share in this house." When they get the answer right, descriptively praise them.

7. **Deal with any questions.** Questions are a positive sign; it means your children are beginning to think ahead. So give some more descriptive praise: "I can see that you're thinking about how this rule will work; that's very [sensible, grown-up, responsible]" (or whatever seems most appropriate for your children). It's a good idea to have talked through any possible problems with your partner and be ready with an answer, such as "Of course, you can keep the same bedtime when it's not a school night." If your children come up with a good point that you hadn't anticipated, you can always praise and buy yourself time: "That's a good question; thanks for raising it. I'll think about it and discuss it with [Mommy or Daddy] and let you know what we decide."

8. **Apply the rule to everybody.** This will not always make sense, but children have an innate sense of fairness, so it helps to make the change something for everybody. For example, say, "We're going to go to bed slightly earlier, too, so we can get up earlier and be in less of a rush in the morning" or "It's not just you and your brother; nobody is going to leave the table without asking permission." That means you will have to ask your partner before getting up to answer the phone or get something from the refrigerator in the middle of the meal. Make sure you don't say something you don't intend to do.

9. **Help the rule along.** At the end of your conversation, ask your children to put the new rule into their own words. Once again, this will help them to own it and allow you to check that they've properly understood. If they are rude or sulky, still use descriptive praise ("Well done, you've remembered the rule"), but ask them to do it again without the sarcasm, rolled eyes, or whatever. If they are still resistant, acknowledge and name the feeling, but still ask again. Praise any step in the right direction: "You looked at me this time when you spoke; that's really polite."

10. **Reinforce.** A couple of days before the new rule starts, ask (rather than tell) your children about the new rule. Help them to think ahead about what has to be done: "I will need to have my bath half an hour earlier, turn off the computer, and lay out my pajamas."

11. **Follow up.** On the starting day, perhaps in the car going to school, think ahead to what will happen tonight. When you're getting into the zone of the change, make certain that you're in the room. It will help focus your child on the preparatory steps and show you mean what you say.

12. **Descriptively praise.** If you have taken the time to set up the new rule, everything will go like clockwork, but don't forget the praise: "You are in bed at the new time; that's really cooperative." If your children are slow or uncooperative, find something minor to praise: "You've stopped typing on the computer; that's a step in the right direction." Offer choices, but make sure all the options you offer are acceptable to you: "Would you like to brush your teeth first or put your dirty clothes in the laundry basket?"

How to Roll Up the Red Carpet

If you have started to say no and have introduced new rules, you already have two useful tools. Here are some more ideas for rolling up the red carpet.

Deal with Your Own Stuff

If you're rolling out the red carpet to assuage your guilt or to overcompensate for some personal failing, it stands to reason that it is better to go to the root of the problem. Returning to Archana, whom we met earlier in the chapter, instead of allowing her to just manage her anxiety by keeping her son under close scrutiny all the time, I asked her to think back to her own childhood.

"My father died when I was about eight," she explained. "He had cancer, but my mother thought it was best to hide this information from us."

"So one minute he was there and the next he was gone," I commented.

"She didn't think we should go to the funeral, either."

"So you had no chance to process or deal with the information."

"And it remained a closed subject because my brother and I didn't want to upset her."

"No wonder you're anxious."

I helped Archana to work on her anxiety with simple breathing meditations and to accept that although her feelings made sense because of her history, her coping strategies today could have a negative influence on how her son saw the world.

Once again, I know it is going to sound strange to leap from child care to dog training, but there are useful parallels. When I went to puppy classes with both my first dog, Flash, and my second one, Pumpkin, the instructor gave me the same message: "Your anxiety goes down the leash." I was concerned that the puppy lunged to play with another puppy. The more tense or angry I got, the more anxious or excitable the dog became.

In just the same way, your feelings and fears are transmitted to your child through your body language and tone of voice. My morning walk with my dog often coincides with parents taking their children to school. Even when Pumpkin is on the leash and is heeling, parents will occasionally shrink away and pull their children behind them. Invariably they apologize but explain that the children are afraid of dogs.

I smile, but I think, *I wonder why!*

Small children live in the moment. It's very frustrating when we're trying to get them out the door, because they don't understand that we have a long list of things to do and places to go. However, it also means they don't bear grudges about ordinary day-to-day things. They think the way your family is organized is the right way—after all, until they go off to school, they don't really have enough experience of the outside world to judge.

So if, for example, you work and they go to Grandma's on Thursday and a babysitter on Friday, that's just the way it is. You don't have to compensate. If you find yourself feeling guilty, you should certainly check that there is not a good reason and that your child isn't truly suffering, but otherwise tell yourself, *This is about me.* If you're calm and relaxed about something, the odds are that your children will feel the same.

Replace Friendship with Respect and Trust

It's fine to be friends with your adult son or daughter, because that's a relationship of two equals who are both responsible for their own lives. However, the relationship between a parent and a child is not one of equals, because you are legally responsible for the child. You also have more experience of the world, the ability to see the bigger picture, and an understanding of the effects in the future of the decisions made today. So there are times that you need to step in and take charge.

If you're a friend one minute and a parent the next, that's not only confusing, it makes it harder for your child to trust you. Which hat are you wearing at any give time, friend or parent? One minute Nicole's mother was hiding her late nights, and the next she was disciplining her. No matter how close Katie might have been to her daughter, she still remained the responsible adult.

Because pretending that an unequal relationship is an equal one creates problems, it is much better to have a relationship based on respect (for your opinions and experience) and trust (that you want the best for your children).

Look for examples of when your children are respectful, such as when they are listening and accepting what you're saying, and make certain that you descriptively praise. For example, say, "You didn't walk away even though you were upset; that is very respectful" or "You asked to get up from the table and you followed our new rule; that was very respectful." Even though it might seem easier to let your children get away with sarcastic tones, heavy sighs, and other passive-aggressive behavior, that's letting them get away with being disrespectful.

Instead, bring the unexpressed emotions up to the surface: "What did that sigh mean?" If they say, "Whatever," stop them and ask, "What would you really like to say?" Follow up their answers with descriptive praise: "That was really grown-up and respectful to tell me your concerns and feelings rather than trying to hide them. Now we can talk about them." Trust normally follows from respect, as long as you are consistent in your decisions and follow through.

Ensure That Age Brings Benefits

Ensuring that age brings benefits further emphasizes the idea of respect by giving precedence to people who are older and have more experience, like grandparents and teachers, but it also gives your children an incentive for growing up and taking responsibility rather than seeking to remain a child.

What do I mean by "age brings benefits"? Let's start with your oldest child. He or she had the benefit of your undivided attention when he or she was small. Therefore, when your next child arrived, he or she could easily have felt sidelined. When I talk to my clients about their childhoods, youngest children will often reminisce about the benefits of being the "baby of the family." Meanwhile, older children will sometimes complain that they fought all the battles with their parents for independence and privileges, but their younger siblings got a "free ride" on the back of their efforts.

You can get around this problem in the future and ensure less squabbling among your children today by giving a few extra privileges to your oldest child. The most obvious example would be a later bedtime, even if it's only fifteen minutes. As your children get older, remember the milestones and generally stick to them. So, for example, if your oldest was not allowed to stay out to midnight until he or she was sixteen, don't let the youngest have that privilege at fourteen. Children like consistency and fairness within the family. In a big, scary, and confusing world, it helps them feel safe and makes it easier to start regulating their own feelings.

Grandparents provide another opportunity to teach this value. You can encourage your children to give precedence to older people by insisting that they open the car door for their grandmother or take a cup of tea to their grandfather. Make certain your children don't talk over older people at family gatherings; teach them to listen to what the adults have to say. You can set a good example, too.

Excuse me for stating the obvious, but one day we'll all be the eldest in the room. So by giving precedence to the older and wiser, we are laying the foundation for respect for ourselves in the future. In this way, we all have a stake in age bringing benefits. In contrast, giving precedence to the youngest means that our best days are behind us, and we can never achieve that preeminence again. That can also be overwhelming for the "golden child" who does not really understand the world or his or her power in it and is forever anxious about losing his or her "shine."

Formal meals, like Sunday brunch or Thanksgiving dinner, provide a simple but powerful way to ensure that age brings benefits. Serve the oldest person first and the youngest last. (I've been the guest at several families where the children were served first, to keep them quiet, and they had almost finished eating by the time the last person had been served and everybody else started eating. Obviously, this does nothing to teach children about delayed gratification.) If a mealtime does not fit in with your baby's feeding routine, give him or her something to eat separately before everybody else sits down and then a little something to chew on while everybody else is eating. The baby can also have dessert with the family but should still be served last, at his or her place in the family hierarchy.

Gain Cooperation

Nagging your children is exhausting and time-consuming and puts a barrier between you and them, and it is also training them to ignore you the first time in the hope that you'll give up or do the task for them. In contrast, gaining their cooperation makes you a team rather than you being your children's personal assistant, running after them on the red carpet (such as putting on their coats when you're trying to get them out the door in the morning).

You are probably thinking that sounds wonderful but impractical. However, if you've been implementing the ideas in this book, you already have a lot of the necessary skills in place. You could use setting up new rules as a way of getting ready in the morning and back it up with lots of thinking ahead so that your children not only know what is expected of them but they also repeat the new rules back to you and own their tasks.

The next item for your tool kit is *Stop repeating yourself.* It is pointless shouting up the stairs, so go to your child. It is pointless talking to his or her back or when he or she is immersed in something else; you need his or her full attention because you want to ask just once, and therefore you need to make it count. So stand and wait until your child stops whatever he or she is doing. Your presence alone—quiet, determined, and calm—will make him or her look up at you. When that happens, use descriptive praise: "You stopped what you were doing and gave me your full attention; that was very respectful."

If your children are doing something really immersive, such as playing a computer game or watching TV, your presence alone in the room may not be enough. If necessary, ask your children to turn down the volume and look at you. Notice every step toward this goal and reinforce it with descriptive praise. Now you are ready to say to them just once: "We're leaving for Granny and Grandpa's at ten; make sure you're ready."

You might need to set up *Stop repeating yourself* as a new rule ("I've decided not to keep nagging you, so I'm going to tell you once rather than keep reminding"), but it is important to stick to your guns. So if, for example, the rule is that your children have to be ready at a certain time with all their gear to go to soccer practice, you will *not* keep reminding them as the time arrives.

At zero hour, if they're still on the computer, you just do something you want to do and say nothing. Wait till they suddenly realize the mistake; at this point, you can either arrive late or decide it's not worth going. If they forget an important piece of equipment, they have to live with the consequences. I know this is tough and may sound hard-hearted, but I'm going to say it anyway: you are not their social secretary or their servant.

It might seem cruel to let your children fail, and they could easily get upset or critical. Stay calm and don't lose your temper or tell them, "I told you so." Fortunately, you have just the tools for dealing with this situation. Acknowledge and name the feelings: "You're feeling angry and annoyed." Follow up by asking why they think you've done this. Use descriptive praise when they give the correct answer, such as "I'm old enough to take responsibility for being on time myself." If you're still finding this hard, tell yourself that self-reliance increases confidence, and there is a big difference between what your children *want* (you running after them) and what they *need* (learning to take responsibility for their own actions). Fortunately, children quickly learn that you will not ask twice and will listen carefully the first time.

Do Less Around the House

Even small children can learn to clean up after themselves, look after their belongings, and do small chores (such as setting the table and carrying their dirty plates to the sink). Before you decide on their responsibilities, it is important to agree with your partner so you can present a united front. If your children are used to being waited on, it is important to acknowledge and name their feelings, especially since they might experience your removing a small part of your care as withdrawing your love. You can overcome this problem by staying with them the first few times so you are giving your support and encouragement (but not doing the task for them). Obviously, the chores will also have to be set up using new rules.

A good rule for cleaning up is that toys have to be put away immediately after your children have finished playing with them. Not only does regular cleaning up keep everything under control and make the mess seem less overwhelming, it can also be presented as a positive: "You'll know where they are next time you want to play with them." You can also have a penalty—for example, once a day you will remove anything left lying around or not in your children's rooms, but they can earn it back by doing an extra chore.

If there are several tasks that might have to be done on different days, you can help your children accept and remember the plan by getting them to create a wall chart. They can design it themselves and draw pictures for particular jobs. You might also consider having stars for tasks completed. (I will cover rewards in a moment.)

Teamwork can make a dreaded chore seem easier. For example, you could help clean your child's room, especially if the mess has gotten out of control. Descriptively praise all efforts, but explain that you're just helping out and that he or she has to put away the majority of the items.

It also helps if there is a regular time to do chores, like after your evening meal, and for everybody, not just the children, to do something useful around the house. You can give your children a choice between two chores: "Do you want to clean out the guinea pig's cage or scrub the pots?" From time to time, swap chores so nobody is left with something he or she hates.

Instill Discipline

Discipline is a really difficult topic, because even though everybody is fervently against child abuse, they're just as strongly in favor of discipline. Sometimes it can be a fine line. Few of my clients are comfortable criticizing their parents, and very few will admit to anything abusive. However, if I ask, "How did your parents discipline you?," they will gladly relate tales of being hit with a belt, locked in a closet under the stairs, sent to their rooms without dinner, and thrown out of the house at sixteen; in one case, a client reported not being spoken to for three months. Being tired or at the end of their rope means that some parents will lash out and occasionally strike their children. Remember, children learn from us, so if you do succumb to administering physical punishment, it will only encourage them to hit their younger siblings or smaller classmates.

I've left discipline almost till the end of this chapter because there are many tools to help you avoid reaching this point (which I hope I've started to explain), and I wanted to stress that most children misbehave because they are full of negative emotions and don't know how to cope. You have learned to help them by acknowledging and naming their feelings.

Sometimes all the new skills and understanding will not be enough, however. You will need to stop your child from misbehaving, and if he or she is too wound up to be able to listen, what should you do? This is when I recommend a time-out. (It's a variation on what I use with adults who have passed the point of having a reasonable dialogue and risk becoming verbally or physically abusive.)

Here's how it works. The child has to sit in one place and has his or her freedom curtailed. Some people call it the time-out chair. The place should be somewhere close to you and easy to monitor so the child cannot sneak off to play. If your child is very agitated and acting out with anger, you might need to stay close. However, there should be no chatting or scolding, just descriptive praise: "You've stopped hitting your brother; that's good," "You've stopped fidgeting," or "You've sat silently for a whole minute; that's very cooperative." I would suggest, as a guideline, one minute of time-out for each year of your child's age—but you will know best.

After a time-out, ask your children to repeat why they needed it and why their behavior was wrong. Descriptively praise when they give the right answer: "That's right; well done." In this way, you end the disciplining on a positive note.

You can often avoid disobedience, stop your child from doing a forbidden behavior, or gain cooperation by using a countdown. Remember, children live in the moment, and it takes them awhile to get their brains in gear; they might also be testing if you really mean it. So tell them, "I'm going to count down from ten, and when I reach one, I want you to _____ [fill in the blank]." However, if you do threaten time-out or some other penalty, it is vital that you follow through, even if your children get upset and throw a tantrum. Otherwise they will neither respect you nor take you seriously.

Reward Rather Than Indulge

You want your children to behave not because they are frightened of the consequences but because they have understood the reasoning behind a rule and have accepted it as right for them, your family, and the community. There is another reason I emphasize rewarding good behavior rather than punishing bad behavior: threatening a dire punishment will make your child angry, rebellious, and less likely to cooperate.

For example, some parents threaten to take something, like a bicycle, away from their children in the hope that this will make them reflect on their bad behavior, but it just causes outrage. This is because the parents didn't give the treasured possession on the condition of good behavior; they just said, "Merry Christmas" or "Happy birthday" or "Congratulations on passing your exams."

So what's the alternative? This is where rewarding rather than indulging your children comes into play. We love our children and therefore want to indulge them, but too much giving, without any strings attached, encourages a feeling of entitlement. In contrast, if you reward good behavior, your children will believe they have earned the treat and will feel good about themselves, too.

We love our children and therefore want to indulge them, but too much giving, without any strings attached, encourages a feeling of entitlement.

There is also a benefit to your marriage in not indulging and starting to reward. Although few parents will agree to the right level of indulgence, most can come up with a reward structure on which they can agree.

What Makes a Good Reward?

You want a simple and immediate connection between the good behavior and the reward (not "Be good for a month, and we'll get a dog"). That's why the best rewards are small, easy to arrange or do, and either free or inexpensive (so money and love are not linked in your child's mind). In this way, your rewards can almost be immediate. A note of caution: I would also avoid using food as a reward—particularly sugary, high-fat, and salty snacks. Not only are these bad for your children's health, they can also set up an unfortunate link between love and food, which is bad for their long-term relationship with food.

Here are some alternatives for what you can let them do:

- Try on your jewelry.
- Go to the park and kick a ball around.
- Paint on the kitchen table.
- Have an extra story at bedtime.
- Help bake a cake.
- Be given extra pocket money.
- Choose what to cook for dinner (from your normal range of meals).
- Have extra screen time (computer, tablet, video game, or TV).

Screen time is a very useful currency. It is in your children's interest to limit their exposure; pediatricians and child psychologists recommend just one to two hours a day (and *no* screen time for children under two years old). They warn that going over this limit increases the chances of a child being less physically active, more aggressive, and harder to put to bed, and it also increases attention problems, anxiety, and depression. However, a survey published in *Pediatrics* magazine monitored 7,400 children ages nine to fifteen and found that one in four kids had more than the daily recommended limit (not including screen time for the older children to do their homework).

Setting up Screen Time as the Currency in Your Household

If using screen time as currency sounds like a good idea for your children, you've already got the necessary skills for setting up a new rule. Here is a recap, adapted for the specifics of screen time:

1. Introduce a date for starting this new rule so your children have a chance to get used to the idea. For example, begin by saying, "On Monday, we're going to be introducing a new rule."

2. Explain the rule.

3. Your children will be upset, but instead of sweeping their feelings under the carpet, be sure to acknowledge them and name them—for example, "You're feeling worried about how it will work."

4. Ask them to guess why the rule is being introduced.

5. Use descriptive praise for any sensible answers, and ask for others.

6. Show your love. One of the reasons for less screen time is so you can do more things together as a family. (If your children don't come up with this answer, please share it with them.) Ultimately, what your children want, more than anything, is your attention and your interest in them.

7. Explain that they can earn extra screen time for doing certain chores around the house (such as feeding the cat or cleaning their rooms).

8. Answer any questions.

9. When the new rule is introduced and they complain about the screen being turned off, identify the feelings, sympathize ("New rules are always difficult at the beginning"), and compensate with some extra attention. For example, dance around the room together to music (with small children) or play a board game or cards (with older children).

10. Be sensitive about your own screen time. If you have buried yourself behind the computer when they are around, it is sensible to limit your own consumption in the initial phases. Remember that children have an innate sense of fairness, and it could be that you're having more screen time than is good for you, too.

Alternative Ideas in Action

John and Marie, whom we met in Chapter 6, had two issues: how to reward rather than indulge and how to be consistent (since each cared for the children while the other one worked). They solved both problems with an app that they downloaded to their smartphones.

"The children get points for completing certain tasks, like getting dressed themselves and being ready to leave for school on time and for general good behavior," Marie explained. "They can also have them taken away if they're naughty or uncooperative. The points can be cashed in for a small treat or saved up for a bigger one."

"It has worked really well because we have a standard system that we both agree on," John commented, "and if someone like Marie's mother is looking after them, we put the system into her phone, and she can add or subtract points, too."

"I overheard the kids discussing whether they should pool their points and buy a toy they'd both play with," added Marie, "so it's teaching them how to cooperate. It has also allowed John and me to discuss how we parent—without it getting too heated. I could show John, in the memory, how he'd been giving lots of points, whereas I had been the one having to take them away. I doubt we could have tackled this subject otherwise."

"Best of all," concluded John, "I can keep track of how the kids have been behaving, even when I'm working away. Before I talk to them in the evening, I can have a quick look at my phone and know what they've been up to. It helps me feel more involved."

How to Put Your Partner First

I once counseled a mother who was prouder of getting her two daughters into an Ivy League college than of going there herself—perhaps because she had sacrificed her own career to concentrate on her children. Unfortunately, our children's failure is our failure, and their pain is our pain. No wonder we want to smooth their way. It is almost as if our sons and daughters are princes and princesses and we want to run ahead to ensure a red carpet has been rolled out in front of them. Meanwhile, we're on the sidelines cheering and taking photographs. With so much pressure to raise kids the "right" way and so much guilt about being a working mother, many parents turn themselves into unpaid flunkies, too.

When a client's daughter was making a one-minute video to support her application to a broadcast journalism graduate program, her mother spent half the weekend running around sourcing material and acting as a second pair of eyes. (Meanwhile, she had made no progress on relaunching her own career or figuring out her postdivorce life.) Unfortunately, red-carpet parenting was her default mode, and she found it hard to know when to let go and when her help was truly needed.

In the past, when men were less involved with parenting, there was an unspoken acceptance that the children would be closer to their mother and that somehow they "belonged" to her. Today, with equal parenting (or as near that goal as possible), I see an unspoken rivalry between parents—especially if their relationship is under stress—to be the "more loved" parent. One partner will criticize the other's contribution to raising the children or will look to one of the children for emotional support. The latter nearly always involves giving special privileges to that child, confiding secrets, and creating alliances so the child will stand up for that parent in arguments with the other parent.

It is only human nature to want to be popular or to show your exasperation with your partner when your children are around. However, making your child your ally will do neither the child nor your marriage any favors. Ultimately, children belong to nobody. They are their own people, and although you are responsible for them while they are minors, they are just passing through your relationship; one day they will leave home and possibly get married and start their own families.

Here is how to stop competing with your partner and start cooperating:

- It is okay to listen to your children when they complain about your partner, but don't agree with any criticism (however justified it might be) or run your partner down. If there are mitigating circumstances or something your children have misunderstood, please feel free to defend your partner. However, it is best to encourage your children to take the problem up directly with the parent against whom they have the complaint.
- If you disagree with your partner about something fundamental, discuss it together behind closed doors.
- Always support your partner on matters of child-rearing policy in public.
- Set aside enough private time together to talk through any disagreements, and present a united front. It will make your partner feel respected and valued.
- If this is hard, resolve to keep talking, listening, and debating.
- No two people think exactly alike. The problems arise when people give up trying to communicate.

Summary

However much you love your children, it's not possible to "carpet" the whole world for them. They are going to fall in love and get their hearts broken. They will be up for a promotion but someone else will get the job. Their soccer teams will sometimes lose. That's why they need to learn to be resilient, cope with setbacks, and become self-reliant.

This will also help your relationship, because the time saved servicing your children can be channeled into nurturing each other. At first, it might be hard getting your children off the red carpet and developing new habits takes time, but it will bring great benefits in the long run and reduce your stress levels. Even better, with your eyes no longer fixed on the red carpet, you will notice each other again, let go, and be free to dance together.

9

What Will Your Children Tell Their Therapists?

We are the first generation to have fully incorporated the ideas of Sigmund Freud and the other founders of modern psychology. We accept the profound effect of childhood on shaping the adults we become. The result is that today's parents face anxieties that never crossed the minds of their parents or grandparents. What if we make the wrong choice about breast-feeding or toilet training? What if our attention slips for a moment and some harm happens to our children that has a lasting effect on their mental well-being?

What passed for a socially acceptable joke in previous generations—like "Hitting my children might not do them any good, but it makes me feel better"—will now bring conversations to a shuddering halt. With our knowledge of the unconscious, we no longer take, at face value, remarks like "It never did me any harm." We are fully aware of the responsibility of being a parent, and this is a great step forward.

At the same time, there has been a parallel revolution in our attitudes to therapy. When I first started working with couples in the mid-1980s, there was a sense of shame about admitting that you needed help. Today we have a much more straightforward attitude: if you need help, it's best to ask for it. The result is that seeing a therapist, counselor, psychologist, or psychiatrist is a much more mainstream activity; whereas thirty years ago I was surprised when clients had had counseling before, today I'm surprised if I'm the first person they've seen. Once again, I think this is positive.

Unfortunately, these advances are not without problems, and today's middle-class, educated parents have a new fear to add to their list: "What will our children tell their therapists?" That's why I've decided to devote a chapter to offering some reassurance and addressing the underlying concerns. Most important, I will explain the difference between a passing trifle (which will soon be forgotten) and something that really could cause serious long-term harm (and potentially be recounted in heartbreaking detail thirty years later).

Despite our greater exposure to therapy, there are still some misconceptions about it. One of the most common is that the main thing you do in therapy is complain about your mother. I wish it were that easy! I have heard thousands of people talk about their childhoods, and very few are critical of their mothers. (It *is* easier for clients to complain about their fathers.) We are protective of our mothers because we idealize them and long for their love and their approval.

My job is to help my clients have a balanced picture and accept that their parents were not perfect. I'm not seeking to *blame*—far from it—but by accepting our parents' flaws, we can begin to accept our own. In the words of the German philosopher Immanuel Kant (1724–1804), "From the crooked timber of humanity, no straight thing was ever made." *We are human; we make mistakes; it comes with the territory.* This is much better than trying to live as an "ideal" person loved by an "ideal" parent (and helped by an "ideal" therapist).

The majority of my clients present a balanced picture of their parents' weaknesses *and* strengths. Even people who are critical are quick to explain the circumstances that caused their parents to fail. In the same way that we love our children no matter what, we love our parents despite their shortcomings.

Now that you are reassured that your children are unlikely to assassinate your character, it is important to also be aware of the behavior that most damaged my clients when they were children, so you can avoid falling into the same traps. These behaviors will not be doing you or your relationship any favors, either. Therefore, I will also cover the effects on your life, as well as on your children and offer advice on how to turn things around for everybody.

Expecting Your Children to Regulate You

How often have you been in the street or the supermarket and heard a parent turn to a small child and tell him or her off, saying something like "Don't make me mad" or "Don't make me lose my temper"? It is so common that it almost goes without notice. We might even smile sympathetically because we've all felt the same way at some point. However, this encapsulates a problem that, unchecked, causes huge long-term problems. As we noted in Chapter 4, it is the parents' job to regulate their children's emotions, not the other way round. So if your children are acting out, it is much better to acknowledge and name their feelings and discover what is causing them to be upset.

In stark contrast, the stressed adult in the street or the supermarket is asking the child to ignore his or her own feelings and tune in to those of the parent. Obviously, if your children are doing something antisocial, like pulling boxes off the shelf, you need to stop that. However, it is much more powerful to ask the child why this behavior is wrong—thereby getting the child to own the reason for stopping—rather than just shouting at him or her. In the first scenario, the child understands that he or she is making extra work for someone else or damaging something that doesn't belong to him or her. In the second, the child is stopping merely as an attempt to appease you—that is, regulate *your* moods.

Unfortunately, there are many ways that we don't take children's emotions seriously, because it makes us feel uncomfortable. If they're crying, we tell them, "Don't be a crybaby," as we were told by our parents. Anger is even more difficult to deal with, and some people will go to great lengths to avoid it (by suppressing it or rationalizing it away). So instead of acknowledging and naming our children's anger, the temptation is to trivialize or dismiss it: "What have you got to be so upset about?" or "Don't be so stupid." Once again, we are asking our children to regulate our emotions, and we avoid having to face our own demons.

The Effect on Your Children

These relatively trivial examples are unlikely to be the source of tearful stories to therapists in the future, but they explain the patterns and what can happen if children are more interested in reading their parents' moods than their own (and therefore suppress a strong emotion whenever one comes up) or do not trust their own reactions to the world around them.

"I never knew what to expect when I got home from school," explained Stacey, thirty-two, who sought help because she was anxious and found it hard to have long-term relationships. "Sometimes my mother could be wonderful and be the best friend ever: we'd clear the kitchen table and make things out of old cardboard boxes, newspapers, and glue. Other times, she would be withdrawn and sullen, and I would tiptoe around the house trying to become invisible so as to avoid upsetting her. She could also fly off the handle over something that didn't really make sense—like I wanted blue wallpaper on the doll's house we were making, and that showed that I was 'selfish' or 'ungrateful.' I was always trying to read the signs and to get it right."

The situation got worse as Stacey got older and was more likely to have an opinion of her own. She was thrown out of the house when she was sixteen and again at nineteen over some dispute that Stacey could no longer remember. As an adult, Stacey recognized that her mother had undiagnosed mental-health issues, but as a child, she thought the tantrums were caused by something that *she* was doing wrong. And that's the big problem: children are completely egocentric, because their brains are not fully developed and they haven't had enough experience of the world, so they will turn themselves upside down and inside out to be accepted and try to fit into even a topsy-turvy family.

In all my years as a therapist, I have come across only two clients who consciously knew, before the age of seven, that their parents were "dangerous." One woman recognized that her father was an abusive bully and, at age six, set herself up as her mother's protector, even though she could not understand the complexity of an adult relationship and the part sex played in her parents making up after an argument. One man, at about the same age, realized that his mother was an "emotional vampire" and would "suck you in, manipulate, and push you away," and he decided to distance himself.

I can't begin to imagine how frightening those realizations must have been to young children who are utterly dependent on their parents for food, shelter, and support—people who also have the legal right to make decisions about their children's lives. No wonder young children would much rather believe the fault is theirs; it gives them the illusion of being in control, and they can try harder, appease more, and disappear into the background rather than face reality.

The Effect on You and Your Relationship

If you expect someone else to regulate you, you are always going to feel vulnerable and anxious, because others can always let you down by ignoring you, getting angry, or downplaying your feelings. You are also going to crave your children's love, and if you fear that love is a scarce resource, you are more likely to compete with your partner to be "more loved."

You can't be aware of your children's emotions and take them seriously without being aware of your own. So think back to your childhood. What were the forbidden feelings? Sometimes they are overtly suppressed—Don't make a scene, or "If you don't calm down there'll be tears before bedtime"—and sometimes they are so much part of how the family operated that nobody had to say anything.

> *You can't be aware of your children's emotions and take them seriously without being aware of your own.*

If you can't come up with anything, think back to your last extended-family gathering. What is acceptable behavior, and what would cause shock and consternation? Now you have probably identified what is forbidden. (There is more help in the exercise section later in this chapter.)

Inconsistent Parenting Styles

Children need consistency, because they can't make sense of the world and their places in it if it is forever changing in unpredictable ways. Unfortunately, some parents switch between two unhelpful, but not particularly damaging, styles to create a toxic pattern that will keep their children's future therapists very busy. What are these two styles, and why is the combination so harmful?

The first is called *intrusive*, or overinvolved. These parents make their children the center of their lives, and therefore nothing is ever too much trouble. I know it sounds great to have someone so completely attuned to your needs, but it comes at a cost.

Gary had to go to the hospital for a back operation, and even though he was thirty-five years old, his mother, instead of just visiting him every day, brought a sleeping bag and moved into the hospital with him for ten days! Apparently, she was worried: "What if he needs something during the night and the nurses are busy elsewhere?" When asked whether it was truly necessary, she replied, "But that's what mothers do." Can you imagine how marginalized his wife felt?

I had another client whose father died when he was just six years old, and his mother never remarried and didn't even have any boyfriends. "Her life revolved around me and my brother," Curtis explained. "We were a tight-knit little unit. As the older child, he became almost a surrogate partner for his mother—something that was reinforced by well-meaning relatives, who told him, "You're the man of the family now." Curtis's mother treated him as the "golden child" who could do no wrong. The relationship between his wife and his mother was extremely fraught, because his mother believed that nobody was good enough for him except her. Worse still, Curtis found it extremely hard to imagine how other people might be feeling or how his remarks or behavior might affect anybody else. After all, he'd spent his formative years being always right, and his needs, wants, and beliefs were paramount (while everybody else's were of little or no consequence).

The second unhelpful style is called *disinterested* or neglectful. In these cases, the parents are too tense in their own lives, or they have too many children and leave the younger ones to fend for themselves. Sometimes an all-consuming job, addiction, mental-health issues, or divorce can make the parents disinterested. In other cases, my clients' parents thought they were doing the right thing or had no other choice; they sent their children off to boarding school at seven because they lived in remote places with no normal schools or they sent them to live with their grandparents or another relative because the parents had to work all the time to earn a living. Distances, poor transportation systems, and cost meant that some of these children would see their parents only once a year. It sounds terrible, but the effect is not as catastrophic as you might imagine.

Patricia, the wife of Gary with the intrusive mother, had been put into foster care by her mother when she was five years old and had had a succession of foster families.

"Some were better than others," she described, "but most were more interested in the money than in being parents."

"You must have felt very alone," I sympathized.

"I had one foster-sister that I'm still close to, but I'm not in touch with anybody else. I just focused on getting through school and getting on with my life."

This strategy had proved extremely successful. She had attended a top university and had worked for an international bank.

In most cases of uninterested parents, children find support, interest, and help from other parties: grandparents, teachers, older siblings, or neighbors who see the void and step in.

Now that I've described the two unfortunate but not disastrous parenting styles, let's examine what happens when they collide and why the combination can be toxic. Unfortunately, many children have to deal with parents who are intrusive one moment and then, because they become exhausted and overwhelmed, are neglectful the next. They make excuses like "After all I've done for my children, don't I deserve some me-time?" It is almost impossible to maintain the level of intensity for intrusiveness—in fact, I rather admire the tenacity of Gary's and Curtis's mothers—so that's why many parents will collapse and become disinterested, feel guilty, and then redouble their efforts and become even more intrusive—until the next time it becomes too much, and the cycle begins again. The result is that they will switch back and forth between two unhelpful ways of parenting, confuse their children, and make their lives significantly more difficult.

The Effect on Your Children

With intrusive parenting and having every whim met, the danger is that the children grow up to view other people as simply a means to an end. In addition, every feeling has to be acted on without regard to the effect on other people. With disinterested parenting, the children are forced to regulate their own feelings by, for example, crying themselves to the point of exhaustion. On the surface, these children seem calm but under the surface, their feelings are intense. They find it hard to trust, and when they grow up, they can have difficulties developing long-term relationships.

With parents who switch between intrusive and disinterested, the children are forced to exaggerate their feelings in a bid for parental attention. These children grow up to become overly aware of their emotions, so that small setbacks seem like the end of the world. Worse still, they haven't learned to self-regulate, and they expect their partners or even their children to soothe them instead.

The Effect on You and Your Relationship

Intrusive parents run the risk of getting their entire sense of identity and self-worth from being a mother or a father, and that's fine when their children are small. But what happens when they grow up and start leaving home? I often counsel parents, particularly mothers, who reach a crisis point when their youngest child is about to go off to college, and they ask themselves, *Who am I?* and *What is my purpose in life?*

> *Intrusive parents run the risk of getting their entire sense of identity and self-worth from being a mother or a father, and that's fine when their children are small. But what happens when they grow up and start leaving home?*

If you are switching between intrusive and disinterested parenting, it will have a damaging effect on your marriage, too, because your partner will not know what to expect when he or she comes home each day. As one male client told me, "I can cope with hostility [because in his wife's opinion, he hadn't done enough] or being ignored [because she was preoccupied with the kids], but what I dread most is the unknown."

I doubt that you fall into the disinterested category; the simple act of buying this book and reading it indicates the opposite. My concerns are that you may be intrusive because you love your children so much. In most cases, this happens because a parent overidentifies with the child, so the child's successes become the parent's successes and sole source of personal validation. Under these circumstances, there is a danger of pushing our interests onto our children or hoping they can fulfill our unfulfilled ambitions. You can avoid this trap by stepping back and leaving enough space for your children to develop their own interests and find their own paths. If your children are getting older and you're facing an empty nest, it is important to find new interests and reasons for getting up in the morning. It is also an ideal time to start focusing on your marriage again.

Labeling

When I ask my clients about their childhoods, I draw up a family tree for each one so I can keep track of the number of siblings, the birth order, parents' divorce, and so forth. Particularly when the clients come from large families, I ask them to describe their brothers and sisters. It is amazing how quickly they come up with a label for each one: "He was the oldest," "She was the baby of the family," or "He was the clever [or naughty or rebellious] one." Sometimes the label is more pernicious: "She was Mom's favorite" or "He was the black sheep of the family."

I doubt that the parents ever described their children in this way, but the unspoken messages, their body language, and the way they treated their children made the labels clear to everyone in the family. Similarly, I sometimes ask my clients who are parents to describe their children, and, once again, I discover labels—for example, "She's a daddy's girl," "He's really sensitive," or "We're really alike, and that makes for a volatile relationship."

When I did this exercise with Heather, forty-eight, I discovered she was the youngest of six children. She had four older sisters: "The eldest is responsible, the next is the rebel, and the one after that is the career. My next-eldest sister was ill, and she died when she was only thirteen years old and was never mentioned again." Next in the family tree came her only brother. "He was the favorite because he was the boy," she said. When I asked Heather about her place in the family, she replied, "I was the baby and the mistake."

"How did you figure that out?" I asked.

"My parents really wanted a boy, so they kept going until they had one—and then came me."

"What was it like being the baby?"

"Everybody is there to look out for you."

That sounds really nice, but it comes at a cost: it can make you rather helpless. When her marriage hit a rough patch, Heather had neither the skills to resolve it nor the ability to ask for help. "Looking back," she recalled, "there were so many of us that help always just arrived. So I suppose I kept my head down and hoped for the best, which is probably the worst thing I could have done."

The Effect on Your Children

Once we hang a label around someone's neck, we remember evidence that supports it and ignore anything that contradicts it. Not only does a label encourage someone to live up to that reputation, it also often says more about the person giving the label. For example, a child called sensitive could be described as in touch with his or her feelings, depending on how comfortable you feel about expressing your emotions yourself. Worse still, these labels stick, and even years later, our choices, interests, and behavior can still be governed by the labels our parents gave us or even the ones they gave our siblings. If your brother was, for example, the "academic one," it implies that you are less academic or maybe even "stupid."

> *Once we hang a label around someone's neck, we remember evidence that supports it and ignore anything that contradicts it. Not only does a label encourage someone to live up to that reputation, it also often says more about the person giving the label.*

It is best to avoid labeling your children, even if the labels are positive. In the past ten years, I've seen more and more adults who were the "golden child" in their parents' eyes because they were labeled as gifted or extremely clever. Indeed, they did well at school, attended top universities, held down good jobs, and have risen to the top of their chosen careers.

There are two problems with being a "golden child." First, your parents' love can seem conditional on doing well, and even an A-minus can seem like not only failure but being unlovable. Second, it can come as a horrible shock when things go wrong and other people, like your husband or wife and your new boss, do not find you quite so golden. What would seem like a setback to mere mortals can quickly seem like the end of the world to a "golden child."

The Effect on You and Your Relationship

If you label your children, you are also likely to label yourself and each other as mother and father. Some partners even call each other that after they have children. As you can imagine, seeing your partner purely as a parent is not very sexy and does little to improve your love life. Getting stuck in one particular role, rather than getting your identity from a variety of sources, can also increase the likelihood of a midlife crisis.

Labeling is part of human behavior. We do it with nations and with public figures, because it makes a complicated world seem simpler. So please don't beat yourself up if you've already labeled your children; it's not too late to change. Awareness is the key. Look for evidence that contradicts your assessment—particularly for the labels "she's just like me" or "he's like his father." It is also better to look for multiple characteristics. A child is not just pretty but is kind and brave, too. Ultimately though, it is up to your children to discover their own identities rather than having these thrust upon them. After all, it doesn't matter which path through life your son or daughter chooses, as long as it is the right one for that individual.

If you are beginning to question your own life path, don't panic. It is natural to wonder, *Who am I?* from time to time and *What do I want from life?*—especially in the wake of one of your parents dying. The problems arise when we try to suppress these questions and get stuck with an outdated label. If your partner is beginning to wonder about his or her identity, this can be really scary, because we find change difficult. However, it is better to listen, offer support, and therefore be seen as your partner's ally than to try to squash his or her concerns and become the enemy.

Warring Parents

All couples argue from time to time. It's fine to do this in front of your children as long as you can also listen, respect each other's viewpoint, and find a compromise or negotiate a settlement. This shows that it is possible to disagree and still love each other. These are skills your children will need with their siblings, friends, and partners when they're older. Unfortunately, some parents can't contain their anger and model the opposite approach: shouting, making personal insults, or trying to punish each other.

Unfortunately, even divorce does not necessarily solve the problem. Instead of fighting in the kitchen, they are fighting over the phone, in text messages and e-mails, and even through the children. The problems are often compounded by new partners, financial disputes, and unresolved pain. I've had clients whose parents divorced more than thirty years ago but still couldn't be in the same room—for a wedding, a christening, or any other extended-family event—because they would cause a scene or still be fighting over who caused the breakup.

The Effect on Your Children

Although we like to imagine that children take divorce in their stride because it is so commonplace today, the long-term effect is substantial. Judith Wallerstein (1921–2012), a senior lecturer in the School of Social Welfare at the University of California at Berkeley, studied 60 middle-class families and 131 children over twenty-five years after divorce and discovered that only 10 percent of the children experienced any relief when their parents' marriages ended; eighteen months later, the majority were still trying to make sense of what happened; and five years later, most children still secretly hoped that their parents would reconcile—even if one of them had subsequently remarried.

The Effect on You and Your Relationship

Family breakdown can make parents fall into *all* the unhelpful traps. They can be so upset by the behavior of their partners that their children feel the need to manage their feelings (and thereby attempt to regulate their parents). Divorcing parents can be so consumed with their own problems that they appear uninterested to their children and then feel guilty and swing to being intrusive to compensate. Divorce also encourages labeling and black-and-white thinking in which each parent blames the other. For example, he is bad for going off with another woman, or she is vengeful for making it difficult to see the children.

The main message of this book is that you should put your partner before your children and not neglect your own interests. However, relationship breakdown is the one exception to this rule. Here I would ask you to put the children first, above your own pain or what seems best for your relationship. I have seen lots of partners who say, "We're splitting up while we're still friends so the children don't have to hear us arguing." It sounds rational, but my experience is that marriage (and trying to get along together despite everything) forms a protective layer around a relationship.

In general, you will interpret your partner's behavior in a reasonably favorable light. If she doesn't phone, it's because she is busy. If he can't look after the children on Tuesday night, it's because his exercise class is really important and helps keep him sane. Unfortunately, family breakdown rips away the protection, and you'll interpret the same behavior in the worst possible light: she didn't phone because she's angry with you, and he's chosen exercise over his children because he's trying to punish you.

Partners break up because they have poor communication skills, but divorce calls for exceptionally good ones. Therefore, if you have any goodwill left in your relationship, use it to resolve your marriage problems and seek professional help. Even if you fail, you could learn to talk and listen to each other. Having really tried will help the partner who is less interested in splitting up to recover better, and it will also help you to cooperate in reducing the effect on your children.

Forbidden Topics

As I've already discussed, humans are made of "crooked timber," and parents make mistakes. Ultimately, it doesn't matter if—from time to time—you expect your children to regulate your mood, switch from intrusive to uninterested, or label your children. Similarly, it's not the end of the world if you get divorced. Children are more resilient than you think. The problems occur when it is impossible to discuss something, especially *your* failings.

If a child can talk about his or her relationship with you and ask, "Why were you mad at me?," and you can tell him or her, "I wasn't mad at you, I was just tired and short-tempered. You haven't done anything wrong. I'm sorry," then your slipup has provided an opportunity to strengthen your relationship. It has also taught your child an important lesson: if he or she is upset, this is a sign that something is wrong and requires attention. It's when a subject is unmentionable that it becomes pernicious.

"I went to see my first diet doctor at age eight," explained Teresa, who is now fifty-eight. "My mother was always making 'helpful' remarks like 'Your new haircut makes your face look thinner.' At mealtimes, she would carefully watch what everybody else was eating but never ate very much herself. On Sunday nights, we would go out to a restaurant, and if I would choose one of the delicious items on the menu like roast duck and gravy—considered fattening—she would give me one of her looks and say, 'The poached fish looks very nice. I think I'll have that. Why don't you have the poached fish too, Teresa?,' and I would give in and go along with her. At the same time that all this was going on, my mother would be eating alone in the living room while my brother and I were asleep. I would sometimes wake up and smell something delicious like pizza being cooked. She also had secret places where she'd hide sweets and chocolates, and I'd sometimes go and take just one, desperately hoping she wouldn't notice."

Although Teresa's mother's weight was only ever slightly above or below what would have been considered healthy for her height, she obviously had issues about her weight and transferred a lot of her anxiety onto her daughter, who spent the next fifty years gaining and losing weight. However, it was impossible for her to talk to her mother about her attitudes toward food or even to debate whether being fixated on one's body image was a good or bad idea.

The Effect on Your Children

Instead of listening to their emotions and acting on them, your children are being taught to ignore painful and difficult feelings and hope that they will go away. Sometimes, for minor setbacks, this can be okay, because sometimes little problems do fix themselves. However, for big subjects—and it's normally the big ones that families ignore—pretending the problems don't exist does not resolve them but only makes them worse.

The Effect on You and Your Relationship

If you cannot deal with difficult subjects, there are only two options: to suppress them, which leads to depression and anxiety, or to run away, whether by shutting down, exploding, or leaving the relationship. Neither option provides a long-term solution to unhappiness.

Therapy is all about making people aware of the unspoken messages and allowing the unmentionable to be talked about. After all, talking about something is the first step to doing something about it. Therefore, if you take what your children say seriously—even if it seems a bit strange because they come to difficult topics via routes that don't seem logical to you—they are unlikely to need a therapist when they grow up, because all the important things have already been aired.

Understanding Your Own Feelings

It is difficult to regulate your children's emotions if you ignore your own. You are also more likely to label someone else, like your children or your partner. Similarly, if you can't talk about something like anger or sadness, your children are going to find it equally hard to do so. All this self-awareness might sound like a tall order, especially if your parents were not emotionally literate. However, you've already started to learn some of the necessary skills:

- **Acknowledge and name.** When your children are upset or irritable, you have learned to acknowledge and name the feeling rather than ignore it. In the same way, I want you to take your own emotions seriously rather than ignore them, pretend they don't exist, or talk yourself out of them. So ask yourself, *What am I feeling? Why?*

- **Keep a feeling diary.** Whenever you have a quiet moment, stop and jot down the most recent feelings and what provoked them—for example, pleasure at a frosty morning, joy when your baby smiled, or frustration when you couldn't get the lid off the jar. Keep the diary for at least seven days. When I do this exercise with my clients, I discover two important things: people underrecord the good stuff and a feeling doesn't last forever but is quickly replaced with another. This is contrary to our fears that if we allow ourselves to be angry, for example, we will be stuck there forever.

- **Accept the feelings but challenge the thoughts.** Even the feelings that get bad press have their advantages. For example, anger provides energy and a sense that something must be done. So please accept your feelings, no matter what. However,

I would like you to challenge the thoughts that might underlie the feelings. For example, your underlying thoughts might turn righteous anger from something proportionate into something overwhelming. Tracey's husband, for instance, had left her for another woman. She felt not only rejected but also angry about there being less money and having to go out to work rather than being able to stay at home with their eighteen-month-old daughter. These are understandable and natural feelings. Yet some of her thinking and language was turning these feelings into levels of rage and resentment that made her consider trying to stop her daughter from seeing her father. "I'm going to lose my daughter," Tracey sobbed uncontrollably. I accepted her anger but challenged the thoughts. "You're not going to lose your daughter. That sounds like social services taking her into foster care. She's going to day care, and you'll see less of her, which may be upsetting, but you're not losing her."

- **Report your feelings.** If your partner or your children do something to upset you, don't suppress or act out your feelings (by slamming doors, sighing, or rolling your eyes). Report them by using the formula from Chapter 7: *I feel . . . when you . . . because . . .* For example, "*I feel* angry *when you* don't wipe your feet *because* it makes more work for me." In this way, everybody is clear what you feel (that it's anger, not rage) and what the causes are.

- **Self-soothe.** Instead of flying off the handle or expecting your children, your partner, or your boss to calm you down, take responsibility yourself. Acknowledging, naming, and reporting your feelings will help. Other ways of soothing include exercising (like running), unwinding (like having a hot bath or a cup of tea), giving yourself a treat (like half an hour reading a book), meditating or doing breathing exercises, and sharing (like speaking to a friend). Be wary of things that seek to remove the feelings, like alcohol or sugary foods, which is called self-medicating and is not the same as self-soothing.

- **Address the problem.** Remember, feelings are clues to help you make your way through life, not something awkward to be avoided. What is the feeling telling you? When you're calmer, you can talk to your children and your partner about their unhelpful behavior or, if it's really about you, address the problem yourself.
- **Remember to be assertive.** You can ask. Your partner can say no, and you can negotiate.

How to Put Your Partner First

One of the themes of this book is that if you're offering a courtesy to your children, you should consider doing the same to your partner. So if you're not going to label your children because of the damage it does to them, I'd like you to refrain from labeling your partner, too. Unfortunately, it is all too easy to interpret other people's behavior in a negative light and create a filter through which you see everything—for example, "He's selfish" or "She wants to control me." In effect, this is labeling your partner as lazy or bossy and finding more evidence to back it up. Before too long, you have a caricature of him or her in your head that makes you exaggerate your upset feelings ("This just proves how I'm taken advantage of" or "I can't even breathe right") and simultaneously discount your partner's opinions ("What right does he have to complain, after all I do?" or "She *would* say that, wouldn't she?").

Here are some ways to challenge your internal labeling of your partner:

- Instead of assuming the reasons for your partner's actions, try asking him or her.
- Avoid leading questions, such as "Did you fail to pick up our daughter because you couldn't be bothered?" This is slightly better than simply making an accusation, but just barely! It will immediately get your partner upset and trigger an argument rather than an explanation. A question is likely to be leading if it requires a mere yes or no for an answer.
- Find an open question. These start with *how, why, what,* or *when*—for example, "Why didn't you pick up our daughter?" or "What happened?" These types of questions suggest that you are genuinely interested in the answer and will give your partner a fair hearing.
- Listen to the explanation with an open mind. If you find yourself slipping into black-and-white thinking (good-and-bad or right-and-wrong), remind yourself that life is more complex. There are many shades of gray.
- Focus on the matter at hand. Thinking about past behavior or worrying about the long-term implications will raise the stakes and encourage labeling.
- Ask follow-up questions. This will help you to truly stand in your partner's shoes and understand the complexity of his or her feelings on the subject.
- Look at your own motivations for something that's controversial between you. What makes you behave in this way? What are your conflicting urges? In most cases, you will find several layers of reasons for your actions, not just one fixed motivation. If you are complex, your partner is probably just the same.

Just as important as not labeling your children is letting them be true to themselves, rather than pressuring them to follow interests or careers that you believe are right for them. Once again, I'd like you to extend this idea and let your partner be his or her own person, not just a reflection of what you'd like him or her to be. I know this sounds difficult, and possibly even threatening, but let me give an example of what this means in practice.

Philip, age thirty-two, had been almost talented enough to pursue a career as a golfer but became a car salesman to pay the bills. Although he had long since given up any ambitions of turning professional, he still looked forward to his weekend round of golf. "Obviously, I don't live for golf because my wife and children are the most important thing in my life, but I can take all my frustrations out on hacking around the course. I'm out in the fresh air, and I can forget everything just concentrating on getting the ball into the hole. I would go as far as saying golf keeps me sane."

In contrast, his wife, Kitty, had her two children, her recently widowed mother, and Philip at the center of her life. "I thought when we had children that he'd put golf to one side," she admitted. "I'm not suggesting that he give it up altogether, but not every weekend. He's up early on Saturday morning and not back until late after lunch, and that's not the end of it. Sometimes he wants to go away on weekends for a team match and the odd Sunday. He's got responsibilities, and it shouldn't always be me looking after the boys."

"The problem is that Kitty doesn't have any outside interests," replied Philip. "I'm perfectly happy to look after the children while she goes out."

"I do go out," Kitty insisted. "I'll have coffee with my girlfriends and I watch my soaps, but I don't let them interfere with family time."

In many relationships, there is pressure to be and think alike, in the hope that this will help a couple sidestep any conflicts. However, as I've explained, it is important to let your partner be his or her own person and to see being different not as a problem but as an asset. Let me explain how this works in practice.

As Philip and Kitty demonstrate, there is a conflict at the heart of many relationships in which one partner pushes for couple time and one campaigns for time apart. However, good relationships need both we-time (so the relationship doesn't wither and die) and me-time (so each of you

> *In many relationships, there is pressure to be and think alike, in the hope that this will help a couple sidestep any conflicts. However, as I've explained, it is important to let your partner be his or her own person and to see being different not as a problem but as an asset.*

doesn't lose a sense of yourself as an individual). The problems happen when you get stuck on one side of the argument and start to perceive your partner as the enemy.

What should you do if the thought of letting your partner be his or her own person, or speaking up for your own needs and thereby being different from each other, seems inherently threatening? Once again, if you've been trying out the ideas in this book, you'll have the necessary skills in hand. I'm talking about assertiveness, which I first discussed in Chapter 2. With assertiveness, you can ask for something and your partner can say no; you can discuss your differences, negotiate, and find a compromise.

In terms of labeling, it is important not to think you know your partner's motivations. For example, Kitty assumed that Philip spent too much time on the golf course because "he doesn't love me and the boys enough," whereas the real reason was that it helped him deal with the pressures of a job he didn't particularly like. Meanwhile, Philip assumed that Kitty wanted him to "hang up my clubs," whereas she just wanted more time as a family and more attention for the boys. Once they stopped assuming and started talking and listening, they were able to compromise. Philip came home straight after the game rather than drinking with his golf partners;

> *With assertiveness, you can ask for something and your partner can say no; you can discuss your differences, negotiate, and find a compromise.*

he also started taking their eldest child (who was interested in sports) up to the club, too. Meanwhile, Kitty started having some me-time, and Philip committed to being home early to look after the boys one night a week.

Finally, if you can stop labeling your partner as a husband or a wife and a father or a mother and see him or her as a person, too, you can probably extend the same generosity to yourself. In that case, you will allow yourself interests outside your relationship and family and find hobbies and activities to help you relax, unwind, and self-soothe.

The child-rearing years last for a surprisingly short time, and having multiple identities and seeing each other as complex, and therefore interesting, people will help smooth the transition back to just the two of you when that time comes.

Summary

The best way to avoid your children needing a therapist is to provide security and consistency so they grow up knowing through both expectation and experience that you will protect them when they are sick, injured, or simply feeling bad, rather than not noticing, not caring about, or misunderstanding them. Nearly every self-defeating strategy—like picking fights, withdrawing into oneself, or pestering for reassurance—is to avoid anxiety or depression and to feel safe (if only for a few moments and no matter what the long-term cost).

The core of my work as a therapist is providing security, so that my clients feel accepted, heard, and no longer out of control. Hardly any of my clients question whether their parents loved them, but that love usually feels conditional or unreliable.

If you're going to take just one idea from this chapter, it should be this: If your son or daughter has a problem or is acting out, it could be in response to you. Although this knowledge will make you feel uncomfortable, there is a silver lining. Although it is really hard to get someone else to change his or her behavior, it is relatively easy to change your own.

Epilogue: Why You Should Put Your Partner First

At the beginning of this book, I introduced a controversial idea: children should come second. I didn't expect you to accept it, but I asked for your indulgence to make my case that putting your partner first is in the best interest not only of your relationship but of your children, too. If you put all your energy into raising the next generation, you will not only exhaust yourself and your marriage, you will also risk identifying so closely with your children that their success is your success and their failure is your failure, and this will put them under unnecessary pressure.

Unfortunately, much of the modern debate about parenting swings between the extremes of being perfect and being neglectful, with basically nothing in between. That's why I reintroduced the idea of being good enough. This describes parents who are there to pick up their children when they fall but who stand back enough to allow the children to make mistakes and discover the world for themselves.

I would not be surprised if, at the beginning of the book, putting your partner first seemed like another demand to add to an already long to-do list. I hope that the idea doesn't seem quite so onerous or impossible now and, most important, that you accept that *it won't harm your kids*.

To recap, here are the central ways of putting your partner first:

- Greet your partner first when you come home.
- Don't let your children interrupt when you and your partner are talking to each other.
- Put a lock on the bedroom door.
- Even when your children are babies, you and your partner should dress up and go out together.

- Put your partner's interests over those of your parents and back him or her in any battle with his or her parents.
- Accept your partner's feelings, because from where he or she is standing, they make sense. Listen, discuss, and don't jump to conclusions.
- Give positive feedback about what is working for you and use descriptive praise to encourage more of the same behavior.
- Don't assume your partner knows what's going on in your head; tell him or her.
- Parent as a team and don't make unilateral decisions or compete to be loved more.
- Don't discuss adult stuff with your children, use them as go-betweens, or create alliances with them.
- Have fun together as a couple, not just as a family.
- Prioritize sex.
- Make children responsible for tasks around the house so that there is more time for you to be partners rather than servants.
- Let your partner be his or her own person.

Before I return to the exercise in the first chapter about priorities, so we can see whether working through the book has brought about any changes, I need to discuss two issues: work and self.

What About Work?

When I do the priorities exercise from Chapter 1, a lot of people complain that their partner puts work first, above the children and certainly above the relationship.

Work is an incredibly complex subject (and probably worth a book in its own right). On one level, your job brings you money to pay the bills, provide for your children, and save for the future. However, it is much,

much more. It is part of your identity. It is also where you make friends and get a sense of belonging. In uncertain times, working hard provides the illusion of security. Finally, the feedback from senior staff and the respect of more junior staff can make you feel competent, worthwhile, and valued. No wonder success at work is closely tied to your self-esteem.

When one partner accuses the other of being obsessed with work, or putting it first, I always hear the same defenses: "You like the vacations, house, and lifestyle it brings," "I'm doing it for the family," "I thought it was the right thing to do." I always ask people to reflect on other reasons they might work so hard. How much of the long-hours culture is really about financial need? How much is related to personal satisfaction? How much stems from old messages from our parents to "work hard and achieve"? And how much is just simple habit?

If the amount of time spent at work (and on work at home) is an issue in your relationship, try this exercise. Imagine that your job is a cake, and divide up the reasons for working so hard. What percentage would you give to each of these four categories: financial need, personal satisfaction, messages from parents (or society in general), and habit? If there are other important reasons, add them to the list. Next, ask your partner why he or she thinks you work so hard, and have him or her complete the same exercise. Afterward, compare your results and discuss them. I would be surprised if you don't have very different conclusions.

Although you may think you're working hard for the family, your partner will imagine you're doing it for yourself. If you truly believe that you're working for the benefit of the family, do you find it hard to ask for things for yourself? Does work provide you with a ready-made excuse for time alone or to get out of tasks that you don't particularly like yet allow you to still feel like a good person? In the same way that some parents fuse their personal interests with those of their children, are you fusing your personal and work interests with those of your partner? It's always worth stopping and questioning the central importance of work. There are other ways of finding meaning in your life, a close circle of friends, or self-esteem than from your job.

Finally, in the same way that children are just passing through and that marriage should be forever, a job is just something on your résumé, and even the most successful career ends in retirement (or the business is passed on to the next generation).

If you're guilty of overprioritizing your work, how can you make your partner believe that he or she hasn't been forgotten? Here are a few ideas:

- Switch off mobile devices during mealtimes.
- Set a time at night after which you will not take calls or respond to e-mails.
- Devote weekends to family time. If you need to do some work, clear it with your partner beforehand, set a time limit, and stick to it.
- Do not take work on vacations. If you must, negotiate a limit, such as one hour a day, and discuss with your partner when it should be.
- Make a greater effort to attend your children's special events: concerts, sports events, parents' evenings at school, and so forth.
- Take time off to cover an occasional child-care emergency.
- Send text messages, leave cards, and make other small gestures that show that even though you might not be there, you're thinking of your beloved.

What About Self?

It is always hard to find a balance between being considerate to others and not neglecting your own needs. If you do suppress your needs, there is a danger of becoming passive (going along with what other people want) rather than being assertive (asking for what you want, listening to your partner, and negotiating if your needs are incompatible). Conversely, if you're determined to get your own way, you risk becoming domineering or manipulative. Short-term, or over minor matters, most relationships can accommodate both passive and domineering behavior, but over time and especially regarding major events, these patterns build resentment and anger.

So where should you put yourself in your list of priorities? Once again, there is no simple answer. It depends on the circumstances and what's at stake. However, if I had to come up with an aspiration (which won't always be the possible solution), I think it is still best to put your partner first. We live in a consumer society that's always stressing self-gratification. We worship strong people who get their own way and make things happen. There's nothing wrong with that, *but*—and it's a big *but*—we can become self-centered and not consider the effect of our behavior on other people. After all, we know how *we're* feeling, but it's much harder to listen to others or take what they say seriously. If you're in any doubt about a particular course of action, ask yourself the following questions:

- Is this something I *want* rather than something I *need*? Double-check your answer, since it's easy to dress up wants as needs. For example, I would question someone who says, "I *need* this vacation in the Maldives." I accept that people need to relax and recharge their batteries, but there are other ways of destressing and self-soothing—like going for a run or having a long weekend break. True needs are tied up with what makes our lives meaningful—for example, a musician has to make music, a writer has to write, and so on.
- Why does this activity or item mean so much to me?
- Have I explained it properly to my partner, or have I assumed that he or she will somehow know?

If your partner is asking for something that seems unreasonable or impossible, ask yourself these questions:

- What is it about my partner's upbringing and life experiences that makes this request particularly significant?

- Is it a need or a want?
- How could I put myself in my partner's shoes to understand more?
- How could we find a compromise that would be acceptable to both of us?

Returning to "What Are Your Priorities?"

Get out the cards that you made for the exercise at the beginning of the book and lay them out in the original order. Thinking about what you've learned and your experiences doing the exercises, do you want to change your priorities in any way?

Self	Partner	Children
Work	Friends	Parents
Siblings	Hobbies	Fitness and health
Fun	Home	Pets
Status	Personal development	
Sex	Intellectual nourishment	

Explain your thinking to your partner and listen (without comment) to his or her decisions. After you've both finished talking, discuss the reasons for your changes or staying the same. If you're going to make changes, how are you going to turn words into actions?

What If I Still Want to Put My Children First?

There is no right or wrong answer to balancing the needs of your children and those of your partner. After all, you know your relationship and your children best. Perhaps you find the idea of priorities annoying or too general, or you dislike ranking. Whatever your reasons for disagreeing,

I hope that my arguments have provided a way of discussing parenting with your partner, have helped you understand each other better, and have removed some of the pressure to be perfect.

Perhaps you have altered your priorities but your partner has not budged on his or hers. In these circumstances, I would suggest approaching the subject in another manner. Take the first three or four areas (or however many are truly important to you) and imagine that your time and emotional energy are a cake (as you did above for work). Before reading this book, how much time and energy would have been devoted to your children and how much to your relationship and the other significant areas? Now, having finished reading and thinking about my arguments, would you slice the cake any differently?

I know about the pressures on parents and the natural desire to do the best for your children, but I hope that the chapters on what children really need, the pitfalls of being a red-carpet kid, and what your children will tell their therapists have provided some food for thought. Your children might still take up the biggest slice of your life, but could you make it slightly smaller? What could be cut from the things you do for your children to provide more time for your relationship? How could you make this aspiration into a reality? To help you with these decisions, I have gathered all the key ideas in the Ten Golden Rules that follow this chapter.

Summary

Juggling priorities is really hard, especially with so many demands on your time. Don't worry if you and your partner don't always agree on how to prioritize work, satisfy your own needs, and bring up the children. Nobody gets the balance right all the time. However, if you have learned good communication skills, you are halfway to finding a solution that will lead to happy children, a happy marriage, and feeling personally fulfilled.

The Ten Golden Rules

1. Don't neglect your marriage; it is the glue that keeps the family together.
2. Being a parent and a perfectionist don't exist easily together. Instead, aim for being good enough.
3. Your main job as a parent is to take your children's feelings seriously, but this doesn't mean giving in to every whim. Rather, it means explaining why something is not possible or sensible.
4. Happy relationships need good communication skills as well as love and connection.
5. There are no right or wrong answers in disputes about how to raise your children. Listen to each other, be assertive, and negotiate.
6. Don't draw children into adult issues or let them take sides.
7. Encourage your children to be self-sufficient and don't become their servants. In this way, you will have more time to invest in your relationship.
8. You need to feel loved by your partner and not just like a service provider. It is therefore important to be romantic, have fun together, and make sex a priority.
9. When there's a problem, try not to label your partner or the children as the cause; look at your own contribution.
10. If something is good enough for your children, it is probably good enough for your partner, too.

Further Reading

By the Author

I Love You But . . . I'm Not In Love With You: Seven Steps to Saving Your Relationship. Deerfield Beach, FL: Health Communications, (2007). How suppressing issues might seem the best way to keep the peace but just stores up problems for the future.

Learn to Love Yourself Enough: Seven Steps to Improving Your Self-esteem and Your Relationships. London: Marshall Method Publishing, (2014). How your childhood affects how you feel about yourself, how to make a fresh start with your parents, and how to deal with your inner critic.

Have the Sex You Want: A Couple's Guide to Getting Back the Spark. London: Marshall Method Publishing, (2013). How lovemaking changes over time in a long-term relationship, how to talk about sex, and how to keep the spark alive.

Resolve Your Differences: Seven Steps to Dealing with Conflict in Your Relationship. London: Bloomsbury, (2011). How to be assertive and how to deal with anger in relationships in which you don't argue enough.

Further Reading

By Other Writers

Gerhardt, Sue. *Why Love Matters: How Affection Shapes a Baby's Brain*. New York: Routledge, (2004). The science behind why regulating your baby's emotions is so important.

Janis-Norton, Noël. *Calmer, Easier, Happier Parenting*. New York: Plume, (2013). How to get cooperation from children ages three to thirteen.

Schwarz, Robert, and Elaine Braff. *We're No Fun Anymore: Helping Couples Cultivate Joyful Marriages Through the Power of Play*. New York: Routledge, (2011). Written for therapists but full of ideas for increasing the fun in your relationship.

Zilbergeld, Bernie. *The New Male Sexuality: The Truth About Men, Sex and Pleasure*. New York: Bantam, (1999). A classic guide to understanding men and sex; my female clients find it really useful for getting inside their husbands' heads.

Acknowledgments

Fiona MacDonald Smith and Sarah Maber, two journalists at the *Times* of London, took me out to lunch, and, during a discussion about what I might write next, jumped on the idea of children and their effect on a marriage. By saying, "I'd like to read that book," each of them gave me the courage to press ahead.

I would also like to thank my agent, Rachel Calder; and my book group members—Gail Louv, Chris Taylor, and Jamie MacKay—who all offered their personal experiences and made countless useful suggestions. I'm grateful to Clare Christian at Marshall Method Publishing for introducing me to Liz Gough. And thanks to my team of associate therapists, Debby Edwards, Claudio Esposito, and Sally Fifield.

My research into the topic was informed by Kate Figes (*Life After Birth*), Gaby Hinsliff (*Half a Wife: The Working Family's Guide to Getting a Life Back*), Rebecca Asher (*Modern Motherhood and the Myth of Equality*), and Nina Grunfeld (who introduced me to the books of Nanny Smith).

Other people whose discussions on motherhood have helped are Hilly Janes, Christine Anstice, and Rachel Alexander, who guided my reading. On fatherhood, my thanks to Richard Groves, Thierry Brigodiot, and Simon Crompton.

Most important, I would like to acknowledge the contribution of my clients. On many occasions, it seems that I learn more from them than they do from me.

Also By Andrew G. Marshall

i love you but . . .
I'M NOT IN LOVE
with you

7 STEPS TO SAVING
YOUR RELATIONSHIP

"The most common question people ask when they hear
about my work is: 'Is it really possible to fall back in love?'
My answer is always the same—an emphatic yes."

ANDREW G. MARSHALL